PENGUIN BOOKS

REVOLUTION IN THE THIRD WORLD

Gérard Chaliand is a French political scientist and author. He has spent twelve years in Africa, Latin America, the Middle East, and Southeast Asia. Altogether he has lived for more than eight months among guerrilla groups in Guinea-Bissau (1966), Vietnam (1967), Colombia (1968), Jordan and Lebanon (1969–1970), Eritrea (1977), Iranian Kurdistan (1980), Afghanistan (1980 and 1982), Central America (1982), Angola (1985), Peru (1985), and the Philippines (1987).

Chaliand is the author of twenty books, of which thirteen have been translated into English. He has been a visiting professor at Harvard, Berkeley, UCLA, and the Universities of Manchester and Sussex, in England. He currently teaches at the French Ecole Nationale d'Administration and is an adviser to the Center for Analysis and Planning for French Foreign Relations.

D0064062

Also by Gérard Chaliand:

ARMED STRUGGLE IN AFRICA (1969)
PEASANTS OF NORTH VIETNAM (1970)
THE PALESTINIAN RESISTANCE (1972)
REPORT FROM AFGHANISTAN (1982)
GUERRILLA STRATEGIES (1982)
STRATEGIC ATLAS (1985)

REVOLUTION in the THIRD WORLD

Revised Edition

Gérard Chaliand

Translated by Diana Johnstone
Introduction and Postscript
translated by Tony Berrett

PENGUIN BOOKS

PENGUIN BOOKS
Published by the Penguin Group
Viking Penguin Inc., 40 West 23rd Street,
New York, New York 10010, U.S.A.
Penguin Books Ltd, 27 Wrights Lane,
London W8 5TZ, England
Penguin Books Australia Ltd, Ringwood,
Victoria, Australia
Penguin Books Canada Ltd, 2801 John Street,
Markham, Ontario, Canada L3R 1B4
Penguin Books (N.Z.) Ltd, 182–190 Wairau Road,
Auckland 10, New Zealand

Penguin Books Ltd, Registered Offices:
Harmondsworth, Middlesex, England

First published in the United States of America by
Viking Penguin Inc. 1977
Published in Penguin Books 1978
Reprinted 1979, 1980, 1981, 1982

This revised edition published in simultaneous hardcover and paperback editions
by Viking Penguin Inc. 1989
Published simultaneously in Canada

10 9 8 7 6 5 4 3 2 1

Originally published in France as
Mythes Révolutionnaires du Tiers Monde by Editions du Seuil.
Copyright © Editions du Seuil, 1976.

Library of Congress Cataloging in Publication Data
Chaliand, Gérard.
  [Mythes révolutionnaires du tiers monde. English]
  Revolution in the Third World / Gérard Chaliand; translated by Diana Johnstone;
[with new] introduction and postscript translated by Tony Berrett.—rev. ed.
    p.   cm.
  Translation of: Mythes révolutionnaires du tiers monde.
  Bibliography: p.
  ISBN 0 14 01.1845 4
  1. Revolutions—History—20th century. 2. World politics—1945– . 3. Guerrilla
warfare—History—20th century. 4. Socialism—Developing countries—History—20th
century. 5. Developing countries—Politics and government. I. Title.
D842.C4513   1989
321.09—dc19   88-29070
                                                                         CIP

Printed in the United States of America
Set in Times Roman

This book
is dedicated to
the Vietnamese people,
to the memory of
my friend Amilcar Cabral,
and above all to
the memory of my mother.

Of the gods we believe, and of men we know, that by a necessary law of their nature they rule wherever they can. And it is not as if we were the first to make this law or to act upon it when made: we found it existing before us, and shall leave it to exist forever after us; all we do is to make use of it, knowing that you and everybody else, having the same power as we have, would do the same as we do.

THUCYDIDES, *The Peloponnesian War* (105 V)

When the axe came into the forest, the trees said: the handle is one of us.

TURKISH PROVERB

INTRODUCTION TO THE 1989 EDITION

This book appeared a dozen years ago. It was written between 1972 and 1975, at a time when any number of myths were being peddled about the Third World, guerrilla warfare, and socialism; over the years it has become a sort of classic. The myths analyzed in it were those associated with various socialisms; with the revolution in many countries of Asia and Africa, where the gap between plans and reality was enormous; with guerrilla movements inevitably headed for victory because their case was just or the struggle popular. In short, this book denounced totalitarian bureaucracy, populism, and the lyrical illusions based on the Wretched of the Earth. The analysis, which was built on seven years of experience on the ground including many months in guerrilla zones, was essentially accurate. However, my training at the time meant that I still peddled two myths, as Richard L. Sklar pointed out in his perceptive review of my book published in *In These Times*. One was the theory of economic dependency, which teaches that the Third World is condemned to stagnate unless it opts for an autocentric philosophy of development. This view of things needs to be heavily nuanced. None of the economists who accepted the validity of the dependency theory had left any room for the possibility of a take-off such as that of South Korea or Taiwan. The second was the conviction, still widely entertained by Third Worldists, that bureaucracy rather than political repression accounts for the perversion of modern socialism. As Sklar wrote, "Bureaucracy and socialism are both badly abused as a direct result of the deprivation of liberty." Last, I taught that the bureaucracy of the countries of the Third World having carried out a radical social revolution, such as that of North Vietnam or Cuba, was the agent of economic development.

Since this book was published, the Third Worldism in which a section of Western youth and intelligentsia basked has gradually turned into a hostile reaction to the Third World, especially when it is revolutionary, or it has faded into indifference. This phenomenon is ambiguous. It is based on a more clearheaded assessment of the nature of bureaucracy and of the blockages of Soviet or Chinese society, and has led beyond Leninism, to the rediscovery of the virtues of democracy in the classical sense of the word. But at the same time, this turnaround, engendered by the crisis, the failures of the revolutionary Third World, or its crimes, gave rise to a new conformism which, as it stopped seeing only the injustices of "imperialism," as was formerly the case, now sees nothing but the crimes of the adversary. This conservatism feeds on a rejection of, or an indifference to, the causes which provoked the crises in the Third World societies. Once the favored home of myths they have become today the symbol of barbarism, as represented by Khomeini's Iran.

The postscript, "Revolution in the Third World Revisited," sets out, with things as I see them today, a global balance sheet of the Third World and Third Worldism and an analysis of the major events of the last decade, together with some suggestions about the outlook.

Over the last quarter of a century, I have been privileged to be present as an observer in over fifty countries in Africa, the Middle East, Southeast Asia, and Latin America. I have spent a dozen years in the Third World including over eighteen months in guerrilla zones or war zones on the three continents. Because I have never belonged to any institution, I had the freedom to move about as I wished, choosing my own itinerary and accepting the uncertainty that goes with it. For the last twenty years, I have lived only by my writings and lectures, and I am grateful to American universities, especially Harvard and Berkeley and above all UCLA, for having invited me as a visiting professor on numerous occasions. I also taught in France from 1980 to 1989 at the Ecole Nationale d'Administration (ENA).

The experience of political and armed struggles gradually led me to emphasize strategic thought—the fruit of which was the *Strategic Atlas* (Harper and Row, 1984)—insofar as I came to feel that an awareness and understanding of the relationship of existing forces was a better gauge of revolutionary change in the Third World than ideological assumptions and received ideas. If, over the years, I have come to adopt a more hardheaded approach, that does not in the least mean that I have abandoned the fundamental beliefs that motivated me: the right of peoples to self-determination, equally valid for Algeria as for Afghanistan, and a certain idea of justice.

It goes without saying that the countries of Asia, Africa, and Latin America will not find it easy, whatever their proclaimed ideology, to produce democratic societies. On the one hand, because their heritage is not the bourgeois democratic revolution produced by the Enlightenment, but classical despotism, be it Manchu China, the Ottoman Empire, or the Spanish Empire in whose empires, human beings were thought of not as citizens but as subjects; on the other hand, Marxism in actual practice has turned out to signify the rise to power not of the workers but of omnipotent and totalitarian bureaucracies. But it would show very little progress in lucidity if one simply returned, after a period of openness, even of illusions about the Third World, to Western-centeredness. It would be pointless to have been concerned about the Third World if one had not drawn a few lessons, first and foremost of which being the understanding of the others. Seen from the viewpoint of morality as well as that of politics, the Third World is one of the West's fundamental problems.

My taste for the ground was born of traveling. I have spent eighteen years of my life traveling and living abroad. When I was growing up, these journeys were made by hitchhiking—charter flights only made their appearance in 1961. This traveling for the sake of traveling, from a taste for adventure and archaeology, gradually led me to become interested in the political problems of the Third World. A few fascinating years at the Ecole des Langues et des Civilisations Orientales in Paris opened up for me a quest for cultures worldwide that I felt was our universal heritage.

These journeys were journeys into wholly different societies not simply into blank space. Not only did I have to learn how to behave in the various cultures, know their codes and signs, but in the course of my surveys, I also had to mix with both the peasantry and the most impoverished classes in the cities as well as the elites (power or not), and especially the leading groups of national liberation movements. It was a time when colonialism was being rejected; generally speaking, relations with liberation movements were greatly facilitated by their adoption of a number of features of modernity: attitude to time, organization of work, language, and the like.

An independent participant-observer, I devoted a considerable portion of my work as a political scientist to national liberation movements. I worked outside any institution, without any financial help either from the state (where French researchers seek funding) or from foundations (where American researchers seek theirs), and I was several times invited by one liberation movement or another to observe how they lived. In this way I was able to observe on the ground the guerrillas in Guinea-Bissau (1964, 1966), the war in North Vietnam during the American bombing (1967), and the provinces of Tolima and Huila in Colombia (1968), and to stay with, successively, Fatah, Nayaf Hawatmehs' PDFLP and Georges Habash's PFLP in Jordan and Lebanon (1969). But it also enabled me to be in Eritrea with the Eritrean People's Liberation Front (1977), in Iranian Kurdistan fighting against the Khomeini regime with A. R. Ghassemlou's Kurdistan Democratic Party, three times in Afghanistan (between 1980 and 1982), both with the Islamic fundamentalists and with the traditionalists, in Central America (1982), in Angola with Jonas Savimbi's UNITA (1986), in Peru to see the Shining Path in the provinces of Ayacucho and Apurímac as well as Lima (1986), and in the Philippines with the New People's Army (1987).

In my writings, guerrilla warfare takes a prominent place, from *Armed Struggle in Africa* (Monthly Review Press, 1968) to *Terrorism* (Saqi, 1987), including *Guerilla Strategies* (University of California Press, 1982), *Report from Afghanistan* (Penguin, 1982), and older works such as *Peasants of North Vietnam* (Penguin, 1969) or *The Palestinian Resistance* (Penguin, 1972). Unlike other Westerners, French, British, or American, I am not an expert on counterinsurrection but on insurrection. I have always experienced guerrilla warfare not from the side of the forces of law and order but from the side of those who are fighting against the state and seeking, usually, to replace it. The range of experiences I have studied covers anticolonialist struggles, Marxist-Leninist movements against independent states, underground movements of minority groups seeking to gain autonomy, and movements fighting a state that claims to be Marxist-Leninist. Like all those who have become theorists of guerrilla warfare—the most widespread form of warfare used in the last forty years—I did not study the technique at school. Herman Melville once wrote: "The sea has been my Harvard and my Yale." The ground has been my university.

For those who know how to be satisfied with the bare necessities of life—provided they come through unharmed—the precariousness of war gives each moment, each creature, each thing, a special value. But I did not deliberately become a specialist in guerrilla warfare and irregular fighting in general. When I suggested to Amilcar Cabral in 1963 that I visit the zones he controlled in Guinea-Bissau, I little knew that I would later become one of the few experts on this type of conflict.

I am not fascinated by guerrillas: one is only fascinated by what he knows from a distance. Guerrilla action has many aspects, and many observers think it is just the matter of wandering about on foot that is more or less difficult and spectacular. But its deeper interest lies elsewhere: in the study of the organization of a society to face up to a violent crisis, in the political and strategic understanding of a leadership or skilled personnel able to grasp the weakness of the adversary, inspire the people, and create the conditions of permanence. All the components that precipitate the unleashing of uprisings—foreign oppression, social injustice, discrimination, crises—are at work as the century draws to a close, and irregular conflicts in the coming years will only increase in number.

As for our murderous world, moving almost blindly, it can only arouse in the man of action or among those who reflect on what men do a vision of tragedy in which the defeated and the victims have—always—been the majority.

—Gérard Chaliand
July 1988

PREFACE

It is nice to sit around listening to stories. It may be gratifying to believe that the "socialist" revolution is at hand in Asia, in Latin America, perhaps even in Africa; or to imagine that it has already been achieved in the Soviet Union, in Yugoslavia, or in China, according to one's learnings; or to argue that bureaucracy is an avoidable evil and that in various places around the globe the proletariat, the historic agent of change, has been or is being "betrayed."

As may be guessed from this beginning, I am interested, in this book, more in exploring myths and realities than in making predictions. The critical task of trying to focus on the facts underneath slogans, platforms, and proclamations is the main job for a participant observer, which I have been for some fifteen years.

Revolution in the Third World—a scientifically inaccurate but convenient title—takes up the political and social problems of Asian, Latin American, and African countries; specifically, the problems of revolution in formerly colonial or semicolonial countries. I have chosen to make the book, which in any case could not be complete, as brief as possible, with a minimum of figures, quotations, and footnotes; at the risk of seeming simplistic, I have tried to use ordinary, clear language rather than specialized terminology, which very often serves only to mask banality. I have referred only in passing to economic questions and issues concerning development, which have so often been studied already. Above all, I have tried, using comparative methods in the light of historical, sociological, and cultural factors, to restore *political* considerations to their rightful place in the study of the Third World—that is, to the number one place.

After a general introduction dealing with underdevelopment and dependency, I take up three main aspects of revolutionary change in the Third World: first, armed struggle, or, to be more precise, the political strategy of contemporary armed struggle in Asia, Latin America, and Africa, with its successes and failures; next, the nature and characteristics of the many national revolutions, which more often than not proclaim themselves socialist, especially in Africa; and finally, the nature and characteristics of the national and social revolutions called communist or socialist—a subject that requires not only concrete examples but also a reminder of basic theoretical notions about "communism" and the transitional phase of socialism which is supposed to lead to it. Having had occasion to see at first hand how ideology tends to twist reality to fit its dogmas, I have tried as hard as I can to keep this book from being subjective. If it turns out that the prospects for real change do not look bright, is it not true that they have always depended not on our wishes, but on the true relationship of existing forces?

A sort of Third World euphoria began to be felt at the close of the 1950s, during the Algerian war, and it was soon given a boost by the radical turn of events in the Cuban revolution in

1960–61. In France, some of those who had at first opposed war in Algeria now demanded, sometimes actively backed, the cause of Algerian independence. More than the first Indo-China war (for which France had not called up draftees), the Algerian "revolution," geographically so close to Europe, came to symbolize the anticolonialist struggle. The works of Frantz Fanon, in particular his *The Wretched of the Earth,* inspired this anticolonialist trend of thought in Europe, and before long it could be found in the United States too, especially among blacks, where it merged with opposition to the war in Vietnam. Third World euphoria was an important characteristic of the 1960s, both in the Third World itself and in the West, especially among students and youth. It developed in the context set by "decolonization," whether by decree or by force; by the emergence of armed revolutionary movements in Asia, Latin America, and Africa; by a controversy between Russia and China, hinging, in the official texts, on problems of revolutionary strategy; and finally, by the rather dreary state of politics in most of the advanced industrial countries of the West.

In speaking of Third Worldism, one cannot ignore the minority fraction of American blacks, who in the late 1960s shared the myth of a Tricontinental Revolution via the figures of Fanon, Che Guevara, and Ho Chi Minh, while at the same time feeding it with their own image. Within some elements of the European Far Left, the final embodiment of Third Worldism may well be found in the recent myth of immigrant workers as representing the potential revolutionary vanguard.

There has been little analysis probing beneath the seemingly inexorable tide of events or beneath the rhetoric of leaders, getting at the actual matters at stake in a given conflict or the actual nature of the independence gained or lost. Over and over again, leaders of African and Asian countries have opted for socialism in words alone, while numerous guerrilla groups have led people to overestimate their strength, their rootedness, and the scope of their operations. Many a transitory situation has been considered or proclaimed irreversible.

Despite certain common traits, some of them fundamental
—distorted and dependent economies, preponderance of traditional rural structures, a high population growth rate—the Third
World, which in fact is an integral part of the capitalist system,
is sharply differentiated. The basic differences hinge on the level
of development of productive forces, not on the extent of poverty.
India is no doubt more poverty-stricken than Tanzania, but there
is no comparison between them in the level of productive forces;
countries like India, with a long-standing and powerful bourgeoisie and fairly significant, concentrated proletariat, are infinitely
more complex societies than those of West Africa, for example.

As to the level of development, Latin America, even though
dominated by a single civilization and language (outside Brazil),
is far from homogeneous. And by the same token, there is not
one Africa but several (even speaking only of tropical Africa),
each with vastly different levels of productive forces, and for that
matter vastly different historical stages, to be found within a single
geographical area or country. A third great area, dominated by
(although not identical with) Islam, stretches from Morocco to
Central Asia, predominantly Arab, Iranian, and Turkish, again
heavily differentiated (consider the differences between Egypt and
Yemen, for instance). Then there is the Indian subcontinent and
Southeast Asia, with the Hinduized, Sinized, or Islamized states
running from Burma to Vietnam, with the sharpest differences
between lowland plains and mountains. The term *Third World*
envelops in a semblance of unity what is in reality a multiplicity
of worlds.

For all the prevailing poverty, the situation is not explosive
in most Asian, African, and Latin American countries. True, all
of them face the same problem: how to achieve real independence
based on autonomous development. This is why it has been possible to call the overall situation revolutionary. But despite appearances and the well-founded impatience of those who are aware of
the problems, the overall situation—for historical or social reasons,
or thanks to partial reforms—is undergoing only very gradual
modification. Outside the context of generalized wars, when the
loosening of the dominant powers' grip may permit a propor-

tionate assertion of autonomy, it is in fact unusual for the social contradictions within a formally independent country to become so acute as to set off a deep nationwide crisis. This occurs only when the grip of a foreign power is added to the crushing weight of a corrupt upper class unable to promote even lopsided growth. This offends everyone, and most of all the modernist petty bourgeoisie (civilian or military) whose access to what it considers its rightful functions is blocked. That is why most of the "revolutions" in the Third World during the past thirty years have been undertaken by the relatively small class of nationalist petty bourgeoisie who are eager to promote development. The classic example of this phenomenon was Egypt.

The revolutions in Asia, Latin America, and Africa have been thought up and led by intellectuals, who mostly came from the petty bourgeoisie. Only a few of them have been far-reaching. These revolutions have sought to overthrow established powers when the latter proved incapable of coming up with any response to the crises wracking their societies. In places where the ruling classes were unable or unwilling to adapt fast enough, the dissatisfaction of the petty bourgeoisie has joined with the humiliation felt by intellectuals; centuries of accumulated contradictions in rural society have come to a head when further distorted by the introduction of capitalism and aggravated by population pressure; and all this has combined to produce revolutionary explosions. Yet this has happened rather less often than the objective situation might lead one to expect—perhaps because the modernist elites are weak or lack real links with the peasant masses, or because the industrial capitalist countries have intervened, directly or indirectly, anxious to preserve their hegemony. Most of the time, for reasons we shall try to analyze, these revolutionary explosions, often restricted to "the top," have resulted only in nationalist regimes with statist tendencies, not in thoroughgoing revolutions affecting the social structure.

This book is the product of seven years of living and traveling in North Africa, tropical Africa, the Middle East, the Indian subcontinent, Southeast Asia, and Latin America. I made the acquaintance of these countries in various ways and circumstances without any help or grant—usually, until quite recently, managing to get along by doing various kinds of manual labor or by living in rural villages where I was doing surveys. In most of the countries, I got to know peasants as well as the kinds of city people a foreigner usually meets—administrators, tradesmen, and the local intelligentsia. My knowledge of a half-dozen languages almost always enabled me to communicate directly with those city people, but I often needed an interpreter in order to talk with the peasants. In quite different circumstances I have also had occasion to get to know the Third World of international congresses, experts, and official meetings. For months, I have also observed and experienced what it is like to live in conditions of guerrilla or all-out war on three continents: living in the insurgent areas of Guinea-Bissau; doing a survey on peasants of North Vietnam while the American bombing raids were going on; living among Palestinian resistance movements in Jordan; investigating guerrilla areas in Colombia. Finally, I have met and in some cases gotten to know various political figures, party leaders, and heads of state—such as Che Guevara, Ben Bella, Julius Nyerere, Modibo Keita, Sékou Touré, and Amilcar Cabral.

In this book, centered as it is on problems of national liberation, armed struggles, and the transitional phase theoretically leading to socialism, I have taken as my examples, from among some thirty Third World countries on three continents, a few that seem to me to provide the best illustrations of historical evolution since World War II. In other words, I have attempted to delineate a sociological approach to armed struggles, revolutionary populisms, and modern bureaucracies.

Los Angeles–Montreal–Paris   G. C.
1972–75

ACKNOWLEDGMENTS

I want to thank Maxime Rodinson, Pierre Vidal-Naquet, and Juliette Minces for their numerous critical remarks; Robert Silvers of the *New York Review of Books* for the confidence he manifested in my project from its earliest beginnings; Elisabeth Sifton of The Viking Press for her editorial work and her long-lasting support; and, of course, Diana Johnstone for her intelligent and sensitive translation.

CONTENTS

INTRODUCTION
the dimensions of development

1. Work and Days

However great the differences among the various societies of Asia, Africa, and Latin America, many share certain basic traits which characterize all traditional rural societies (including the rural society of Europe before the industrial revolution). To start with, there is always, in Asia as well as in Latin America, a strict hierarchic order. Big landowners are in some way connected, through family or favors, to top administrators. There is sharp competition for jobs that bestow prestige, even when they are not directly remunerative. Family ties, in the broad sense of the term, underlie village economic and political life. Since the best safeguard for the future is to be related to a powerful family, marriages are the expression of a social strategy with specific aims. But even the humblest family offers each and every member a refuge which can always be counted on, which represents security in the face of all human and natural adversity. (Those who find themselves suddenly outside this traditional world, immigrant workers in Europe, for example, are able to appreciate fully all its reassuring and protective warmth.) Poor peasants, even though strongly aware of their poverty, see themselves as having a place in the order of things, and can only dream of escaping, along with their families, from their humble status

Awareness of belonging to one's village—center of security and continuity—while stronger in some societies than in others, is a reality, and in regard to outsiders the village will show a cohesion which rarely fails: a refusal to give information or to betray the secrets of the group. At times, however, violence breaks out along class lines. Just have one bad harvest come along on top of, say, the overbearing harshness of a landowner or the exorbitant demands of usurious moneylenders or the government, and riots may break out; if the situation is ripe, these may lead to peasant rebellions in which all manner of hatred and humiliation, patiently accumulated, bursts forth in unbridled savagery.

In the village, whether in the Near East or in Southeast Asia, men work according to the seasons and to whatever jobs are provided by the major landowners, usually getting into debt with the usurer, generation after generation, without ever being able to make any real change in how they live. Life continues to be bounded by the village horizons, and as for the state government, even if it serves to initiate and coordinate important public works, such as irrigation and flood control, it is mainly feared because it puts on pressure through taxation and conscription. Child mortality is high, life expectancy low; the peasant is usually worn out by the age of forty and ill with some form of parasitosis. Only within his family can the landless peasant or small landholder win recognition; if he has a lot of children—male—he enjoys prestige. His wife will also be more highly regarded for producing numerous sons, but her chance to gain respectability or even prestige comes with age and the desexualization of growing old. When she has raised her sons and married them off, she commands their households and inflicts on her daughters-in-law the humiliations she used to suffer. What is demanded of women, besides giving birth to males, is that they not transgress two strict rules: to be virgin when they marry and to be faithful afterward. Sexual taboos, related to religious or magical beliefs, occupy an important place in the moral code. While less tightly bound by such constraints than women, men are also subject to a code of strict prohibitions. The order and especially the security of the group depend on it. The family respects the rules of religion and social morality, the rites for the dead or belief in gods. Village life depends on resignation on the part of the underprivileged, as well as overall submission and deference to the hierarchic order as dictated by age, sex, and so on. On account of this very rigidity, there are frequent outbursts of violence for all sorts of reasons—whether over minor violations of property rights or in response to some other real or imagined offense—proportionate to the usual stifling submission to social rules imposed by the group.

What is called "modernizing" the rural world is a highly complex task. By definition, it implies upheavals aimed at more or less totally changing the traditional social, economic, and cultural structures. The economic structures can be *modified* in a fairly short time—by expropriation, redistribution, collectivization, or by introducing new techniques and ways of organizing work, so long as the process is carried out with thoroughness and determination. But the gradual transformation of the superstructures—that is, of all the factors that decide a people's idea of their social reality—calls for patient, constant, and intense effort. This kind of effort in turn requires an ideology capable of introducing a new rationality, and without this, modernization is impossible. Modern social and economic organization, whether capitalist or "socialist," requires a capacity to calculate the future and plan it, up to a certain point. This implies a certain notion of time and the future. Traditionally, in rural societies the foreseeable future amounts to no more than the cycle of the seasons, as farming follows the rhythm of sowing and harvesting, summer and winter, dry season and rainy season. Even here, forecasts are uncertain, what with nature's whims. So the very idea of controlling time is foreign to such societies. We can more rightly say that our relationship to time, which probably stayed about the same from the age of the Pharaohs to the dawn of the modern era, has drastically changed in the Western world under the influence of industrialization. But traditional rural society is completely caught up in a much slower rhythm (such as is still reflected in Indian or Egyptian films). It views temporal change only in terms of the simple alternations of day and night, the seasons, and the eternity between birth and death. No traditional rural society can have anything but a fatalistic and non-Promethean notion of the world, for its subjection to time, as well as to what it considers the way things are, is virtually total. Modernization means changing that way of thinking.

Every nation or country of Asia or Africa, with the exception of Japan, was subjected to colonial or semicolonial domination between the middle of the nineteenth century and the Second World War. The formidable expansion of capitalism, creating a world market that in turn brought about the direct or indirect domination of Africa, Asia, and Latin America by a few Western industrialized nations, found its classic expression in European colonialism. Each industrialized capitalist country tried to lay hands on sources of raw materials and at the same time tried to grab or at least control as much territory as possible in order to keep the others out. Faced with this mounting "white peril," only Japan, thanks to its isolation and to a determined ruling elite, managed to avoid the fate of other countries by undertaking, from 1868 on, a crash program of industrialization.

Economically speaking, the main result of Europe's colonialism was to create, for the first time in history, a truly worldwide market. But in the process of introducing modernizing elements (including, indirectly, the weapons which can be used to escape from it) industrial capitalism inevitably disrupts the economies of the dominated countries. This disruption is behind what is commonly called underdevelopment. In fact, there is no such thing as underdevelopment without distortion of a traditional economy and a growing dependence on advanced capitalism. But industrial capitalism creates underdevelopment by breaking the traditional order and balance while for the most part retaining the old production relationships. Finally, deterioration of the terms of trade is a clear consequence of the underdevelopment resulting from capitalist domination—terms of trade between industrialized and underdeveloped countries being set less by the law of supply and demand than by power relationships.[1]

The colonial economy is the extension of the capitalist economy insofar as colonial territories are put to work solely according to the needs of the mother countries, out of the way of competition from rival states. Deliberately complementary, the colonial economy is limited to certain sectors, such as mining and plantation crops, and the commercialization of its products remains in the hands of large European firms, whose commercial networks are oriented toward the very Western countries that forced their colonies into monoculture. (Thus at the end of the 1950s, Indonesia was producing 40 percent of the world's rubber, Ghana one-third of the world's chocolate, Brazil 45 percent of its coffee.) The colonial countries depend on the colonizing or dominant nations buying these products (at prices imposed by the latter) since this commerce accounts for almost their entire income. Throughout the colonial period, this system ruled out any accumulation of capital within the colonial countries.

It was by relying on the traditional ruling classes they found in the Third World that the capitalist countries first managed to impose their military and political domination. Exploitation colonies, where the whole point was to drain as much wealth as possible toward the mother country, had two basic forms of administration: the British system used native governments and old-time chiefs to exercise authority; the French system allowed

---

[1] By terms of trade I mean the relation between the prices of import goods and export goods. There is deterioration in a colonized or underdeveloped country's terms of trade when prices of the goods it must import rise faster than the prices of the commodities it exports to industrialized nations. Since the latter set the prices, this deterioration is scarcely surprising.

the natives to occupy only the lower levels of jobs. But this difference was only secondary. In both cases the colonial system sought its allies among the same traditional ruling strata.

Settlers' colonies, which were nonexistent in Asia (except for the special case of Israel), in Africa constituted a different sort of situation, one that gave rise to sharp conflicts (as in Algeria, Rhodesia, South Africa, Angola, Mozambique, and Kenya). In this type of colonization, the European minorities occupy the dominant social or economic positions and benefit either directly or indirectly from the work of the colonized people whose land has been expropriated. Not only the loftiest levels of Europeans, but also the "poor whites," minor civil servants, office clerks and workers, have the advantage of high pay, high at least in comparison to the natives, and above all enjoy a privileged status on the basis of their ethnic origins. This type of colonization leads to the most complex and violent conflicts of all.

The introduction of capitalism by way of colonization has of course profoundly transformed the societies of Asia and Africa —most notably in creating new social classes. The dislocation of traditional agriculture, the transfer of common land to private ownership, and, especially, urbanization create the conditions under which these classes are formed, and they develop as the capitalist mode of production is gradually introduced: a small bourgeoisie, and, finally, an industrial or agricultural proletariat. Along with population growth, the two developments whose effects on social change are most significant are probably the introduction of private land ownership (previously unknown in many societies and always of minor importance prior to European interference) and the emergence, by way of the government administration, of a new, educated elite from the petty bourgeoisie.

Without doubt it is the new elite who are mostly sharply aware of the phenomena of colonialism and who resent it most bitterly. In fact, the government apparatuses which have absorbed much of this administrative petty bourgeoisie frequently became the center of opposition to colonial domination. Intellectuals and semi-intellectuals working in junior positions, able to speak the colonizer's language, and more or less familiar with his culture, are in a good position to learn a great deal both about the colonizer's character and methods of control and about his own ruling class's betrayal and corruption. Humiliated in regard to their national identity, they are at the same time eager to take over the functions they consider their due. This explains the role of the army in a number of Arab countries, or that of junior officials in tropical Africa. The situation is different in settlers' colonies, where the European settler population has mostly kept natives out of junior administrative posts. There, the national movement may be taken in hand either by liberal professionals or by very modest sectors of the small bourgeoisie. Sometimes, once independence is granted and the traditional ruling class is back in power, these new administrative or military elites who have felt largely excluded from the privileges of power, may try to throw the rulers out. And they may momentarily try to enlist the support of the masses.

If victorious, a significant part of the petty bourgeoisie manages to use its control of the government apparatus, whether through the army or a single party, as the means to develop, *to its own profit,* the capitalist mode of production (nationalized or not). This process is the essential domestic feature of decolonization.

One of the last—and lesser—social effects of colonization is the creation of a proletariat. The obligation to pay taxes in cash, deteriorating living conditions in the countryside, population increases—all this leads a large number of peasants to look for work in town. But, since few jobs are available, the proletarianization remains limited, and the workers often retain their ties with their village.

On the psycho-cultural level, probably no historical phenomenon of modern times has been so traumatic and so destructive of the mental structures of entire societies.[2] Everywhere, but most especially in nations whose own history dated back to

---

[2] See Fanon's psycho-cultural analysis in the chapter on violence in *The Wretched of the Earth* (New York: Grove Press, 1967), as well as Albert Memmi's keen analysis in *The Colonizer and the Colonized* (Boston: Beacon, 1970).

antiquity—China, Egypt, Vietnam, Persia—the onslaught of Europe on colonialism stunned, bewildered, and overwhelmed the traditional elites. In terms of relationship of forces, no satisfactory response was forthcoming to the challenge of industrial capitalism, except in Japan. In a sense, answers were no longer adduced from traditional sources and, instead, began to be inspired by Western models (and Marxism, despite its universality, is an integral part of the West). In the same way, when it came to trying to shake off European domination, it was the major ideology of nineteenth-century Europe—nationalism—that was called upon.

But the first response to the shock of colonialism, in all societies with a traditional state organization, was to take refuge in tradition as an ideology of resistance, to exalt the past and preach patience while waiting for better times. This was a response strongly influenced by the scholar elites and clerics representing religious values (two categories often taken for one). In Vietnam, as in China, Confucian scholars when they criticized their kings and emperors who bowed to foreign power did so in the name of Virtue, and dreamed of restoring sovereigns worthy of "the mandate of heaven." In Muslim countries, the men of the faith who represent the Oumma (the Islamic community) preached loyalty to the traditional religion and way of life. Following defeat or occupation, this rigid clinging to old values became the basis of a kind of ideology of resistance. Soon a second response would develop, this time put into motion by a westernized bourgeoisie, which advocated adopting parliamentary or republican forms of government along European lines in order to modernize the country, and which set up modern political parties. Thus the Young Turks made their appearance in the Ottoman Empire in 1908, China became a Republic in 1910, Egypt adopted a modern code of law. But just as a foreign occupying power is not disturbed by the attitudes of the scholars and priests, in the same way nothing in a given society is changed by a democratic facade set up by its bourgeois elite. It is much more complicated. The peasantry watches, powerless, as its economic conditions are changed; it tries to preserve both its subsistence economy and its traditional values, and thereby appears even more passive than usual. The village tends to close in on itself more than ever, turning its back on foreigners and outsiders, colonizers and their deputies. But it is in the cities that the most obvious contradictions arise. There the colonizers rub elbows with the colonized; native bourgeois, grown wealthy through trade with the West, live side by side with minor officials and clerks, impoverished scholars grimly aware of their plight (and, too, of the plight of their people), and jobless or semiunemployed peasants who have become part of the urban proletariat.

Within certain elements of urban society, the trauma of colonialism has caused the deepest hurt. Before he ever lifts up his head or turns to open revolution, before getting directly or indirectly involved in national liberation, the colonized person in Asia or Africa is first of all a person who is ill at ease with himself. Usually he unconsciously accepts the white colonizer's standard of values, and consequently suffers from feelings of shame, inferiority, and humiliation. When his social circumstances allow, he tries to imitate the colonizer, adopting his norms and way of talking, but all this is vain, since his very skin gives him away. The aggression he suffers from the white world is not compensated by any defense or justification from his own people, who on the contrary, put pressure on him to adjust and conform. The colonized city-dweller of a certain social level is both attracted to and repulsed by the white world; he is in servitude to an order which is not his own; yet he sees no way out.[3] If he strictly conforms to the colonizer's culture and standards he may be rewarded with signs of approval and satisfaction from the white world. But at the same time, he becomes ashamed of his own people, with whom he cannot but identify, which automatically drags him down to their level. Looking at his own people from

---

[3] For all his claims to negritude, Leopold Sedar Senghor, a remarkable poet as well as President of Senegal, in part of his poetry nevertheless expresses a loss of personal identity that shows up in lines like: "Seigneur parmi les nations blanches, place la France à la droite du Père" ("Lord, of the white nations, place France at the right hand of the Father").

both the inside and the outside, he continually recognizes traits of his own that he is trying to mask; his own people bear open witness to what he is truly deep-down inside, to the self he has tried to stifle. In the depths of his being, acknowledged or ignored, his greatest affliction lies hidden—self-contempt. Having repudiated himself, and in fact by repudiating himself over and over, day after day, he has been stripped of his identity; he no longer knows who he is. And to the ideology of revolution—nationalist, by definition—falls the therapeutic task of cleansing that shame, providing a new identity, a new face, of restoring dignity. Formal independence is only a halfway measure, so long as Western cultural standards continue to bear down.

But meanwhile, coming after the first two anticolonial responses, another more radical attitude has found expression in bureaucratic, Leninist versions of Marxism in variant forms— Chinese, Vietnamese, Korean, and, more specially, Cuban. This has made it possible, among other things, to lay the foundations of national revivals in a number of countries.

2. The Prospect: A World Both Poorer and Less White

No study of the Third World could hope to gauge the future without studying demographic projections.

World population, estimated at nearly four billion in 1968, will top six billion at the close of the century, at which time Asia, Africa, and Latin America will account for approximately 80 percent of the human race, compared to 65 percent in 1965 (and Asia alone for 68 percent).

If North America, with slightly more than 6 percent of the world's population, takes in nearly 40 percent of world income (as it did in 1970), while Europe and the Soviet Union, with 22 percent of the population, take in 38 percent; then that leaves more than 70 percent of the world's population with only 22 percent of its income. By region, the proportions are:

Nation	Percentage of Population	Percentage of Income
Africa	8.0	2.5
Middle East	4.5	2.0
Latin America	7.0	5.0
Asia (from Pakistan to China)	55.0	12.0

Obviously, demographic, political, and social problems will become most critical in the vicinity of China.

The Third World's lack of economic self-sufficiency, the stagnation, even regression, and pauperization that plague it have been amply documented time and again. But let me briefly summarize the brutal facts:

The industrialized countries of the West, with less than 40 percent of the total population of the capitalist world (by which I mean the industrialized countries *and* the Third World, excluding all "socialist" nations), take in more than 85 percent of total capitalist world income. The United States alone takes in half. It used to be that colonial and semicolonial countries were seen to have three functions: first and foremost as suppliers of raw materials and agricultural products; second as areas for capital investment; and third as market. Today, however, they are only secondarily significant as areas for capital investment. American business prefers to invest in Europe, including backward areas, such as Spain and Greece (though private investments in Latin America are still considerable). While certain raw materials have been replaced by substitutes, for instance synthetic rubber; minerals and petroleum, on the other hand, continue to be essential and account for about 40 percent of the export earnings of the underdeveloped countries. For the most part, investments are concentrated in these sectors.

Interestingly enough, the geographical distribution of American investments does not correspond to the geographical distribution of repatriated profits. While receiving nearly half of U.S. foreign investments in 1965, Western Europe contributed only a little more than a fifth of the repatriated profits the rest of the world turned over to the United States. Latin America took in $1.1 billion between 1965 and 1968 and payed out $5.4 billion in profits, for an overall loss of $4.3 billion, while for Europe, the figures add up to a gain of $800 million. In short, it is as though the poor countries, through the intermediary of the United States, had been financing part of the development of Western Europe and the United States itself.

According to liberal theories, the poor countries were suffering from a lag in development that was caused strictly by internal factors, principally lack of capital, and increased investment was seen as the basic condition for what W. W. Rostow called economic takeoff. However, for Marxist-oriented economists, underdevelopment is not so much a lag in growth as a structural blocking of it, due to the industrial nations' domination, distorting the domestic economies of the Third World. Seen in this light, underdevelopment could only lead to more underdevelopment, except in a very few countries whose growth remained heavily dependent on the West.

Underdevelopment is not an internal phenomenon due to the set structures of Third World countries, but a product of the world capitalist system and an integral part of it. There can be no way of overcoming it except by putting an end to dependence itself and to the structures of the dependent relationships. We can better grasp now the extent to which development is not an economic problem to be solved by injections of capital, but rather a *political* problem.

The Third World as a whole is not advancing but, rather, is tending to fall still further behind. F.A.O. figures indicate that the growth in farm production has barely kept up with population growth, at an annual rate of 2.9 percent. In all the years between 1952 and 1969, there was no increase in per capita output.

Of course, agricultural output is not the whole of production, and some countries come out even, or ahead, thanks to their raw materials, especially petroleum. This factor often accounts for the variations in growth within the Third World. But for the population of the Third World as a whole, the relatively higher growth rate makes little difference, and between now and the year 2000 the number of people in a state of "latent hunger" is projected to go from two to four billion.

The failure of foreign aid or multinational assistance, and the failure of existing institutions and structures to come up with solutions, was clearly brought out at the United Nations Conference on Trade and Development (UNCTAD) held in Santiago in 1972. Robert McNamara, President of the World Bank, argued that development as we now experience it is unacceptable, for the gains made have not been distributed fairly among nations or among population groups within nations. His conclusion, however, that we shouldn't waste our time trying to place the blame for this situation, or worse, wear ourselves out in fruitless confrontations between rich and poor countries, evaded the heart of the problem. Several months later, in an important speech opening the General Assembly of the International Monetary Fund and the World Bank, Mr. McNamara, who, while surely more a reformer than a conservative, can scarcely be suspected of trying to make things look worse than they are, said in his assessment of the development outlook for the decade, that the goal set for a 6 percent growth rate for underdeveloped countries during the decade could not be reached. And even if it were—which is out of the question —the living conditions of the majority of the 2 billion human beings who inhabit the poor countries would not noticeably change, for in present conditions, an increase in national income does them no good. In fact, growth naturally tends to be concentrated in the modern sectors of the economy and scarcely touches the levels of the population with the lowest incomes. At least 40 percent of the overall population of the Third World, 1.5 billion people, are virtually destitute. However, Mr. McNamara added, the underdeveloped countries could considerably reduce the glaring inequalities in income without paralyzing the incentive to increase productivity.

The action program suggested by Mr. McNamara, in its effects at least, was not far removed from a genuinely revolutionary approach; but his proposed reforms have virtually no chance of being put into practice:

—to try to increase the income of the poorest 40 percent of the Third World population by setting up national development plans that include specific measures for that purpose;

—since poverty is closely tied to unemployment, to make an all-out attack on joblessness and underemployment through urban and rural public-works projects, such as building roads leading to markets, low-cost housing, reforestation, irrigation and drainage.

—to make the institutional reforms indispensable to the redistributing of economic power: agrarian reform, tax reform, credit revisions, and so on.

—to organize public funding better, since expenditures for public services, which in principle means health, transportation, water supply, education, etc., all too often profit the rich more than they benefit the underprivileged.

In reality, effective political and social brakes on such reforms can be found in the very nature of most of the Third World's existing regimes. Far from envisioning even partial reforms along those lines, most of the states concerned have been incapable of directing foreign investments toward economic sectors in a manner consistent with the interests of economic development.

In Latin America, to take just one continent, in the decade of the 1960s, growth of GNP (taking into account population growth) was at 2.3 percent annually, a lower rate than the one set in 1961 by the Alliance for Progress, which was already modest in its expectations. Behind this overall average rate were varied situations: a few countries made progress, while most of the others stagnated or fell behind. Outstanding in the first category were Brazil and Mexico, where large industrial firms had made heavy investments since they were both already industrially advanced and politically safe, along with a few others, such as Costa Rica and Panama. The second and by far the largest category included Paraguay, Ecuador, Honduras, Argentina, Chile, and Uruguay—countries in which per-capita agricultural production remained stable or even dropped, as in Peru, Argentina, Chile, and Colombia. Industry made small improvements, but except for Chile during the Allende period in the early 1970s, and to some extent Peru, structures were not even slightly changed anywhere. Simultaneously, because a large fraction of domestic savings was turned away from productive sectors, and the need grew to reimburse foreign capital that had already been invested, it became necessary to rely heavily on foreign financing, which in turn increased indebtedness. At the current pace, the $20 billion or so of debts in 1970 will probably reach $100 billion well before 1980.

During the same decade, the GNP in Southeast Asia (again taking population growth into account) rose at an annual rate of 1.7 percent. There was some increase in a few export crops, such as rice and jute. Industrial production increased and diversified, but almost exclusively in the realm of processing of export goods. At any rate, this growth affected only the few countries that got the full benefit of American aid and investment: Taiwan's and South Korea's exports increased by 38 percent and 21 percent respectively. But all these economies—especially those whose rapid growth took place thanks to foreign capital and markets (primarily American)—are extraordinarily fragile and dependent. Also noteworthy is the complete absence of any kind of reform, especially agrarian reform, in the part of the world where it is most called for. A very minor percentage of investments went to agriculture, on which two-thirds of the population directly depend for their living. Finally, one can observe in the countryside a growing gap in the standard of living between rich and poor, since the "green revolution" has mainly profited landowners—this is particularly the case in the Philippines and in India—who are able to make investments.

In short, the industrialized capitalist states control Asia, Africa, and Latin America to their own profit. Their control keeps production, political, and ideological relationships static, and development becomes impossible. Development, far from being a technical problem for economic experts (who at best can introduce improvements or stopgaps here or there, but who cannot make structural changes), is above all a political problem. Moreover, it is the extreme gap between rich and poor people in Third World societies that brings this problem out in its full dimensions.

Most existing institutions and structures in the underdeveloped countries get in the way of any real development. They are kept in place thanks to the alliance between Western capitalism and corrupt local ruling classes. This combination—domination exercised by the industrial capitalist countries, and the inability (or refusal) of the local ruling classes to free themselves from that domination—accounts for the stagnation of the Third World.

Technical improvements and partial reforms can alleviate the most serious contradictions, but they cannot overcome the pervasive crisis affecting the Third World. To escape from underdevelopment, these countries cannot count on foreign currency earned by exports, for the exchange is too unequal. They can only count on the mobilization of their own material and human resources. And in some countries, these resources do not amount to much; the very possibility of change is limited, unless perhaps within a regional grouping. The national economies remain specialized, and specialized, moreover, according to the needs of industrialized countries. The orientation of investments keeps the Third World dependent on the West, which provides the essential markets. (It should be noted that foreign aid usually also indirectly subsidizes the industrial capitalist countries that give it, to the extent that much of it is given not freely, but for the purchase of equipment manufactured by the donor country. At least three-quarters of foreign aid winds up back in the country that "gave" it.)

The New Delhi Conference (1971) set 1 percent of the national income of the industrial countries as the proportion that should go to aid the Third World. In fact, that aid has dropped from 0.83 percent in 1961 to 0.69 percent in 1965, and even further in the 1970s. But these statistics do not stand for any precise reality, since aid rarely helps in any real sense of the word.

According to Tibor Mende, an expert whose authority is based on many years' work in international organizations concerned with these problems, real aid amounts to 0.2 percent of the national product of the rich countries. As for private philanthropic aid to the Third World, in economic terms it is only a drop in the bucket.

For twenty years, "aid" has everywhere proved incapable of changing the situation in which the people of the underdeveloped countries find themselves. India, which was supposed to be a model of accelerated and democratic development, has scarcely managed to make any changes at all in the living conditions of most of its peasant population. Exceptionally, a few countries, such as Brazil, Iran, and Ivory Coast, have managed, although in a dependent and precarious way, thanks to abundant resources or progressive reforms, to register a more than negligible degree of growth over the last few years—but the fruits have scarcely benefited the majority of the population.

In the last analysis, aid serves the trade interests and still more the strategic and political designs of industrialized capitalist countries. In maintaining and spreading influence, aid is, after all, the cheapest thing at hand. United States aid in the course of the 1950s and 1960s went especially to Formosa, South Korea, and South Vietnam. France directs its aid mainly toward the franc zone. Such "aid," whose free portion constantly drops, deepens the indebtedness of the poor countries and drives more and more of them to the point where they can see no prospect ahead but that of chronic debt.

3. The Emergence of Third Worldism

Right after World War II, the world was characterized by a political bipolarity which lasted until the early 1960s. Subsequently, divergences turning to outright rivalry between China and the Soviet Union—along with the gradual loosening of absolute Soviet hegemony over what is conventionally called the Socialist camp—the Gaullist questioning of the Atlantic order, and American recognition of China introduced a new era in international relations. During these two periods, spread over thirty eventful years, occurred the liquidation of the colonial empires and the emergence of Asian and African nations previously under the wing of a few Western countries.

Abruptly in September 1945, Ho Chi Minh proclaimed to the crowds in Hanoi the independence of Vietnam. The following year, formal independence was granted to the Philippines by the United States (which actively helped to put down the Huk rebellion soon after). A similar process took place in Malaya, where British troops gradually managed to put down a Communist rebellion supported by the indigenous Chinese, and then granted independence to the Malay Muslim upper classes. India obtained independence in 1947, and the tensions which the British had sharpened between Hindus and Muslims led to a splitting of the country in two: the Indian Union and Pakistan (West and East, the latter now having become Bangladesh). Indonesia, after a violent struggle against Dutch rule, gained independence in 1949.

This was the year of the most important event in the colonized or semicolonized world since the end of World War II: the triumph of the Chinese revolution. Here was a major upheaval involving one-fourth of the human race, joined in a single homogeneous nation, heir to a rich civilization, whose peasantry had always been unusually hard-working and resourceful, and what is more, with a really first-rate intelligentsia

During this time, France, pushed out of Vietnam by the Japanese invasion, and trying since 1945 to get back in by force of arms, got bogged down in a colonial war in Indochina which led to its defeat at Dien Bien Phu in 1954. The Korean War of 1950–53 ended in partial victory for both sides. In fact, around 1952–54, less than five years after the Chinese revolution, situations stabilized and the first postwar period came to an end.

For the most part Asian countries gained their independence during the years right after World War II, but things were not the same on the African continent. The 1955 Bandung Conference of Afro-Asian Nations, while essentially an Asian conference, nevertheless marked the first appearance on the international political scene of a world that only yesterday had been completely under the sway of Western powers. Meanwhile, France, only a few months after Dien Bien Phu became involved in another colonial war, this time in Algeria.

In 1956 Britain and France, in conjunction with Israeli forces, responded to Egypt's nationalization of the Suez Canal with their last major colonial expedition. It was a fiasco. North Africa, except for Algeria, gained independence, and, in 1957, the Gold Coast was the first colonial state of tropical Africa to become sovereign, taking the name Ghana. In 1958 a revolution in Iraq overthrew the Hashemite dynasty set up by the British, while Guinea, by answering no in a Gaullist referendum in 1958 on adherence to the French Community, became the first independent state among France's West African possessions. Soon after, thanks to the war of liberation carried on by the Algerian Front for National Liberation, all of the African territories under French domination, with the exception of French Somalia (essentially the port of Djibouti) and the islands of Reunion and the Comoros, won formal independence. British decolonization, after the episode against the Mau Mau uprising in Kenya, proceeded steadily from 1957 to 1965, with only one serious hitch, the secession of Rhodesia. The ups and downs of decolonization in the former Belgian Congo between 1960 and 1965, notably the short-lived secession of Katanga, were accompanied by bloodshed and violence.

The sudden expansion of national liberation movements of the Communist type lasted from 1945 to 1954—with two defeats, in the Philippines and Malaya, one victory, in China, and two half-victories, in Vietnam and Korea. The national liberation movement of the anticolonialist type, with no social goals in particular, blossomed until the beginning of the sixties, at which time virtually all the colonies had formal independence. The second phase of Western efforts to check Communist (or Communist-sympathizing) movements began with South Vietnam, reaching the point of direct intervention of American troops in South Vietnam (1965), the bombing of North Vietnam, and the more limited although serious American interventions in Laos and Cambodia. Nineteen sixty-five was also the year when a coup d'etat against Sukarno in Indonesia made it possible to liquidate a regime friendly in Peking and the largest Communist party in "free" Asia.

In the Middle East, while Dr. Mossadegh's efforts to carry out an oil policy in accord with Iranian interests failed, in Egypt Colonel Nasser managed to score a point by nationalizing the Suez Canal. The Americans, blinded by their anti-Communist obsession, failed to take the proper measure both of Egypt's longing for national dignity and of the limits of Egypt's petty-bourgeois nationalism and consequently pushed Egyptian leaders toward the Soviet Union. The example was subsequently followed by other Arab countries—Syria, Iraq—faced with a United States policy of vigorous support to Israel, Jordan, and Saudi Arabia.

In these confrontations, Africa played only a very minor role. With the exception of the Congo (now Zaire), events there were scarcely a matter of concern to the United States, which in any case had not worked out a clear African policy. Meanwhile France intervened in Gabon in 1965 and in Chad in 1970 to safeguard the neocolonial status quo.

In the Western Hemisphere, the United States responded to Castro's Cuban revolution with a blockade, an invasion at the Bay of Pigs, and plans for a Latin American Alliance for Progress. The Cuban missile crisis in 1962 was the clearest sign of the limits of what the United States was ready to endure in its traditional area of domination. Counterinsurgency training centers turned out nearly 20,000 Latin American experts to be used in Colombia, Guatemala, Bolivia. In 1964, a coup d'etat in Brazil brought pro-American military men to power. The following year, the United States intervened directly in the Dominican Republic. Finally, the Americans actively lent a hand in liquidating the Allende experiment in Chile.

Meanwhile, following the Bandung Conference of 1955, a

certain number of countries attempted with questionable success to create a stance of nonalignment, independent of both the main blocs. This attempt, at least in the foreign policy field, owed its conception to Yugoslavia, which, as a Communist country that broke away from Moscow, was in a unique position. Yugoslavia's most faithful allies were then Egypt and, especially, India. During the 1950s, indeed, India enjoyed great prestige, due to a variety of factors: it had become independent under the aegis of Gandhian nonviolence, idealized by international public opinion; it enjoyed a British-style parliamentary democracy (though this concealed a cruel and violent world of pitiless social stratification); Nehru and his neutrality between the great powers were enormously popular; finally, to many people, especially in the United States, India embodied an original attempt to seek a third way (which others saw as illusory) between capitalism and socialism, which might provide a model for democratic development in the face of "totalitarian" China.

But in fact, until the late 1960s, there was virtually no way to escape the world's bipolarity. Egypt as well as India found themselves allied with the Soviet Union. In the meantime, however, alliances and alignments managed to loosen on both sides.

In Africa, Guinea's no in the 1958 referendum was a rejection of colonial rule that only the Mau Mau rebellion and the Union of the Cameroon Populations had foreshadowed by armed struggle. Guinea's initial policies raised short-lived revolutionary hopes, which sympathizers soon transferred to Mali, where adherence to "scientific socialism" was proclaimed in 1961. Algeria won independence in 1962, after a lengthy armed struggle, and became a land of refuge for most of the revolutionary movements of Africa and even Asia. In the Portuguese colonies, the armed struggle was initiated in Angola in 1961 was taken up with undeniable success in Guinea-Bissau in 1963, and Mozambique followed in 1964. In South Africa, some nationalist groups responded to the Sharpeville massacre by organizing urban terrorism (1961–64) which attracted a certain amount of attention. In Brazzaville, street demonstrations led to the collapse of Fulbert

Youlou's neocolonialist regime in 1963. The following year, Zanzibar wiped out the "feudal" regime of the Arab landlords, and in 1964 a revolution overthrew the conservative regime of Marshal Abbud in the Sudan.

Looking at Africa some years later, one sees that political movements—for instance in Senegal, Niger, and Cameroon—which sought to oppose the new nations' formally independent regimes have failed. Much the same can be said of the predominantly ethnic or religious movements in southern Sudan and Biafra. The situation is better in Chad and Eritrea, whose movements are supported by Arab countries. South Africa is solidly controlled by white racists; Rhodesia has lined up with South Africa. Only the nationalists in the Portuguese colonies have, under difficult conditions, kept up their struggle with relative success —notably in Guinea-Bissau and in Mozambique until 1974.

Most of the regimes which used to be considered somewhat revolutionary have been eliminated by coups d'etat: Nkrumah's in Ghana, Modibo Keita's in Mali, Ben Bella's in Algeria (although the Ben Bella regime was replaced by a similar one). Others which survived do not look revolutionary today—Guinea, Egypt. The People's Republic of the Congo continues to go through "socialist" metamorphoses while its economy remains in the hands of foreign interests. Compared to what generally prevails on the continent, Tanzania, with Somalia, stands out as the only country where corruption is not the main characteristic of the regime, even though in fact the country's "socialism" can boast of very few Socialists other than its President, Julius Nyerere, and a few one-time officials who have been dismissed.

With the Cuban Revolution, Latin America finally made an appearance on the contemporary world stage with something other than the usual travesty of endless *pronunciamientos* and *juntas*. The idea that the apocalypse of continental revolution was imminent, through creation of guerrilla *focos* drawn on the Cuban model, and the illusion that the revolution could actually take power within a short time, became widespread. The early 1960s saw a whole series of guerrilla bush fires suddenly flare up and then die down, as numerous as they were fleeting, along with a few movements of greater scope: the Venezuelan Armed Front for National Liberation, the "Independent Republics" in Colombia (1964), the Guatemalan guerrillas. The failure of the foco theory was brought home dramatically by the death of Che Guevara in Bolivia in 1967, shortly after the Organization of Latin American Solidarity had met in Havana. For a time, the hopes of those who had acknowledged the failure of rural guerrilla warfare based on focos were turned toward urban guerrilla warfare, in Brazil and especially in Uruguay. Meanwhile, no condemnation of the 1968 Soviet intervention in Czechoslovakia was forthcoming from Cuba; Cuba's economic problems steadily worsened, culminating in the semifailure of the *zafra,* the predicted 10-million-ton sugar crop (a failure predicted by several economists well before the Cuban leadership decided to launch the campaign for it, incidentally). A few insurrectional groups are still fighting on in Latin America against heavy odds. More than a dozen years after the Cuban revolution the only significant social changes that have taken place occurred thanks to a very special Chilean experiment, crushed in the military putsch of September 1973.

The Middle East was late in finding a place in revolutionary Third World mythology, on account of the petty-bourgeois nationalism of even the most vociferous Arab "revolutionaries" (as in the Ba'ath parties). Interest in that area developed only with the appearance of the Palestinian resistance movement, after the military defeat suffered by the Arab states in the war of June 1967 enabled the Palestinians to assert their own identity. Until the main body of its military forces were wiped out by the Hashemite monarchy in Jordan in 1970, this basically nationalist movement for the most part mimicked in form and rhetoric the whole range of Third World revolutionary struggles from the preceding decade, without ever managing to come to grips with its own peculiar situation.

In Asia, Third Worldism—whose distant sources are the Chinese revolution and Dien Bien Phu, that Waterloo of colonialism—is connected to the war in Vietnam, especially following direct American intervention in 1965. The war in Vietnam embodies the very model of the Third World myth: a war of the people victoriously resisting the most powerful imperialism. But it is more than that, not only by its exceptional nature, but because it is one of the major factors that determined the limits of American hegemony.

4. Neocolonialism in Tropical Africa

In tropical Africa, several new social groups made their appearance during the colonial period: the agents of colonial power (whether political or economic), educated elites of the modern type, wealthy planters, traders, small businessmen, and salaried employees. A new stratification began to form, and the process was considerably hastened by independence. (The rural sector, while influenced by such developments as the introduction of a money economy, remained closer to traditional patterns. Some rural communities lived from subsistence farming, some from growing export crops, while still others, in between, produced food for the domestic market.)

During the colonial period, traditionalism embodied the kind of resistance to the colonizer which first and foremost consisted of rejection and refusal. The first agent of modernization was the political party, an organization new to Africa, created by modernist elites to mobilize the population with a view to independence and sometimes, to development. But on the whole, the first years of independence were marked by a return to a pseudotraditionalism, born partly from a real need to develop an African identity, but also from the leaders' desire to ward off social unrest and class conflict. A manipulation of tradition made it possible, by extolling African "communal democracy," to mask the social antagonisms, but then showed up once independence had been achieved. The notion was that the African peasantry's communal democracy should make it possible for Africans to adopt modern collectivist forms of organization with relative ease. This particular myth concerning the African peasantry was promoted by both the Senegalese and the Malian leaders during the period of Modibo Keita's "socialist" experiment, and the theme has been taken up once more by the Tanzanian leadership. This evaluation is based on the assumption that the traditional village community has been, in its essence, preserved. It is indeed true that most farming land in Africa is collectively owned. Small family production continues within the framework of the village community, plots being allotted to families for use. However, if collective ownership of the land remains the basis of the rural system, it is nonetheless marked by sharp social differentiation. The traditional structures survive in appearance and in prestige, but they are largely emptied of their former economic and social content. The increasing use of money, the harvesting of new crops, and the appearance of salary systems have undermined the old arrangements. Besides, the old-time villages were not egalitarian, even if they were only slightly stratified; while there was no such thing as private ownership of land, the existence of "patriarchal slavery" is proof enough that social differentiations were no less real for being less obvious.

It appears that in the sort of barter economy that prevailed in West Africa, native bourgeoisies could not develop under the system of direct administration as they did under the indirect colonial administration found, say, in the wealthier territories of Nigeria and the Gold Coast. Import-export trade was controlled by foreign capital, and most local trade was in the hands of Lebanese (in West Africa) or Indians (in East Africa). Commercial activity in the hands of Africans was limited to small trade or transportation. A few coastal countries like Ivory Coast had a bourgeoisie of plantation owners, but in general the demand for national independence arose among the petty bourgeoisie, the lower-ranking employees in the colonial administration. Indeed there was no other social category in tropical Africa capable of playing that role. In places where a planter bourgeoisie or an embryonic merchant bourgeoisie actually existed—as in

Nigeria, the Gold Coast or, to a lesser degree, Ivory Coast—the administrative bourgeoisie linked up with them. And in those quite numerous regions where the tribal chiefs held onto their powers, alliances were generally formed with the bourgeoisie. There too, independence was followed by an accentuation of strong social differences (less so in the poorer countries of the interior). In the less prosperous countries such as Guinea, Mali, or Tanzania, the nationalist movements created by the petty urban bourgeoisie did not have to ally with any merchant or rural bourgeoisie since there were none, and sought instead by way of mass parties to guide if not to mobilize the peasantry. This process was accompanied by a weakening of the power of the tribal chiefs.

In the 1970s, Africa looked politically much the same as it had around 1960, when most of the continent became independent. A score of regimes had come and gone, replaced by other regimes whose basic orientation, with few exceptions (Ghana, Mali), was no different from that of their predecessors. Rarely did a change of regime lead to any radical social modifications worth noticing (Congo, Somalia). No large-scale, coherent revolutionary change has been wrought in social or economic life. Rhodesia, South Africa, and South-West Africa are still controlled by racist government, while Portugal has had nearly fifteen years of colonial war in its "overseas provinces."

The average annual growth rate for the whole of the continent during the first decade of African independence is about 2 percent after adjustment for population growth. An even greater dependence on the West than one finds in Asia or Latin America is characteristic of Africa, whether in the area of financial and monetary control, in the predominance of foreign firms, which is virtually absolute in tropical Africa, or in matters of language and culture. The deficits in the balance of payments and in state finances keep growing, while the Africanization of economic management is extremely slow. Regional disparities keep widening. While the states of the interior stagnate, a more rapid, though entirely dependent, growth can be seen in the coastal countries where plantation farming has recently been developed

(Ivory Coast, or Liberia, whose average annual growth is around 5 percent), but that growth is very unbalanced and fragile. The return flow of profits on foreign capital is, needless to say, far greater than the flow of capital investment and aid.

The political and social uses of foreign aid in tropical Africa make it an instrument of corruption, a basic neocolonialist trait. Here it can be seen that aid aims at reinforcing a leadership group linked by self-interest to Western capitalism. This group, drawn from among the officials who led the independence movements, governs on behalf of their personal interests from the moment when formal independence allows them to consume a large part of the national income. This administrative bourgeoisie accumulates capital but it seldom invests, and then only in the sectors that pay off quickest, such as real estate. The theme of "national union," once used in the struggle against colonialism, is now used to cover up conflicting interests and social contradictions.

Aside from the balkanization and underpopulation of the region, certain traits of African society are in themselves enough to retard development. On the whole, the peasantry enjoys a tradition of fairly easy work; the staple food crops of yam and cassava require only a few dozen days' work per year. The general irresponsibility which prevailed under the colonial regimes, when each and every task was considered a form of servitude imposed by the colonizer, the prevalence then of forced labor—all this made people produce as little as possible in order to give the minimum to the settler or the colonial state, and this could only develop strong negative attitudes toward productive activity. In addition, the family structure has been and continues to be favorable to parasitism. Salaried employees in African cites find themselves looking after any number of relatives who, although of working age, live by sponging off them. This sort of solidarity, while relieving problems of unemployment and underemployment, reduces the possibility of savings—and investment—if it does not rule them out altogether.

Of course, barely fifteen years ago Africa was almost entirely under colonial domination. A step has been taken: formal independence. Some states have even tried to escape the direct economic grip of foreign capitalism by undertaking a series of nationalizations. But nowhere has a leadership emerged able (or really wanting) to avoid strengthening the administrative bourgeoisie, or to control if not get rid of its economic and political power.

The overwhelming majority of African countries had independence handed to them. Among the former French colonies, for instance, all the regimes (other than that of Guinea) were set up by France within a neocolonial framework. Could they have made other choices or behaved differently than they did? Is it shocking that the leadership segments of these regimes are corrupt? On the contrary, the paradox would have been if they had adopted the sort of revolutionary austerity needed to promote development centered on local needs. Still, without there being any qualitative change, nearly half the original regimes have been overthrown; Brazzaville in 1963 is the rare case of urban masses participating in a violent political action.

The creation of the Organization of African Unity (OAU) in 1963, and the way it has operated ever since, merely reflects these realities, even though the OAU, at least at the start, favored a revolutionary rhetoric. According to the opening statements at Addis Ababa, the OAU set out to fight "against colonialism, neocolonialism and imperialism." In fact, very few African states provided aid to the liberation movements in the Portuguese colonies, for example. In early 1964, *The Spark* of Accra published a study on the role of the Committee of the Nine, set up at the Addis Ababa conference to coordinate aid to national liberation movements. It came out in this report that in fact, the committee had not devoted even the tiniest fraction of its budget to military aid; 63 percent of the money at its disposal went to propaganda and 37 percent to operating expenses. Only three or four countries have agreed (temporarily) to grant asylum to opponents of governments in power. And despite the decision to boycott South Africa, numerous states have kept up trade relations with the land of apartheid, while Ivory Coast has gone so far as to suggest a continent-wide normalization of relations with Pretoria. Furthermore, it is obvious that the boycott was basically a symbolic gesture of hostility. The extent to which the political forces attached to the idea of true African independence carry no real weight may be seen in their utter failure to bring enough pressure to bear on the Western nations (United States, Britain, France) to get them to revise their policies toward South Africa.

Voices were raised in Africa even before the Addis Ababa conférence in an attempt to discuss the real problems, but in the euphoria of newly achieved independence, they no doubt seemed premature. On the whole the problems have remained disguised. For example, the notion that African states are "proletarian nations" has tended to conceal the existence of ruling classes enjoying broad privileges. Leopold Sedar Senghor asserts that there are no classes in Senegalese society, but rather "three technico-professional groups: the liberal professions, wage-earners, and the peasants (including shepherds, fishermen, and craftsmen)." He states that if there is a bourgeoisie in Senegal, it is made up of civil servants, clerks, and workers whose earnings are far higher than the peasants'. In varying degrees, all the independent states of Africa are marked by well-developed administrative bourgeoisies which grew rapidly after independence.

To illustrate this process, we have taken as an example the year 1964 (barely four years after independence) in the states formerly colonized by France, for which we possess particularly good statistics. (It should be noted that only three—Ivory Coast, Ghana, Cameroon—did *not* have an unfavorable trade balance.) Consuming a large share of the national income, the petty bourgeoisie, having gained access to the apparatus, thanks to its education, strengthens its economic hold—the state serving as its instrument of accumulation. To see what this class consumes, how parasitic it is, and why it is not working harder to develop a self-reliant national economy, we might compare imports by these fourteen countries of goods and equipment useful to the overall development of society with luxury imports. The latter imports are by their very nature unproductive and benefit a minority of less than 3 percent of the population. For the fourteen countries, the total of a few of the most obvious unproductive items amounted to twice that of a few of the productive necessities essential to improvement in agricultural production, on which more than three-quarters of the population depended.

IMPORTS of 14 AFRICAN COUNTRIES
in millions of C.F.A. francs (1964) *

Alcoholic beverages	7294.2	Tractors	3741.5
Private motorcars	5592.6	Machine tools	2478.1
Gas for private cars	3561.6	Fertilizers	1517.8
Perfumes & cosmetics	1269.1	Farm tools & equip.	1200.0
Total	17,717.5	*Total*	8,937.4

* SOURCE OF FIGURES: *Marchés Mediterranéens et Tropicaux,* No 1054 Paris, 1965.

But the contrast between what the governments spend on themselves and what they spend on their countries is even more striking. In the 1964–65 budget in Senegal, routine government expenses amounted to 33,975 million C.F.A. francs; by main blocks of outlay, this was divided as follows: public debt 4.1 percent; highest governmental bodies (National Assembly, president's office, Economic and Social Council) 2.8 percent; administrative ministries 37.8 percent; economic ministries 16 percent; social and cultural ministries 24 percent; joint expenses 14.9 percent. By type of expense, the cost of government personnel accounted for 16,050 million C.F.A. francs, or almost half the total (with equipment 19.5 percent; upkeep 5.5 percent; and miscellaneous expenses counting for 28 percent of the total). The report of the Senegal Commission of Finance and Planning, from which these figures are drawn, concluded: "We are spending twice as much for personnel as for actual operations and maintenance. This distribution obliges us to reconsider the structures of our budget. . . . Because operational expenses are currently running higher than revenue, we have been unable to put a single franc into investment, while at the same time we have constantly had to borrow to finance the plan."

The case of Senegal was not unusual; in all the other states as well, the budget for supplies and equipment was insignificant compared to the budget for operational expenses, while everywhere outlay for personnel was very high. In Cameroon, operating expenses for the year studied were 18,550 million C.F.A. francs, while equipment was only 1409 million. Construction and building purchases for government and military offices amounted to almost half of this already very low figure. The government insisted that the operational expenses were "strictly in line with what is necessary to assure normal operation of government services," and it is true that at the time an effort was needed to put down a revolutionary uprising led by the Union of Cameroon Populations. Nonetheless, the appropriations for government operations seemed disproportionate in such an underdeveloped country (in millions of C.F.A. francs for fiscal 1964–65): Foreign Affairs 567; National Economy 320; Finance, Planning and National Equipment 1120; Armed Forces 3600.

In the Central African Republic, a report introducing the finance bill remarked that austerity "is the rule in French-speaking Africa, but while many came to that decision only by the unfortunate path of revolutions or abortive coups d'etat, it is good to see that in the Central African Republic, national solidarity and the political maturity of the population allow the government to reorient its activity along those lines." But all these assertions were contradicted by actual events, including a military coup d'etat. In 1964, operating expenses accounted for 81 percent of all public expenses, compared to 74 percent in 1963; and yet "the appropriations retained [were] 1200 million below the requests of the various parties," and cost of personnel amounted to 58 percent of the budget. In Congo, the cost of the 10,931 employees or agents of the government accounted for 62 percent of the budget—this out of a total population of about 825,000. In Ivory Coast, personnel accounted for 58 percent of the budget; less than 15,000 officials, or *less than 0.5 percent of the population* of Ivory Coast, which counts 3,750,000 inhabitants, absorbed the lion's share. (Only in 1972 did the unbalanced state of the budget lead to "austerity" measures, cutting back luxury expenses in the higher ranks of the administration—slightly reducing the number of official cars, for example.) In Dahomey, Madagascar, and Togo the figures were very similar.

These somewhat boring, but devastating, figures show the place occupied from the start by the administrative bourgeoisie and the use it makes of public funds. This situation provides one of the fundamental explanations for the perpetual imbalance of most of the independent nations of Africa, as well as for the instability of most of their governments.

PART ONE:
THE POLITICAL STRATEGY OF ARMED STRUGGLE

The general principles of guerrilla warfare are and always have been fairly simple. Clausewitz, to start with modern treatments of the subject, although he only touched on it in passing, offered a precise description and analysis of its necessary conditions and rules.

In the Clausewitzian conception, people's war, formed with the awakening of modern nationalism in Europe, is a peasant war of national resistance to an aggressor. In the twentieth century, the nationalist element continues to be fundamental, but it may be reinforced, if not motivated, by social issues which has been the case in the most important revolutionary wars (China, Indochina). Western industrial capitalism induced certain local upper classes, especially landed aristocracies, to collaborate in extending their hegemony; thus a war mobilizing the people was intended to shake off two yokes at once, the priorities depending on the country's status: semicolonial in the case of China, meaning the struggle against the Kuomintang was put first; colonial in the case of Indochina, where the fight against the French came first. (In both cases, Japanese aggression was also an important factor.)

The contemporary contributions to the general laws of people's war, essentially Chinese and Vietnamese, appear in fact to be not primarily military, but rather political. What is new is not so much the use of irregular troops or units to harass a more powerful enemy until it is worn out (if not wiped out), but rather the political organization of poverty-stricken peasants, moved to action by hunger for land, justice, and dignity. Credit must go to Mao Tse-tung for having grasped the full importance of the peasant question in a backward country—not only grasping it but making its primacy clear and understanding all its ramifications. And to the Vietnamese must go credit for having managed to build a political-military infrastructure within the peasantry itself which a whole array of modern technology (to which, incidentally, they also managed to adapt) could not succeed in breaking. Finally, Mao Tse-tung and Vo Ng-uyen Giap systematized the concepts as well as the political and military precepts of a people's war in our time.

Compared to these two, the classic examples of modern people's war, all other guerrilla efforts, whether in Latin America, Africa, the Middle East, or Southeast Asia, are minor; but a comparative study of a certain number of selected cases is instructive.

Armed conflicts in Africa may be classified in three types, sharply differentiated by their settings, their goals, and their chances of success:

Anticolonialist ones waged under a "national" banner: the Algerian war for independence is a classic example here. This category covers the "national" liberation wars in the Portuguese colonies of Angola, Guinea-Bissau, and Mozambique, and the conflicts—even if embryonic or strangled in the cradle—in South Africa and Rhodesia, although they are somewhat in a class by themselves, because control in both countries is exercised directly and along race lines by local white communities rather than by colonialists.

The efforts (most of them poorly coordinated and brief) made by organizations in formally independent countries: the Union of the Populations of Cameroon, which drew its initial strength from the liberation struggle against French rule in 1957–60; the SAWABA in Niger; and various groups in Zaire, such as the National Committee of the Revolution of Mulele in 1964–65.

Basically ethnic or religious struggles (or both), with sometimes revolutionary overtones, within a formally independent country (vice versa: in Africa anti-imperialist or supposedly revolutionary struggles often have ethnic or religious overtones). This category covers struggles begun by minority groups such as in South Sudan, Biafra, the National Liberation Front of Chad (even though the movement likes to consider itself national), and Eritrea.

Obviously the national liberation struggles directed against colonialism are the most likely both to arouse popular support and to attract at least some international backing, and for this reason it is instructive to take a closer look at two important examples from North and West Africa.

But in an eminently political type of war, what matters is for the rebel forces to survive; the mere fact of not being destroyed is a victory in itself. Guerrilla warfare makes it possible to present the political issues in violent and unambiguous terms not only to the masses in whose name the fight is waged, but to the adversary as well. As a rule, national liberation wars are conflicts between oppressed peoples and "democratic" mother countries which send armed forces to repress the rebel movement. If the guerrilla force manages to grow or merely to survive—once it has gained the political support of part of the population—then, with time, the cost of the war, the growth of peace movements, the weariness of the public (or even the armed forces), and sometimes the clearsightedness of leaders in the mother country make a negotiated settlement look like the lesser evil. But the defeat of the mother country is essentially political. The French defeat at Dien Bien Phu, if it had occurred in a noncolonial war, would have meant merely the loss of a major battle; the Viet Minh had merely defeated the French expeditionary corps, not the able-bodied forces of the entire French nation, who were in fact reluctant to be involved in the conflict. Similarly, the Algerian FNL did not defeat the French army, but offered practical proof that Algeria's status as a colony (partly disguised by the myth that it was an integral part of France) could not be maintained.

Compared to this type of situation, the case of Portugal in Africa was, until 1974, special, in that the mother country did *not* have a democratic regime; news was censored; opposition within Portugal to the government was gagged or eliminated.

armed
struggle in
Latin America

1. Guerrilla Inflation: The *Foco* Theory as a Theory for Failure

While some conservatives (in France, for example, during the Algerian war, and the United States during the Vietnam war) have insisted that any revolutionary war can be defeated (thus successfully mixing up the political issue with military questions), a considerable fraction of the Far Left has simultaneously spread and elaborated the myth of the invincibility of guerrilla warfare. Examples were available to support either of the two theses. Among theoreticians and upholders of counterinsurgency, much was naturally made of how the Greek resistance was wiped out just after World War II, or the Huks in the Philippines as

well as the British Army's patient destruction of guerrilla movement in Malaya. Supporters of guerrilla warfare—or of people's
war—for their part cited the example of the Chinese revolution,
the first Indochina war which ended with Dien Bien Phu, the
success of Castro's guerrillas; and last but not least, wasn't the
National Liberation Front of South Vietnam holding its own
against the most formidable military power in the world? The
failures in Greece, the Philippines, and Malaya were far away,
in space or in time. So the myth was able to spread—thanks
largely to the diffusion of Mao Tse-tung's military writings, the
easy victory of the Castroists in Cuba, the stir caused by Frantz
Fanon's work, first in Latin America and then in Africa just after
Algerian independence (although the victory of the Algerian
Front for National Liberation was political and not at all military). All too rarely was the distinction made—a decisive distinction—between wars of national liberation waged against a foreign, colonizing or aggressor element, and class struggles in the
proper sense of the term within a given society. This is not to
deny that the two elements might not be combined in some cases.
Nevertheless, within the last decade, the number of failures, the
number of times that meager guerrilla forces in underpopulated
areas were stamped out, the many retreats and reversals in one
place after another, did not go unnoticed.

A few further general remarks are necessary. In Latin America the echo, if one may call it that, of most guerrilla wars was
far greater than the actual scope of the operations. Verbal inflation was the characteristic of "revolutions" which for the most
part were made up of a few dozen combatants without much in
the way of support, at the most a few hundred men. In the past
fifteen years, only a few guerrilla movements in Latin America
have in either scope or durability amounted to more than minor
uprisings (Colombia, Venezuela, Guatemala, Uruguay). That the
echo could be amplified so many times no doubt has something
to do with Western ethnocentrism: the revolutionaries were white,
"one of us," closer on the cultural level (the Mexican revolution
of 1910 is in varying ways an integral part of the Western sensi-

bility). And last but not least, the personality and physical appearance of Che Guevara, that "twentieth-century condottière," as he called himself in his letters, gave young people an idol with whom identification was both more direct and more appealing than with Ho Chi Minh, for instance.

The Cuban revolution did not spread to the Latin American continent, despite appearances which might have led one to believe that something of the sort was about to happen. In fact, even though there is a tradition of violence in Latin America, social revolutions, even limited, have been rare: Mexico (1910), Bolivia (1952), Cuba (1960) and, a short time ago, Chile (1970). These are rather few, considering that between about 1930 and 1970 one hundred twenty heads of state were replaced by other than constitutional methods. The failure of the Bay of Pigs invasion induced the Cubans, along with all Latin Americans anxious to promote revolution, to underestimate not only the difficulty of mobilizing people by and for guerrilla warfare, but also the determination of the United States, a determination later shown during the Cuban missile crisis in 1962, in the intervention in the Dominican Republic in 1965, and, with greater discretion, in the antiguerrilla campaign and the Chilean counterrevolution. With the passage of time, it has become obvious that it was virtually impossible to coordinate revolutionary forces on a continental scale in Latin America; that, in fact, there was no revolutionary Third World able to make itself felt in an organized way on the global chessboard, nor any "socialist camp" anxious to aid some hypothetical revolution on a continental scale, nor even some revolutionary state somewhere as attentive to the development of the revolution in Latin America as to its own national interests.

Castro's easy victory (what other recent guerrilla force can pride itself on coming to power after only two and a half years of fighting?) had originally given rise to the underestimation of incumbent governments and their repressive organs—backed up in case of need by specialized American forces—and to an overestimation of the people's readiness for revolution. Yet on the face of it, conditions looked favorable; most Latin American governments were inefficient and unstable, and some were heavily oppressive; none seemed designed to promote economic development or the modernization of political and social structures. The Alliance for Progress was a flop. What with the deterioration in terms of trade, Latin America's share in world trade had fallen in less than fifteen years to 5 percent. Income distribution was among the least egalitarian in the world, while the need for agrarian reform was unmistakable. So it was that among certain revolutionaries, encouraged by the Cuban success, hopes were high that by launching guerrilla operations, conditions could be created for radical change.

How was this guerrilla war to be waged? Revolutionary warfare in its modern form is not easy to summarize, but roughly speaking it includes three distinct phases. The *first,* a defensive phase, during which the revolutionary organization takes root among the people, is usually long and requires essentially political preparatory work. When the underground organization and its infrastructure have become strong, the *second* phase begins: now it becomes a matter of weakening the adversary little by little, to season one's fighting units while continuing steadily to extend control over the population. When a point of balance has been reached, the *third* phase consists in developing offensive operations with bigger and bigger units. Schematically, this is what happened in China, then in Indochina, and was in the process of happening in 1965 in South Vietnam when American troops intervened massively to save the Saigon regime.

The general lessons to be drawn from the experience of all the revolutionary wars that have enjoyed any degree of success, can be summed up in two basic points: 1. The objective and subjective conditions must be as ripe as possible, the most favorable situation being one of foreign domination or aggression, enabling the revolution to mobilize the broadest segments of society toward a goal that is both national and social; and 2. The organization of the guerrilla force—and, above all, its clandestine political structure, linked to the population—must be such that it will eventually allow the military guerrilla force to recruit, develop, and endure. These characteristics have essentially been lacking in Latin American guerrilla efforts—even in Colombia, which was the scene of the most widespread violence since the Mexican revolution. But another major reason for the failures of Latin American guerrillas just after the Cuban revolution lies in their attempt to put into practice the foco [1] theory, first formulated by Guevara and systematized by Régis Debray. Based on what seemed to him to be the lessons to be drawn from the Cuban revolution, Guevara, in his book *Guerrilla Warfare*, in 1960, argued that guerrilla fighters can defeat a regular army; the basic terrain of guerrilla war in Latin America should be in the countryside; and especially (and here lies his originality) revolutionaries need not and must not wait until all the objective conditions are right to launch their struggle, since the foco, the mobile focal point of insurrection, is able by its very existence to create them. In other words, Guevara called for imitation of the Cuban example and attached no basic importance to what made it special.

But if guerrilla warfare brought to power the group of survivors who came ashore in the *Granma,* the point is that there was no question *then,* in 1956, of setting up a socialist regime in Cuba that depended on many other factors.

Aside from the neutrality of the United States from 1956 to 1959, there were the varying degrees of participation in or benevolent neutrality toward the Castroist guerrilla effort—especially in Cuba's cities—on the part of people from diverse social backgrounds quite happy to see the end of the Batista tyranny but who did not wish or foresee the direction Castro took in 1960–61. It was only well after his conquest of power, in fact, that the radicalization became perceptible which was to lead to changes in Cuba's social and economic structures. The element of surprise, not to say misunderstanding, which allowed the revo-

---

[1] E. Guevara, *Guerrilla Warfare* (New York: Monthly Review Press, 1963).

lutionary Cuban leadership to make their revolution more and more radical, could not happen again.

Nonetheless the Cuban example gave rise throughout Latin America to both a revolutionary enthusiasm in some sectors of the urban middle classes and an ultravoluntarist strategy, which was inoperative if not downright suicidal. It is, at any rate, true that the activities of the Latin American Communist parties (few of which had much of a following anyway) had scant prospects to offer. Between 1962 and 1965 a few of them, in order not to be found lagging behind (in Venezuela, Colombia, Guatemala), took part in armed struggle, while they went on trying to arrange for the possibility of being accepted on the national chessboard as a legal political force. Simultaneously, it became obvious that the Soviet Union had no desire whatever to be stuck with supporting yet another Cuba.

The weakness of the foco theory, according to which one headed straight into armed struggle without any serious mobilization of the population, was precisely that it cut off the guerrilla fighters from popular support. This was amply demonstrated time and again: in the failures in Paraguay (Movement of 14 May 1959); Colombia (Workers-Students-Peasants Movement, MOEC, in 1961); Ecuador (Revolutionary Union of Ecuadorian Youth in 1962); the Dominican Republic (Revolutionary movement of May 14, in 1963); Argentina (1963, 1964, especially in the Tucuman region); Peru (the 1965 guerrilla efforts of the MIR and the ELN, which briefly tried to take root in the population); Brazil (repeated attempts throughout the decade); Honduras; Mexico; and finally Bolivia, with Guevara—not counting the many groups that came apart before even managing to get to the mountains. Even the groups that did (or still do) amount to something, whether rural (Venezuela, Guatemala) or urban (Brazil 1969–71, Uruguay), were on the whole cut off from the masses. Out of some fifteen countries where serious guerrilla activity broke out at least thirty times, only a few guerrilla centers are still remaining in a half-dozen countries. Among the most long-standing are: in Venezuela, the National Liberation Armed Forces (FALN), led by Douglas Bravo; in Guatemala, the Revolutionary Armed Forces (FAR) of Cesar Montes; in Colombia, the National Liberation Army (ELN) of Fabio Vasquez, as well as the Revolutionary Armed Forces of Colombia (FARC), more or less connected to the Communist party; in Nicaragua, the Sandinist National Liberation Front (FSLN) of Carlos Fonseca Amador; the Tupamaros in Uruguay; and the armed Trotskyist groups in Argentina. Mention can be made in passing of recent organizations in Brazil (heavily decimated) and Mexico (only in the most remote states, such as Sonora and Guerrero, where the Emiliano Zapata Armed Front of National Liberation and the Revolutionary National Civil Action operate, among others.)

Guevara's death in October 1967 provided a spectacular symbol of the failure of Cuban-style guerrilla activity inspired by the foco theory; but in reality the inadequacy of that theory had already been proved, even before its strategy was worked out systematically by Régis Debray in his book *Revolution in the Revolution*. Debray's work—which caused a considerable stir, what with the prestige of the Cuban revolution, Che's personality, and the theoretical weakness of guerrilla leadership in Latin America—analyzed four forms of action and organization: "armed self-defense"; armed propaganda; guerrilla bases; and the classic vanguard party. The initial weakness of the foco [2] is that it is without popular support for a more or less considerable length of time. It has only itself to rely on. But it is important to have a clear idea in advance of the social lay of the land before trying to take root. The point is to figure out ahead of time, by first-hand knowledge of local situations, which are the sectors within the peasantry that can be aroused and mobilized; it is best to know about the obstacles before running into them. Otherwise, guerrillas are doomed to survive only through their mobility in virtually uninhabited areas—like a lonely eagle on a mountain

---

[2] Sections of the following passage appeared in my review of *Revolution in the Revolution*, published in *Esprit* (Paris), November 1967. This review was considered too critical and consequently was turned down by several left-wing and Far-Left publications in France. And my criticisms seemed irrelevant to high Cuban officials in the euphoria of the conference of the Organization of Latin America Solidarity (OLAS, Havana, August 1967), where I was invited as an observer. But Debray has since published an autocriticism of the thesis of his entire book.

peak. And communication between a guerrilla group of urban origin and the rural peasant population is no simple matter. In Peru, where the guerrilla movement was crushed, it had no middle-level political organizers who came from the country or who were otherwise familiar with the peasants' day-to-day problems and able to talk with them in a language that touched them directly. Few could speak Quechua, and few had a thorough knowledge of the Indian problem.

Nor did Debray make any mention of another major problem: that of the cities and how to win them over politically. If coordination is not worked out between guerrilla activities and urban political struggle, the guerrillas are doomed forever to mark time in the countryside. It is certainly possible to start with a numerically weak foco, but it is still necessary to end up with mass organizations and careful political work, notably among workers and students.

Debray concluded that "guerrilla warfare is the crucible from which the party will be forged" and that "the people's army will be the nucleus of the party, not the other way round"—a conclusion influenced by the fact that for most Latin American Communist parties, survival of the party apparatus had long since become the supreme goal at the expense of the revolution itself. But it is important not to let one dogmatism be replaced by another.

If the Leninist conception of a vanguard party made up of professional revolutionaries suggests a certain voluntarism, the Cuban conception of a vanguard cut off at the start from the population it intends to involve and lead into the struggle is going as far in the voluntarist direction as it is possible to go. And it is for this reason that any number of focos have not begun to worry about setting up a future party, for they have ceased to exist before reaching the stage of grappling with that problem.

Even the urban guerrillas of Latin America did not prove immune to focoism, despite their desire to avoid it. However, it was the Tupamaros of Uruguay who, contrary to the Cuban model and with all due respect for local factors, managed to set up the best-structured revolutionary organization on the continent. Nonetheless, a decade of guerrilla activities led only to a right-wing military reaction in Uruguay and a strengthening of the extreme Right in Guatemala. (In 1973, the Tupamaros undertook a general revision of their strategy, recognizing that the weakness of their links to the population had been the cause of their setbacks the year before.) In Venezuela, various constitutional governments little by little pushed the several guerrilla fronts there on the defensive. And the current crisis in Colombia can be explained more by the inability of the National Front to carry out reforms than by successful pressure brought by the various guerrilla groups.

Even putting aside international conditions, Latin American guerrillas lacked a strategy or a clear view of their national problems. Guevara noted in his diary two months before his death, "Not one peasant has yet joined the guerrilla group." Most of the time, the fighting groups knew little of the social milieu they intended to mobilize and almost always lacked middle-level organizers suited to do so. That lack of understanding extended to national factors as a whole. In this respect, the revolutionary myth of Latin America continentalism is rather similar to the myth of Arab nationalism. In both cases one can point to a common language, history, and cultural substratum, but in both cases there also exist significant disparities in the level of economic and cultural development which produce centrifugal influences. Continentalism may well be an exalting idea for parts of the intelligentsia, but for the peasant massess it is all the more abstract, in that integration on the national level is still so far from realized.

And lastly, in at least four countries where guerrilla action has taken place (Bolivia, Peru, Ecuador, Guatemala), the Indian question is of prime importance and requires special attention.

No large-scale rural guerrilla action is possible without the adherence of at least part of the Indian masses. Only Hugo Blanco,[3] in Peru, succeeded in mobilizing Indians, which he did in the early 1960s in the Valley of la Convencion. But then, he

---

[3] See his *Land or Death, the Peasant Struggle in Peru* (New York: Pathfinder Press, 1972). So far, only Blanco has raised the Indian question.

spoke Quechua at least enough to get along. In the Indian world, so violently crushed by physical poverty and so profoundly destructured, the Spanish of the white man only awakens distrust.

Compared to these major factors influencing political development in Latin America, the (usually indirect) intervention of the United States in counterinsurgency operations is of minor importance. True, the United States training center in Panama has turned out more than 20,000 specialists in counterinsurgency who are sent throughout Latin America. In Venezuela and Colombia, local armies have made successful use of these specialized corps. But success is due primarily to the weakness of the guerrillas' support structure and the flimsiness of their links with the population.

Considering the basic political strategy of revolutionary war —in which factors of time, space, and costs are of vital importance—it is impossible to disregard the scant taste exhibited in Latin America for patience, for the sense of the long haul on which revolutionary war depends. The space of revolutionary action, whether geographical or social, is almost always very limited, with so few sectors of society involved that the state and its machinery are never short of reliable allies. And high-level leaders, whose knowledge and prestige are needed to keep the struggle going, feel obliged both by the thinness of the ranks and by social pressure, by machismo, to risk their lives in combats which should not require their presence. Guevara, Camillo Torres, Luis de la Puente, Guillermo Lobaton, Fabricio Ojeda, Carlos Marighello, Yon Sosa, Inti Peredo, to mention only the best known—these grave losses are themselves a sign of the fragility of Latin American guerrilla movements. (By comparison, in a dozen years of war, only one of the fifty members of the central committee of the South Vietnamese National Liberation Front fell into the hands of the enemy.)

A certain number of other sociological traits common to most Latin American societies also need to be mentioned. While these would be secondary in a major war, with the revolution held together by a central revolutionary ideology, these traits weigh against successful action in other circumstances: verbal inflation, accompanied by slight ability to keep secrets; lack of group cohesiveness, worsened by an obsession with authority (what Latin American in charge of a dozen others resists proclaiming himself *comandante*?); machismo and fascination with death (largely products of the Hispanic tradition). The only group which seems to a large extent free of these traits is the Tupamaros, which developed out of a modern urban society with an industrial sense of relationship to time.

In short, the basic weakness up to now of guerrilla movements in Latin America has been their political inability to give rise to a disciplined organizational apparatus connected to a nationwide support structure. Nowhere in Latin America is there any sign that such an apparatus is being developed. In fact, the guerrillas' only serious outside support, Cuba, after Guevara's death gave up the idea of the imminent apocalypse of continental revolution and reduced its aid—at the same time agreeing to respect the positive aspects of regimes like that in Peru, whose reformism it would not have failed to criticize only a short time before. This change is no doubt due to Cuba's domestic economic and political problems, but is also due to the scant success of the guerrilla movements which, fifteen years after Sierra Maestra, have mostly proved to be ephemeral.

But if the guerrilla movements have not directly brought decisive changes in the continent, the Alliance for Progress has also failed; so have the Communist parties. Indirectly, the focos have brought many transformations. Nationalist feeling, as always directed against the United States, and kept alive in the cities mostly by the petty bourgeoisie, grew stronger in the decade following the Cuban revolution. This trend influenced, among others, a large number of junior military officers, who awakened to the idea that the ruling classes were corrupt and ineffective, ineffective in modernizing and developing the country and ineffectual in preserving national dignity. In this sense, the modernization experiments of the Peruvian military regime since 1968 are the result of the guerrilla movements of 1965.

Still, in the past ten years only three or four Latin American countries have undergone any noticeable economic or social changes. Elsewhere the problems that once gave rise to guerrilla movements are still there, the same as ever—indeed, worsened by the population explosion (the projected population of Latin America will be 380 million in 1980 and more than 600 million at the end of the century).

Yet at least for the foreseeable future, it is likely that contrary to the famous slogan of only a few years ago, there will not be a Vietnam in Latin America. The conditions are lacking, not for the launching, but for the successful conclusion of armed struggle. In the last analysis, the historic opportunity for Latin American revolutionaries to start with an organization and build up a broad support structure in the masses has never really existed. In reality, revolutionary wars were a phenomenon that came out of the context of World War II, with the considerable weakening of Western domination and with the experience of Japanese military occupation. It was that world crisis which made possible not the creation of an organization and a certain support structure, which already existed, but the victorious emergence of the Chinese revolution. From that crisis the long battle of the Vietnamese people drew its initial strength.

2. *Violencia* and Guerrillas: The Case of Colombia

Events during the last twenty-five years have made Colombia the classic case of armed violence in Latin America—by virtue of both the scope of peasant participation and the rural implantation which enabled a variety of guerrilla groups—Communist, Castroist, and pro-Chinese—to survive there.

Colombia has a long tradition of violence and armed struggle. More than ten civil wars broke out in Colombia during the nineteenth century, and *bandoleros* and *bandolerismo* are a long-standing feature of the national scene. In recent history, only the Mexican revolution offers an example of domestic violence comparable to Colombia between 1948 and 1958, when an estimated

100,000–300,000 persons fell victim to civil war; banditry spread through the provinces, followed by the formation (spurred by Communist organizers) of "independent republics"—such as Marquetalia. Since 1964, when the political guerrillas were decimated, three zones of insecurity continue to be held by guerrilla groups of divergent persuasions. None of these groups has been liquidated, and none has managed to enlarge its zone of influence. Underlying all this violence, what is the situation of Colombian society, especially rural society?

Larger than Texas and California combined, Colombia has only 22 million inhabitants. It has a coastline of 913 miles on the Pacific Ocean and 1094 miles on the Caribbean. East of the mountains, the inland *llanos* or plains, covering more than two-thirds of the country, are almost uninhabited. The economic and political life of the country is concentrated in the west, on three great ranges of the Andes, the Western, Central, and Eastern Cordilleras, separated by the Magdalena River and Cauca River valleys. The population of Bogotá, the capital, perched in the Eastern Cordillera, has more than quadrupled in thirty years, jumping from 450,000 in 1940 to more than 2 million in 1970. With ten cities counting more than 100,000 inhabitants, Colombia is relatively decentralized compared to neighboring Venezuela and Peru.

Every sort of climate is found in Colombia—not, as in Chile, going from north to south, but depending on the altitude. At the lowest level lies thick tropical jungle; temperate crops grow at a higher altitude; higher still, sparse mountain pastures are finally topped by glaciers. Enough coffee is grown in the middle range to make Colombia the second-largest producer of that crop in the world. The country also produces cotton, bananas, sugar cane, rice, tobacco, and hops. There is no lack of other resources: gold, platinum, emeralds (number-one world producer), and petroleum; 80 percent of the oil production belongs to North American companies, and Choco Pacific and Co., with North American capital, takes care of mining the emeralds, platinum, and gold. Barely 20 percent of the GNP comes from industry, meaning that Colombian economy continues to depend heavily on its coffee, half of which goes to the United States. If the price of coffee drops one cent a pound in New York, the Colombian economy stands to lose $8 million. (In fact, the price of coffee fell from 80 to 48 cents a pound between 1954 and 1964.)

The Caribbean coast of Colombia is a world of its own—a gay, dancing Caribbean world far removed from the bleak sadness of the Andes. The mulatto and black population here gives a special character to the region, which has remained untouched by the violence elsewhere in the country. Unlike the other Andean countries (Ecuador, Peru, Bolivia), Colombia is not largely or predominantly Indian. About half the population is racially mixed, Indian and white, but Spanish-speaking; 20 percent are white (almost all of Spanish origin), since the Catholic church—whose influence is stronger in Colombia than in any other Latin American country—did not encourage European immigration. There are only a few descendants of Germans from the Rhineland and Bavaria; about 23 percent are mulatto; 5 percent are black; the remaining 2 percent, Indians, continue to be decimated.[4]

It is usual to think of Latin American societies as not being racist—but this judgment is made by people who are often unfamiliar with these countries. It is true that the Mexican revolution of 1911 and the Bolivian revolution of 1952 saw an improvement in the social position of the *mestizos,* those of mixed Indian and Spanish ancestry; but the existing gap in Peru, say, between the highland Indians and the Lima bourgeoisie is enormous and unbridgeable. As for Colombia, the fact that the rural population is mestizo and Spanish-speaking narrows the gap but does not eliminate it. The general process of social stratification in the colonial era, in Colombia, as in the other Andean countries, was related to the problem of land appropriation. The mestizos then and now have been relegated to inferior social positions. While

---

[4] An excellent book on the Indians of Colombia is R. Jaulin, *La Paix blanche* (Paris: Seuil, 1971).

the white Hispanic elite, owning the land and controlling the administration, the army, and the church, deliberately avoided intermarriage and looked down on manual labor as unworthy of well-bred people, the mestizos became the producers. And today the Colombian upper class and politicians are as white as ever.

What racial mix that exists occurred mainly in the earlier period of the conquest. The Spaniards broke up the structure of their communal organizations by decapitating them from the start, in order to make way for colonial and Catholic rule. And in contrast to the strong cultural resistance put up by the Maya, the Chichba and other Indians of Colombia quickly adopted the language of their conquerors. By way of the church,[5] the influence of Hispanic society managed to penetrate the "native"—soon to be mestizo—communities (actually the proportion of white ancestry among those called mestizo is often slight). While the political administration imposed control and corporal punishments, the church provided the consolation of resignation and spiritual escapism. When Bolivar's struggle won independence from Spain in the early nineteenth century, nothing changed in the living conditions of the country people.

The importance of the church's role in Colombia is strongly expressed in one very important document: a concordat signed in 1887 between the Vatican and the Colombian government.[6] The concordat granted the church a powerful statutory role in two fields: in its relations with the state, which allow the church to exercise a direct influence on the government; and in its control over education, which clinches its influence on the population. Throughout the long reign of the Conservative party, from 1886 to 1930, the Archbishop of Bogotá used to pick Colombia's president. An anticlerical reaction eventually found expression in the Liberal party, and President Alfonso Lopez undertook a separation of Church and State, but this has remained only theoretical,

[5] Gustavo Perez and Isaac West, *La Iglesia en Colombia* (Bogotá: Ediciones Tercer Mundo, 1962).
[6] See T. Lloyd Mechan, *Church and State in Latin America* (Chapel Hill: University of North Carolina Press, 1934).

for the church is solidly implanted in each and every village. As an example, the Rev. Salcedo's Accion Cultural Popular in the late 1960s had a transmitter broadcasting programs to two and a half million listeners, as well as 30,000 volunteers crisscrossing the countryside and a newspaper, *El Campesino*, which reached 750,000 peasant families.

Despite the centuries-old conversion to Christianity, the peasants still hold to significant magico-religious beliefs, but no doubt in strong interaction with Christianity, as the spirits and supernatural elements are highly moralizing—in any event, their religious beliefs contribute in one way or another to the maintenance of social control over them. The mechanics of the popular doctrine are such that, according to the sociologist Fals-Borda, the peasants believe in the actual physical existence of a scale to weigh sins and good deeds. In 1950, he reports, in the course of an anthropometric survey, many peasants refused to let themselves be weighed, saying, "If I weigh myself on earth, I won't be weighed in Heaven." [7]

The passivity and resignation born of four centuries of colonial and semicolonial experiences were still profound in rural Colombian society at the time of the "violence," and to a large extent still are. Within the church itself a dissenting school of thought has developed, though, devoted to the ideals of social justice which were expressed in the Medellín Congress, for instance, but its strength should not be overestimated. For all the church's enormous influence, it is worth noting that even in Colombia, where priests are quite numerous by Latin American standards, there still are not very many of them: less than five thousand secular priests and about twenty thousand men and women in religious orders.[8]

In the late nineteenth century, both major Colombian po-

---

[7] In his excellent study, *Campesinos de las Andes* (Bogotá: Ediciones Tercer Mundo, 1961).
[8] *Pontifical Yearbook 1968*. For the whole of Latin America, in fact, there are only 43,000 priests, compared to almost 48,000 for France alone; counting the religious orders the total is 183,295, compared to 164,030 for France.

litical parties, Conservative and Liberal, sought the backing of the peasants. This opening up of electoral politics to the peasants was the work of the *gamonales*, minor local celebrities whose position in rural society enabled them to influence the voters. For those who "voted right," they obtained jobs, favors, and rewards, and became the protectors of their clients. Little by little, splits between villages developed along party lines, all the sharper because they were cut off from each other by the mountian topography. This *localismo* reinforced the peasants' conformism and kept existing structures stable. The turn of the century was marked by the Thousand Days' War (1899–1902)— during which Conservatives and Liberals fought each other fiercely and enabled the United States meanwhile to annex the Panama Canal Zone from Colombia. From then until 1948, except for a brief outbreak around 1930–31, Colombia enjoyed domestic peace.

The average daily wage in the Colombian countryside is less than a dollar, and the work is only seasonal. Many peasants who own their own pathetically small plots (some less than an acre) live at bare subsistence level. The agrarian reform begun in the 1960s, which gave title deeds to less than 20,000 families, has not changed the telling statistic that 3 percent of landowners own 70 percent of the land. Every other adult is illiterate, while a third of the school-age children do not go to school. Life expectancy does not exceed forty-five years. The individualism created by possession of one's own plot of land is evidently strong, since there is no sign of mutual aid or work undertaken jointly at the village level; even brothers fail to pitch in to work together on lands they inherited from their parents. Hierarchic relationships are strongly marked, and the state is looked to for everything—for the legacy of colonial centralism persists.[9] The citizen is in fact a subject in a framework of values which is still colonial. The peasant is expected to vote the way his boss

---

[9] Robert H. Dix, *Colombia: The Political Dimensions of Change* (New Haven: Yale University Press, 1967).

does, since political allegiance is dictated not by economic self-interest, but rather by personal, family, and village relationships. Depending on the village, people are traditionally Liberal or Conservative; personal choice has nothing to do with it. This setting is obviously favorable to political bossism—*caudillismo, gamonalismo* and *caciquismo*—while it encourages an indifference to politics which is characteristic of the modern Colombian peasant.

A government job is the prime ambition of every Colombian who has managed to acquire the rudiments of an education, and this is scarcely surprising in a society where manual labor and trade have always been looked down on. The state's decision-making bodies are highly centralized. Together, these factors lay the groundwork for the growth and survival of caudillismo in politics, which is a personalized relationship based on ties of protection and loyalty. What is striking about Colombia (and many other Latin American countries) is *the immaturity of the nation state,* or in other words, the lack of national integration within the society itself. Colombia's ruling classes see themselves as part of a cosmopolitan elite of civilized men faced with ignorant masses; they do not view these masses as citizens making up a nation. And this absence of social integration is just as striking in the city as in the countryside. The urban middle classes—which have grown considerably during the last three decades and now make up about one-fourth of the country's population—depend to a large degree on the state; having only recently come up in the world, they are often more conservative than the modernist elite and put great stress on *la fachada* (appearances). Their political influence is bound to increase in the years to come.

The long, long reign of the Conservatives was brought to an end in the 1930s when A. Lopez Pumarejo became the first Liberal president. Yet despite his promises of reforms, not much changed. In the 1940s Jorge Eliecir Gaitan came on the scene and, as president, opposed what he denounced as "the oligarchies." When he was assassinated in Bogotá on April 9, 1948, an explosion of spontaneous violence was touched off: for three days Conservative party offices and headquarters were wrecked by angry crowds and at least 3000 persons were killed. (These disturbances were known as the *Bogotazo*.) The violencia quickly spread to the countryside, where it raged for a decade. In its first phase, from 1948 to 1953, it reached its fullest extent, sparing only the coastal regions and the southwestern tip of the country (the Narino region and a large part of Cauca). Then, after a coup d'etat led by General Rojas Pinilla in 1953 which effected a short truce, the country was shaken by a second wave (1953–1958) affecting mainly the western and central regions: Tolima, Huila, Caldas, Valle. There was a considerable increase in banditry, and the government's repression was marked by extreme cruelty. That second wave can be said to have continued, to a lesser degree and concentrated in the same places, until the time when the "independent republics" were set up.

Between 1948 and 1953, an estimated 20,000 Liberals took part in the violencia. Conservative villages sought to avenge Conservatives killed during the Bogotazo, while Liberal villages sought to avenge the assassination of Gaitan. The Liberal villages had to fight against both Conservative villages and troops sent in by the Conservative government, whose repression was merciless. The clergy, traditionally Conservative, refused to accord Christian burials to Liberal peasants. In some parts of the country, the army lost control of the situation, and the combatants settled scores with the utmost savagery, in a manner that recalls the Balkan conflicts in the last days of the Ottoman Empire. A number of Colombian authors have attributed the extreme cruelty exhibited by all sides during this conflict to the severe sexual repression which was characteristic of many Hispanic American societies at the time. (The largely black and mulatto populations in the coastal regions were much more tolerant.) According to Hobsbawm, the violencia was also used by a segment of the rural middle class—which felt stifled by Colombia's rigid social structures—in order to improve its standing. Economic hardship had forced many small landowners to sell all or part of their land notably in the three main coffee-producing states, which are marked by their "minifundios"—Caldas, Tolima, and Valle; these were among the most affected areas, along with those where landless peasants were especially numerous.[10]

However, despite being so widespread and long-lasting, the violencia never turned into a revolutionary movement on a national scale. Guerrilla groups organized spontaneously, but their aims did not go beyond their limited area of operations. Most of these groups, while made up of Liberals, had nothing to do with the party leadership. Caudillismo and caciquismo marked each of them, and rivalries between them were frequent. In 1952, Communists and certain Liberals attended a national guerrilla conference which tried to get the people to take up the call for agrarian reform, but this drive was never coordinated, and the rivalry was sharp between the 10–15 percent of the armed groups which were Communist and the Liberals.

After 1953, some guerrilla groups agreed to the amnesty measures proposed by the government, others frequently turned to banditry,[11] and about a third of them kept going. But these last, with their lack of organizational cohesion and their ideological weakness, eventually also ended up in banditry and, in the long run, brought many latent social conflicts out into the open.

La violencia properly speaking came to an end after the deposition of General Rojas Pinilla by a junta in 1957 and the creation, one year later, of a National Front coalition government made up of Conservatives and Liberals. This coalition was based on three principles which are inscribed in Colombia's constitution: an alternation of the presidency between parties (from 1958 to 1974 four presidents held office, two of them Liberals and two Conservatives); cabinet and administrative posts distributed to

---

[10] Eric Hobsbawm, "Anatomy of Violence," *New Society* (London), April 11, 1963. Much has been written about *la violencia*, some of it of very high quality. See G. Guzman, Fals-Borda, et al., *La Violencia en Colombia* (Bogotá: Ediciones Tercer Mundo, 1962); R. Pineda, *El Impacto de la Violencia en el Tolima* (Bogotá: Universidad Nacional de Colombia, 1960); I. Gutierrez, *La Rebeldía Colombiana* (Bogotá: Ediciones Antares, 1962); G. Guzman, *La Violencia en Colombia* (Bogotá: Ediciones Tercer Mundo, 1968).
[11] See Richard L. Maullin, *The Fall of Dumar Adjure: A Colombian Guerrilla and Bandit* (Santa Monica: RAND Corporation, 1969), which recounts the activities of the chief of a guerrilla band supported by the Liberal party which provided cover for a long time, until he was killed by the army.

achieve a balance between Liberals and Conservatives, whoever the president; a two-thirds vote, instead of a simple majority in Congress, required to pass laws and amendments.

With time, the differences between Liberals and Conservatives have diminished and the right wing of the Liberal party is very close to Conservative positions.

This effect of the bipartisan system has made it all but inevitable that left and right wings should form within both parties; of these the most important is the left-wing Liberal Revolutionary Movement, led by A. L. Michelsen, who was elected President in 1974. In addition, The National People's Alliance (ANAPO), of the former dictator, Rojas Pinilla—whose daughter is very active—amounts to an important opposition movement taking a populist type of line. So the National Front works, but in mediocre way, paralyzed by the power-sharing imposed by the conservatism of most of the country's elite. In most national elections, abstention from voting runs around 60 percent.

If population growth maintains its current pace (3.2 percent), which is highly probable, Colombia will increase from 21 million inhabitants (1970) to 55 million by the end of the century, and the working population will also double. But if the creation of new jobs does no more than stay at its current rate of increase, Colombia will still have 4 million unemployed ten years from now—a third of its working population. Seventy percent of the population still lives off farming (while for more than fifteen years Colombia has been importing food); according to an International Labor Office report, the active Colombian farming population, estimated at 2.5 million in 1970, will rise to 800,000 persons by 1985, half of whom will not find work, making what the report calls "the unacceptable current situation" even worse.[12] The industrial growth rate during the past twenty years has averaged 6 percent, but to keep from falling behind, 25,000 jobs will have to be created every year. Nationwide, 5 million new

---

[12] Seven hundred thousand Colombians have left the country in search of work, mainly in Venezuela (1972).

jobs will be needed between 1970 and 1985, since every year 300,000 persons go onto a job market which cannot absorb even a third of them.

Obviously the problem of agrarian reform is still a major, if not *the* major problem in Colombia. Aside from the new lands brought under cultivation since 1961 when the Colombian Institute for Agrarian Reform (INCORA) was founded (an amount which is in any case not all that extensive), the reform has involved about 100,000 hectares of private land and 20,000 families. Compared to agrarian reform, effected in Peru, say, with more than a million hectares expropriated in a single year, the Colombian experiment appears homeopathic. A rational organization of farming in Colombia is possible only by changing ownership patterns, a measure which would run counter to the interests of the big landowners. The situation is still basically the same as it was in 1960, when 636 landlords owned more than 7 million hectares, while 800,000 peasant families were landless [13] and the average size of a peasant holding is 1.5 hectares. Despite the exodus from the countryside, the rural population is increasing by 1 percent annually, so that conditions have tended to worsen.

It is this context that the Colombian guerrilla movements have developed. The Worker, Student and Peasant Movement (MOEC) founded in 1959 by former Communists and young intellectuals, tried in 1961 to set up a guerrilla base in the Cauca region, not far from Marquetalia, and it counted on getting support from former guerrillas who had degenerated into *bandoleros*. It failed, however, decimated alternately by the army and the bandoleros. Then, around 1962–64, Communist organizers began to have a decisive influence in Tolima province, where there had been only isolated cases of peasants seizing land, and guerrillas during the years of violence had had no urban allies. Guerrilla leaders had owed their authority to the values of traditional

---

[13] On the agrarian problem, see Dale W. Adams, *Colombia's Land Tenure System: Antecedents and Problems* (Madison, Wisconsin: University of Wisconsin Press, 1966).

society, but in the late 1950s and early 1960s a new generation arose, molded by this earlier guerrilla experience. Active repression was carried out by the army between 1958 and 1962, thanks to U.S.-trained special elite counterinsurgency units, and the number of *guerrilleros* was estimated at some ten thousand—which is considerable, compared to any other Latin American guerrilla movement. In 1964, peasant self-defense zones called independent republics were created in Tolima and Huila, where more than thirty thousand peasants had been expropriated during the violence, while the peasants in predominantly Liberal areas organized farm labor units and self-defense groups.

But the Colombian Communist party (PCC) soon gained a preponderant influence, and the PCC held to the position that it was possible to create the conditions for peaceful development within the framework of the Colombian state.[14]

Founded in 1926, the PCC had spent its early years in sectarian isolation—except for a short period in 1930–31, when armed groups sprang up to defend agrarian demands made in a zone under party control known as Viota the Red. Subsequently, the party, with an estimated membership of some twelve thousand by 1965, exercised its relatively weak influence mainly in the trade unions and the university. But now these "independent republics," while put together in a rather confused and haphazard way, were under party influence. Numbering ten in all, the main ones were in Marquetalia, Sumapaz, Rio Chiquito, El Pato, Tequendema, Viota, and Guyabero.[15]

In 1962, the Colombian army, under the direction of General Ruiz Novoa, who was then minister of war, began under its counterinsurgency program to apply the so-called Lazo Plan, and scored unquestionable successes for the next three or four years. The first phase involved creating special units adapted to

---

[14] Theses of the Eighth and Ninth Congresses of the Communist party of Colombia.
[15] On the origins of the Socialist movement in Colombia: Robert J. Alexander, *Communism in Latin America* (New Brunswick, N.J.: Rutgers University Press, 1957).

counterinsurgency, strengthening all the armed forces, improving psychological services in order to reduce the latent hostility of the population, and, finally, launching a civic-military action aimed at helping improve economic conditions in the countryside. The army had only a very minor success in the civic-military action, but began using more than two-thirds of its men in police operations and raids. The air force obtained helicopters from the United States through its Military Assistance Program. The army, the gendarmes, and the police were put under a unified command, and mobile intelligence groups were set up. In many regions the population was extremely hostile, but elsewhere—notably in the Quindio regions—the people were fed up with banditry and gave them a better welcome.

Following the March 1964 elections, the decision was taken to wipe out the "independent republics." The plan, again under the direction of General Ruiz Novoa, was carried out in three stages, aimed first of all at striking Marquetalia: [16] an economic and military blockade; psychological warfare, bringing in communal-action organizers and other agents to spread alarmist reports; and intensive bombing.

On June 17, 16,000 *lanceros*—elite counterinsurgency troops whose officers had been trained in Panama—made their assault. Five days later the zone was occupied, but many of the guerrilla forces, under the leadership of a peasant named Manuel Marulanda (whom the Communist party was to name to its Central Committee), managed to pull back, and in July, a manifesto from the Marquetalia guerrillas announced that the strategy of self-defense was abandoned in favor of a people's war of movement. Thus was the self-defense theory advocated by the PCC a demonstrable flop.

Since that date, the PCC has been abundantly criticized by the Far Left in Colombia. It has been reproached for its compromises with bourgeois liberals during the 1930s, for its initial opposition to the candidacy of Jorge Eliceir Gaitan in 1945,

---

[16] Richard Maullin, *The Colombian Army and the Guerrillas* (Santa Monica: RAND Corporation, 1970).

and for its attitude after the *Bogotazo* in 1948, when it backed the National Union Front formed shortly after Gaitan's assassination. Criticisms have also been voiced on more recent issues—not only the self-defense strategy, but the fact that it used the guerrillas' struggle as a trump card in its bargaining with the government to safeguard its own legality. In fact, the guerrilla groups that emerged from the "independent republics" (under the name of the Revolutionary Armed Forces of Colombia, FARC, have been virtually inactive since the end of the 1960s. Since 1967, the PCC, under the leadership of its secretary general, Gilberto Vieira—who has been in office for more than twenty-five years—has emphasized a strategy of electoral politics, declaring that in the case of Colombia, legal channels provide an adequate means to wage the revolutionary struggle.

Colombia's diplomatic relations with the Soviet Union were restored in 1968, and it would seem that large segments of FARC cut back their activity after that date. In Tolima and Huila, four groups were operating until recently—the region is considered an "insecure zone," but it is safe to move around during the day—those of Marulanda (killed in a clash in 1970), Ciro Trujillo, Janunio Valerio, and Cartagena. Their rootedness in the countryside assured them of close contacts in the local peasantry (not very numerous) and an excellent knowledge of the terrain. The Colombian army was unable to crush them completely; put on the defensive, however, these surviving units have never managed to extend their areas of influence and, on the contrary, now amount to little more than pockets of guerrilla activity. There has been a notable drop in armed clashes.

In 1965, a group of eighteen men, led by Fabio Vasquez, founded the National Liberation Army (ELN), which is generally considered a pro-Castro group. Set up by militants with urban backgrounds, the ELN—after six months spent scouting out the terrain, preparing the peasants politically, setting up support bases, and forming information and liaison groups—succeeded in securing a small peasant base in Santander province. At first, Latin American revolutionists paid no attention to the ELN. The Cubans did not invite it to their Tricontinental Conference (in

1966), for example. But subsequently, Havana switched its attitude, and the ELN, which advocated a policy that was hostile to legal and peaceful methods, was represented at the Conference of Latin American Solidarity in 1967.

It was no doubt the fact that Camillo Torres joined the ELN in January 1966 that caused it to become widely known. Coming from a bourgeois background, both a priest and a sociologist,[17] Camillo Torres was one of the most remarkable revolutionary figures in Latin America. He had first become aware of the economic and social impoverishment of the lower classes while making surveys, especially on the outskirts of Bogotá. The more he spoke out against the situation, the more he grasped the political implications and came into conflict with the ruling-class circles around him. A professor of sociology and chaplain at the National University, he was eventually obliged, on account of the stands he had taken, to give up his positions in 1964. Camillo Torres then traveled through various regions of Colombia, holding huge meetings with the wretchedly poor people of the cities and the countryside. Disowned by the church hierarchy, for a time jailed and then freed, Camillo Torres gave up the frock, held more meetings in the provinces, was again jailed and released, and then founded the United Front during the summer of 1965, through which he tried to bring together all the various factions eager to change the social order. The church joined with the press in attempts to destroy the semimessianic image that public opinion was building up around the revolutionary priest. Politically isolated and with no real organization to back him up, Camillo Torres disappeared in November 1965 to join the ELN, and issued this call: ". . . The people no longer believe in elections. The people know that legal channels have been exhausted. The people know the only way left is to take up arms. The people are desperate and ready to stake their lives in order that the next generation may not know slavery, in order that their children . . . may be educated, housed, fed, clothed and above all that they

---

[17] Camillo Torres, *La Proletarizacion de Bogotá* (Bogotá: Ediciones Tercer Mundo, 1961).

may have dignity. In order that they may be independent of American power . . ."

Six weeks later, on January 15, 1966, Camillo Torres was killed in a clash with a military patrol; the ELN had protected him that poorly. And yet, Camillo Torres had succeeded in achieving what very few other Latin American revolutionaries had been able to do: to sound a responsive chord among the poor and underprivileged masses, both in the cities and in the countryside. From May to September 1965, wherever Camillo Torres spoke the biggest town squares were packed with crowds to hear him talk— about expropriating the *latifundistas,* about nationalizing natural resources, about a people's government—and always in a language suited to the people he was addressing.

But if Camillo Torres succeeded in heightening awareness among the classes he was trying to reach, he did not manage to create a mass organization. Nothing held together the people who spontaneously responded to his message except his charismatic presence. Once Camillo Torres was gone, the ELN could not find any other figure able to articulate on a nationwide scale the deepest aspirations of Colombian society. The ELN guerrilla groups were unable to extend their field of action beyond Santander and Antiocha provinces, even though they were supported by Cuba in 1967 and 1968. The movement seems to have been shaken by leadership crises between 1969 and 1971. It made its biggest splash on January 15, 1972, when about 150 guerrillas took over the villages of Remedios, Santa Isabel, El Tigre, and Otu for several hours, looting the banks, setting fire to the law courts, letting people out of jail, stocking up on food and medicine, and making speeches to the population.

A third guerrilla base was created in 1967 in Upper Sinu, Cordoba province, by "pro-Chinese" militants who had left the PCC on account of its revisionist positions. Cordoba province, located in the Western Cordillera, was practically untouched by the violencia, but it is an area of *latifundia.* In 1966, some of the future guerrillas had gone up into the mountains where they set up free schools, provided medical services, built bridges, thus gaining the peasants' confidence and organizing cooperatives.

Then armed struggle was begun. The army has still not succeeded in strangling this guerrilla nucleus, but it has hemmed it in.

According to official figures, 134 guerrillas were killed and 200 were captured throughout Colombia during 1970. But on the whole, combat is rare, and a sort of relative status quo breeds a sense of security on both sides, so long as the "forces of order" and the guerrillas stay within their respective domains. In the long run, this decay is not to the advantage of the guerrilla groups.

And therein lies the real problem. If one takes into account the facts that 40 percent of Colombia's rural population is clustered less than an hour's drive from towns of at least 10,000 inhabitants, that there are thirty cities with more than 30,000 inhabitants and four with between half a million and two million inhabitants, it becomes clear that no guerrilla movement can really amount to anything in Colombia without a coordination between urban and rural areas that none of the current groups is in any position to set up.

And in fact, it has been not so much the guerrilla groups that brought on the recent crisis in Colombia as the National Front, by its do-nothing policy. Signs of discontent—violent protests and spontaneous riots, indeed—have broken out all over the country less to support the guerrillas than to protest against government policy. The main threat to the National Front in recent years has come not from the guerrilla groups but from the National People's Alliance.

First-hand information is lacking on which to base a chronology of the phases or even main events in the history of these guerrilla groups, now down to a few hundred men largely out of contact with any people beyond the areas in which they move. The most active groups seem to be those of the ELN, but they are holed up in sparsely populated and isolated areas, while the army's systematic blockades and sudden strikes generally keep them on the defensive.

The National Front was able to put an end to the violencia and for the most part reduce guerrilla activity to a low, modest level, but it has not gone to the roots of a crisis which benefits the very social classes which keep it going. When all is said and done, the forces which imposed the National Front do not appear able to assure social peace for any length of time. The possibility cannot be ruled out that the army, like other Latin American armies, may get around to thinking that the civilian elites that have led the National Front for almost twenty years are incapable of developing and modernizing the structures of Colombian society.

The Colombian army has not often intervened in politics.[18] When it did so in 1953, it did not have any political power. But since then the army, and notably its junior officers, has been politicized. It was the army that played the major role during the violencia, by effectively combating the various guerrilla movements and setting up a civic-military action program which brought it face to face with the social reality of the country.

In the countryside, ownership patterns, with their high percentage of small landholders, and above all the highly hierarchical and paternalistic work relationships have kept a coordinated peasant movement from developing, despite the decades of violencia and struggles—and also, what with *the low organizational and political level of the guerrilla groups*. This country, which at one time was the showcase of the Alliance for Progress, is going through a crisis which should produce some reforms. The rapid urbanization, the employment crisis hitting levels of society where people were hoping to be integrated into the modern world, the prevalent feeling within the petty bourgeoisie of being left out of the whole decision-making process, the rise within the middle classes of a nationalism which could turn against a large part of the established ruling classes, whose values are more cosmopolitan than national—all this adds up to the likely participation of significant sectors of the petty bourgeoisie, both civilian and military, in the forthcoming evolution.

---

[18] Vernon L. Fluharty, *Dance of the Millions* (Pittsburgh: University of Pittsburgh Press, 1957).

2

revolution in Africa

1. The Algerian Experience and the Illusions of Fanonism

In strictly military terms, the Algerian war ended in defeat for the Front for National Liberation (FNL). On the eve of the signing of the Evian Accords in 1962 which ended the war, only a few thousand men were still holding out, mercilessly hunted down and barely managing to survive. There was nothing similar to the solidly held NLF zones in South Vietnam on the eve of the cease-fire there.

The case of Algeria is interesting in several respects. However strong the rebel leaders' nationalism, the Algerian Revolution —as it was called by the FNL during the war—did not keep its promises to install a radical revolutionary government, as some observers had reckoned it would. Once it was independent, Algeria [1] did not become another Cuba. Frantz Fanon's by now familiar analyses, especially in his *Studies on a Dying Colonialism,* had suggested that the armed struggle itself, aside from providing the Algerians with a violent therapy against humiliation would be able, with no program beyond the prospect of independence, to work profound changes in certain historical, social, and cultural factors in the life of the country. Fanon saw irreversible changes occurring in such matters as the status of women and the place of youth in society. On-the-spot observations made in Algeria since its independence show, however, that such changes, even if they cropped up during the war years, were superficial and lacked any ideological ground in which they might have taken root in day-to-day life. Traditional ways of thinking are not changed by armed struggle, unless armed struggle *as a movement* promotes a modernizing and revolutionary ideology, one which, while exalting the sense of national identity, can also prune the socially and culturally conservative elements out of the national tradition and free the energies òf the greatest number of people. Just as Fanon [2] overestimated the spontaneity of the peasants, and of the masses in general, he also overestimated the usefulness of organized violence as a channeled form of aggressiveness. The need for an idealogically well-equipped vanguard that could give a revolutionary social content to the battle for independence did not seem to him of fundamental importance—contrary to the lessons that can be drawn from that entire historical period.

Algeria's colonial status was special and it made Algerian society in every way one of the world's most dispossessed societies —politically, economically, culturally. In contrast to Morocco and Tunisia, where the national government, the existence of the state, although under foreign domination was not legally denied,

---

[1] G. Chaliand and J. Minces, *L'Algérie Indépendante* (Paris: Maspero, 1972).
[2] The best article on Fanon is by Nguyen Nghe, "Frantz Fanon et les problèmes de l'indépendance," *La Pensée,* No. 107 (1963). See also Irene Gendzier, *Frantz Fanon, a Critical Biography* (New York: Pantheon, 1972)ʹ.

Algeria had merely the status of a French department. Algeria was a France populated by mostly second-class citizens who had less voice in national elections than the 10 percent of the population that represented the European colonial power. Denied representation, denied their very identity, the Algerians—officially referred to as "the Muslims"—were also legally barred from studying their own language, Arabic, in the public schools. The settlers, a million full-fledged French citizens referred to as "the Europeans," took over three million hectares of the best land in the plains for farming, while in the cities they filled most of the jobs, notably in the civil service, which were thereby closed to "the Muslims."

Very few colonized societies have been broken down so fully, and the extent of the damage naturally proved to be important in the formation of the Algerian national movement. This movement, begun first among proletarianized emigrants, wavered for a long time between the goals of independence and substantial improvements in the colonial laws that governed Algeria. Ferhat Abbas, leader of the Union Démocratique des élus du manifeste algérien and representative of the Algerian bourgeoisie (rudimentary, by the way), who was later to become president of the Provisional Government of the Algerian Republic, stated in 1939 that "there is no Algerian nation, no Algerian *patrie*." Yet little by little the sense of national identity crystallized, especially among the urban petty bourgeoisie, and the repression in Setif in 1945, which caused several thousand deaths, sped up the process considerably. The national movement, mainly represented by the Movement for the Triumph of Democratic Liberties, nevertheless kept on a legalistic and reformist course under the leadership of Messali Hadj, while a fringe group, the *organisation spéciale,* decided, after trying repeatedly to win over the Movement, to undertake armed struggle. The Front for National Liberation was born.

On November 1, 1954, a series of attacks against the French power took place at various points on Algerian territory. The insurrection was launched by a handful of virtually unknown men, some of whom had been living underground for years (and consider what that implies in the way of a support structure). Even if they were not themselves of the lower classes, they were implanted in their native regions, mainly in the Aurès mountains, Kahylia in the east, and Algiers regions in the center. The peasant population was quick to support them, for they strongly resented their colonial situation, and a decade of nationalist slogans, together with the neighboring independence movements in Tunisia and Morocco, had sensitized many people to the Nationalist issue.

The insurrection was not, however, the expression of a uniform political apparatus, nor was it tied to a commonly held underlying revolutionary theory. November was an act of rejection of the French colonial system; what it aimed at was Independence. The ranks of the FNL, filled at first with activists of very humble origins and populist leanings, from 1956 on began to swell with cadres of all the different nationalist organizations, anxious to take part in a struggle that, it turned out, was going to be possible after all. But this mixture was bound to strengthen considerably the petty-bourgeois and socially conservative nature of the FLN. The wishful thinking about maintaining the primacy of the political over the military, of the "interior" over the "exterior," expressed at the Soummam Congress in 1956 organized by Abane Ramdane (he was physically liquidated by the Provisional Government some years later), was quickly out of date.

Militarily, the FNL reached its high point in early 1957. The French, taken by surprise, had at first underestimated the nature of the insurrection and its chances of success, and the measures they had taken in 1955 were insufficient to stop its growth. Calling up "available" reserves in 1956—a move made by the Republican Front, thanks to special powers voted by the French Communist party, among others—was nothing but a makeshift response. But in 1957 and 1958 the war in Algeria began to be waged in earnest. And by 1958–59, with the Challe Plan, the battle was, in fact, won by French troops.

In 1957, the French repression of the insurrection in Algeria's cities—especially during the Battle of Algiers—led the FNL militants to head for the countryside in large numbers, while the leadership went abroad, notably to Tunis. Little by little, as their bureaucratic machinery was set up outside the country, a gap grew between the FNL's political and diplomatic leadership and the increasingly isolated fighters in the Algerian countryside (the French set up electrified barriers along the borders). A crisis eventually developed between the "interior" and the "exterior," which the Provisional Government tried to resolve by creating the Army of the Frontiers, led by Colonel Boumedienne—an army which was later to turn on its creator. Meanwhile, the French forces were striking harder and harder against the rebels: the Front's peasant forces were shattered in 1959; some two million peasants were driven into camps (out of a total population of ten million); and hundreds of thousands of refugees fled to Morocco and Tunisia.

People have often said that there was a "peasant revolution" in Algeria, since most of the fighting men were country folk. But in fact the peasants' military role in the war of national liberation was never transformed into a lasting political one. Agrarian reform was not included in the list of initial goals of the struggle. Algerian nationalism, in the modern sense of the term, was in fact forged in the cities and spread by the urban petty bourgeoisie. Algerians were fighting primarily to recapture their identity, for the simple right to be Algerian. By the last years of the war there was no longer any peasant army under FNL leadership, much less geographical zones under its control. The peasants never had the experience of forming a governmental body to represent them, as the peasants in Guinea-Bissau did, for example; they never saw land change hands, as the farmers of South Vietnam did. Frictions at the top between the leadership of the rural regions, the Provisional Government, and later on, the Frontier Command went on over the heads of the militants, not to mention the masses, who continued to have complete faith in their leaders. Between 1957 and 1960, the urban masses were pretty much left to themselves, while the peasantry alone bore the brunt of the war. But just when the rural fighters, decimated by French "pacification" efforts and massive relocations, saw the action die down, the movement was taken up by the cities, which beginning in December 1960, forcefully demonstrated their refusal to accept colonial status. In strictly military terms, only eastern Algeria (*willayas* I, II, III) and to a lesser extent the central area (*willaya* IV) still had an organized support structure of any importance. When the cease-fire came, the FNL's leadership crisis inevitably burst into the light of day, since its only unifying factor had been the goal of independence.

Seven years of war had not enabled the FNL to develop a harmonious leadership, not to mention an ideologically armed party in the Vietnamese style—and this is easily understandable in the light of Algerian circumstances. (Incidentally, independence movement's anticommunism was strengthened by the fact that the Stalinists in the Algerian Communist party, just like the French Communist party, did not give priority to Algerian independence and up until 1956 called for "a real French union.") The Algerian revolution thus did not come to grips with its independence until it was right in the middle of a major crisis, torn by a burden of contradictory hopes. The masses wanted social justice and a better life—after seven years of a war that had cost the lives of hundreds of thousands of Algerians. A power struggle soon overtook the various factions of the FLN, and the question the FLN had never clearly faced was finally raised: what was the social content of Algeria's independence to be?

2. The Independence of Guinea-Bissau and the Heritage of Cabral

An unprecedented event took place in the autumn of 1973. A Portuguese colony—looked upon by Portugal as one of its "overseas provinces," along with Angola and Mozambique—unilaterally proclaimed its independence, which was soon recognized by a number of countries.

"Portuguese" Guinea, a small country of 14,000 square miles wedged between Senegal and the Republic of Guinea on the West African coast, has a population which in 1960 the Portuguese put at 521,336 [3] and which is estimated by the African Party for the Independence of Guinea-Bissau and the Cape Verde Islands (PAIGC) at 800,000. (The results of the most recent Portuguese census in 1971 have not been published.) Whichever figures are correct, Guinea-Bissau, with 15–20 inhabitants per square kilometer, is densely populated, by African standards. Unlike Angola and Mozambique, it has no important mineral resources (although oil prospecting is going on), and the country's economy has depended essentially on peanut and rice exports, until recently controlled by the Companhia Uniao Fabril. Contrary to the other "provinces," Guinea was a thoroughgoing colony.

Portugal first established itself on the West African coast in the fifteenth century, but the conquest of the hinterland began only after the Berlin Conference of 1885 and was still continuing after World War I. Portuguese Guinea was subject to "native law," under which more than 99 percent of the population were classified as "natives" with no rights. Less than 1 percent of the Africans were considered *assimilados* and given Portuguese citizenship with theoretically equal rights. In the Cape Verde Islands, more than six hundred miles away, the population of about 200,000 mostly mulatto inhabitants were as a group considered *assimilados,* and the Portuguese used some of them as junior civil servants in the other colonies.

In 1956, Amilcar Cabral and a few companions, including Aristide Pereira and Luis Cabral, founded the PAIGC in Bissau. Amilcar Cabral, a mulatto born in Guinea in 1925, was an agronomist who had studied in Lisbon, where he had founded a Center of African Studies with a few other African intellectuals who were shortly to spark national liberation movements in other Portuguese colonies—Marcelino Dos Santos in Mozambique, Mario de Andrade in Angola—assimilados like Cabral. Around 1955 Cabral came back to Africa—first to Angola, then to Guinea-Bissau—working as an agronomist, which enabled him to

---

[3] Including 2263 Europeans, 4568 racially mixed persons, and 1478 "assimilated" blacks.

get to know the rural areas. About this time he published *Taking Stock*, a remarkable monograph on Guinea-Bissau.

The party was, of course, clandestine, and at the start, was made up mainly of intellectuals or semi-intellectuals, workers in the port, and urbanized youth with no particular professional training (to Cabral goes the credit of having understood the importance and availability of those marginal young people). The party spent its first three years setting up cells in Guinea's main towns. But on August 3, 1959, a strike in the port was harshly repressed and some fifty demonstrators were killed. The Portuguese political police broke up many of the party's cells, and the party leadership withdrew to the Republic of Guinea—which had gained independence the year before—to reevaluate its strategy.

The party in exile concluded that while there was no chance of carrying on an urban struggle in Guinea-Bissau, the countryside offered ground in which it could hope to take root. A school was set up in Conakry to train young cadres for six to eight weeks at a time, to build a political support structure inside Guinea. This basic training, which later developed into more or less continuous training, aimed with the help of a simple and repetitive terminology at instilling a new way of approaching problems, based essentially on the idea of a shared countrywide struggle against colonial domination. The cadres would go back to Guinea-Bissau to start the clandestine work of mobilization, seeking out sympathizers among the people, isolating the agents of Portuguese rule, preparing people's minds for the battle, making sure who could be trusted to help.

When this work was undertaken around 1960, it was no simple matter, for Guinean society is complex: about a third of the population is Muslim (Mandingues and Foulas), while the rest are animists (Balantes, who make up the majority, Pepels, Mandjaques, and others). The Muslims, in particular the Foulas, live in a traditional chieftain society. Originally nomadic herdsmen, they still own a large part of the country's livestock, although their economy has broadened to include peanuts and trade. When the Portuguese first colonized the hinterland, the Foulas, an aristocratic society, collaborated with them and in return obtained certain privileges; along with the Cape Verdeans (and to a lesser extent the Mandingues) they became the indirect instruments of Portuguese rule over the animist population. The animist groups, in contrast, were unaccustomed to marked social stratification; moral standing gained with age made the old men the village authorities. They lived mainly from rice-growing and scarcely engaged in trade at all. Like the other ethnic groups, they were bound to forced labor and payment of a head tax, but on top of that the Portuguese now imposed Muslim chiefs on their villages.

The reason for the success of the PAIGC, or more precisely for the success of Cabral's strategy, is that these realities were taken into account. Far from overestimating peasant spontaneity in the manner of Fanon or Guevara, Cabral patiently built up a political support structure within the population, and notably the animist sectors, more sensitive as they were to the issues and easier to mobilize. The case of Guinea-Bissau is in this respect comparable to the Chinese and Vietnamese strategies.

Thanks to this clandestine preparatory work, the battle could openly be joined in early 1963—not at the frontier with a few commando raids, but in the very heart of the country, by guerrillas at home among the local population.[4] The fighting began in the south, quickly opened in the north, and the Portuguese were prevented from concentrating their forces so as to cordon off the adversary within a given perimeter. The Portuguese command soon realized that its troops had lost control of about 15 percent of the territory. A year later, despite a large-scale offensive, the Portuguese could not regain a footing on Como Island, in the south. By 1966, the PAIGC had succeeded in extending its control over close to half of Guinea-Bissau, despite the increase in Portuguese troops from 10,000 in 1962 to 25,000 in 1966 (35,000 by 1967), all armed with NATO equipment. Starting in 1964 and 1965, the

[4] G. Chaliand, *Armed Struggle in Africa* (New York: Monthly Review Press, 1969). B. Davidson, *The Liberation of Guinea* (Harmondsworth, England: Penguin, 1969).

party set up a new political and administrative structure in the "liberated" regions. At the village (*tabanca*) level, committees of five (two of them required to be women) were elected in each community by all the villagers, with the party in charge. (Any of the five could be removed by the village assembly.) The committee chairman served as the village's principal political officer, while the deputy chairman was responsible for the militia and the other three members took care of administrative and social matters, supply problems, and production. On this basic structure, the political, and administrative organization of the liberated regions was started, filled out later with Zone Committees (grouping several villages), Regional Committees (North, South, and East), and finally National Committees of the liberated areas. In addition, mobile political action brigades were created to organize the people and train them. Village militias, coordinated by the local armed forces, became responsible for their sectors (the three fronts—North, South, and East—are each divided into sectors), while the People's Armed Revolutionary Forces (FARP) constituted the PAIGC's liberation army in the full sense of the term. By carefully building up these arrangements, the PAIGC was able to lay the foundations of something like a national government throughout much of the country.

In short the party succeeded in proving its strength against obdurate reality—getting the peasants to join in; changing social structures by improving the conditions of women (by such measures as banning forced marriages) and young people (who make up most of the village militia); improving living conditions by building public-health stations and schools, etc. In expelling colonialism from the liberated zones, the party put an end to the economic relationships that had prevailed under Portuguese management; the money economy temporarily vanished, replaced by "people's stores" where villagers trade rice for basic necessities. All military, social, and economic activity came under the control of the party; each infantry group, incidentally, had a political officer who, among other things, was to ensure that good relations were maintained between the troops and the people, to keep them "as close as the bones and the flesh."

By 1968 the party had achieved its maximum expansion, militarily controlling two-thirds of the country (according to its own communiqués). Things had been continually going in its favor. Into this difficult situation and on the heels of a half dozen Portuguese chiefs of staff, Lisbon sent General Antonio de Spinola, who had made a name for himself in Angola, and who now became Governor of Portugese Guinea for a four-year term (later renewed). General Spinola held this post until the summer of 1973, when he was replaced by General J. Bettencourt Rodrigues (commander of the eastern zone in Angola from 1971 to 1973).

During Spinola's term, mostly after 1969, the Portuguese undertook a serious counteroffensive based on an approach and methods that were new to them: a military strategy based on good communications, pacified zones, strategic hamlets, helicopter-borne operations or rapid incursions into regions held by the other side; and a political strategy aimed at winning over the population. According to the Portuguese, this policy was based on principles of social justice, respect for traditional institutions and Guinea-Bissau's various ethnic groups, economic and social development, increased African participation in administration, and domestic security.

In August 1970, the Governor—General Spinola—convened a First Congress of the People of Guinea, made up of traditional chiefs, religious leaders, and "big men" from the villages representing the various ethnic communities in the country. The gathering had been preceded by several regional congresses bringing together the chiefs of the different ethnic groups. Addressing this First Congress of the People of Guinea, General Spinola said, in substance, that social justice meant the absolute equality of all persons before the law, fair sharing of wealth and equal chances for progress regardless of ethnic origin, and respect for traditional African institutions because they reflected the people's culture, and because progress which failed to respect the people's moral values deprived them of their dignity. Addressing the Second Congress of the People of Guinea in May 1971, General Spinola exhorted the delegates to mobilize their people to increase production, and called for a cooperative type of system.

In short, the PAIGC's activities had forced the Portuguese to revise their *conceito de civilizar,* their notion of how to "civilize" the African natives. In fact—and this was new—it was no longer a matter of imposing a way of life considered superior and of refusing to accept as "civilized" anyone but the "assimilated." Portuguese policy now went so far (much farther than in Angola or Mozambique) as to claim to take into account the desire of each population group to retain its own particular identity and culture. But at the same time, Portuguese policy tended to "tribalize" the ethnic groups, fragmenting Guinean society as much as possible, and on the whole, the Portuguese simply encouraged each ethnic group to concentrate on development within its own region. (In the Cacheu region, as all along the northwest coast, the Portuguese set up a "peace zone," populated sparsely and exclusively by Mandjaques; they called this the *chao* policy—the policy of concentrating an ethnic group in its own zone.) This amounted to putting a brake on the unification policy of the PAIGC.

Simultaneously, and while they were intensifying the war, the Portuguese carried out what they called their Better Guinea policy, which consisted of a series of measures aimed at improving living standards among the populations under their control—distribution of high-yield rice; construction of dikes to reclaim land (600 hectares were thereby brought under cultivation in the Mandjaques' chao); installation of new markets in small villages, especially in the Foula region, in the east; construction of several thousand homes; a decree guaranteeing purchase of the entire peanut crop (1970). At the local administrative level, they granted the traditional authorities improved status and greater responsibilities. And, lastly, they tried to expand the school and public-health network, mainly in the "reorganized" villages (*aldeamentos*) with their military schools. At the same time, the Portuguese were resettling Guinea's population into strategic hamlets (in 1970, 500 "reorganized" villages were provided with a militia), and *Comandos de agrupamento operacional* were set up to promote economic and social development. The Portuguese also set forth a policy of "Africanization" of the war, setting up units of several thousand men under the command of Portuguese officers. But their main effort went into intensifying the war. Air raids were stepped up over the "liberated" zones; helicopter-borne operations were sent in to demoralize the population; and a network of tarred roads was built (a constant feature of guerrilla warfare is that it induces the central government to build a highway system—in this way too it helps to modernize the country). But it was air power that played a major role, supplying isolated military posts and harassing PAIGC forces as soon as they were spotted (no point in the country is more than forty-five minutes from Bissau by plane); the Portuguese Air Force used Fiat G 91 R4 and American T6 GM fighter bombers, the French Dornier D027 and Alouettes II and III reconnaissance planes.

Thus during a half-dozen years of war, the Portuguese organized a three-pronged counteroffensive consisting of an intensified and "Africanized" war, involving population shifts and resettlement; a more indirect governmental administration supportive of traditional collaborationist elites, with a tribal policy careful to respect customs and eager to separate ethnic groups into geographically defined zones; and economic development. The results of this counteroffensive are hard to measure and vigorously disputed. While it is unlikely that most Guineans went over to the Portuguese side, as General Spinola declared in 1973, it is quite probable that most of the population found itself under Portuguese control (it might be added that in the course of the conflict 80,000 persons took refuge in Senegal). For Portuguese forces seem to have managed to hang onto the Bissau region, the Mandjaque region in the northwest, most of the east (Foula), the towns, and the Bissagos archipelago. The scope of the measures and projects undertaken by the Portuguese gives some idea of how strong the pressure was from the PAIGC. Of course, it was easier than it would have been in Angola or Mozambique for them to institute reforms, because there was no white settler class around to feel its privileges threatened. And with some success, they consolidated the Portuguese position in certain rural regions and in the towns, hoping that eventually the political and military organization of the PAIGC would break up, and meanwhile striking at the liberated regions to demoralize their people and force them either to flee or to seek Portuguese protection.

In Portugal itself, despite the growing disaffection of most Portuguese with the war and despite outright student opposition, the government seemed for a while to be keeping the lid on by improving the conditions of military service (higher pay, social benefits, family allowances, and opportunities for training and promotion). The efforts of simultaneously fighting three colonial wars for more than a decade with about 150,000 men was no small matter for a small nation with such a backward economy. But Portugal was aided in this by three external factors: its membership in NATO; its policy of letting foreign investors into its rich "provinces" of Angola and Mozambique, which paid for a growing share of the war; and the Azores agreement signed with the United States.

And yet in spite of the Portuguese counteroffensive, the PAIGC managed to maintain its positions, to harass its adversary, to destroy a whole string of fortified posts, and to launch spectacular operations even into the outskirts of Bissau and Bafata (1971). Above all, continuing to develop its strength in the liberated zones, it succeeded in consolidating its own structure—unique among African national liberation movements. And lastly, it developed a successful diplomatic strategy.

The starting point of the PAIGC's diplomacy offensive was Amilcar Cabral's factual analysis: "The situation that has prevailed in Guinea-Bissau since 1968, resulting from the country's liberation struggle under the leadership of the PAIGC, is comparable to that of an independent state with part of its national territory, in particular its urban centers, occupied by foreign military forces." The object was not, as it was for other African liberation movements, to set up a provisional government, but to make diplomatic use of a situation acknowledged by dozens of foreign observers of varying nationalities and political opinions.

Leaving no stone unturned to make the world aware of his people's struggle, Cabral led a delegation of the national liberation movements of the Portuguese colonies to see Pope Paul VI in 1969; in Scandinavia, especially Sweden, he helped to strengthen the movement to provide humanitarian aid to the oppressed peoples of the Portuguese colonies. He pled his cause at the United Nations and in liberal circles throughout North America. In Western Europe, only France refused to let him in.

The PAIGC eventually scored quite a number of impressive international successes. In April 1972, a special United Nations mission visited the liberated regions in the southern part of the country—an event without precedent. This mission's reports led the United Nations Committee on Decolonization to recognize the PAIGC as the only "true and legitimate representative of the peoples of Guinea and the Cape Verde Islands." Next, the U.N. General Assembly passed a series of resolutions confirming recognition of the PAIGC as the sole legitimate representative of the peoples of Guinea and the Cape Verde Islands, and calling on all states, governments, and national and international organizations, as well as U.N. specialized agencies, to strengthen their aid to the PAIGC and to deal exclusively with it. This was also absolutely unprecedented. Lastly, in the course of the same year, the Security Council unanimously adopted a resolution condemning Portuguese colonialism and calling for an end to the colonial war in Africa, withdrawal of the occupation troops and the opening of negotiations. Such a unanimous vote concerning Portugal was also unprecedented, Portugal's usual allies having voted against her, while for the first time, the PAIGC obtained observer status at the United Nations.

Meanwhile, the political development of Guinea-Bissau had continued apace. As of August 1971, the High Council of Struggle, the party's highest body, decided that measures should be taken to organize general elections in the liberated regions during 1972, aiming for the first legislature in Guinea-Bissau. After an eight-month campaign of information and discussion (January–August 1972), elections took place from the end of August to mid-October 1972. Representatives to the People's National Assembly were elected by regional councils from among their members by a two-thirds majority. Each regional council was itself an assembly of representatives elected by the people of all the sectors comprising the region. For the occupied zones where it was not possible to hold elections, the PAIGC named provisional representatives. Any man or woman was eligible to be a candidate who was at least eighteen years old; engaged in productive work or with a clearly defined profession; had never in any way collaborated with the Portuguese; had not committed any civil or political crime.

The final results of the elections, as published in late November 1972, were:

POPULAR ASSEMBLY ELECTIONS

	Registered	Votes Cast	Yes	No
Inside the country	83,000	77,515	75,163	2,352
Outside the country *	4,517	4,517	4,517	
Overall results	87,517	82,032	79,680	2,352
* Militants, cadres, students				

SOURCE: PAIGC.

Those elected included 273 members of the regional councils and 120 members of the People's National Assembly.

On January 20, 1973—between the elections and the proclamation of independence—Amilcar Cabral was assassinated in Conakry by members of his own party. It appears likely that the Portuguese had given certain party cadres reason to hope that they would be granted independence on condition they got rid of the Cape Verdeans who comprised a significant part of the PAIGC leadership. If the political crisis marked by that assassination—followed by an attempted kidnapping of Aristide Pereira, the party's new secretary general—had gone deep, if ethnic problems had really outweighed everything else, the PAIGC would have split. But, in fact, the party's unity was saved. In July 1973, the PAIGC held its second congress inside the liberated areas, with 138 delegates and 60 observers taking part. A permanent four-member secretariat was formed, with Pereira as secretary general and Luis Cabral as deputy secretary general; the two secretaries were Francisco Mendes and J. Bernardo Veira (both having been in charge of armed struggle on a whole front). It was this congress which decided to convene the People's National Assembly in order to proclaim the creation of the state of Guinea-Bissau.

This outcome was primarily the work of Amilcar Cabral, who was surely the most remarkable revolutionary figure of contemporary Africa. Thanks to his political talent, he made a decisive contribution to a well-structured political party, linked to the population. His knowledge of the terrain and his overall vision enabled him to grasp the elements of the conflict and weigh them properly. As an organizer, his achievements include not only the party but also the political and administrative structures of the country itself. As a military theoretician, he was able to grasp and bring out the importance of the clandestine political support structure, and he contributed through his writings, especially *Theory as Weapon* (Havana, 1966) and *National Liberation and Culture* (Syracuse University Press, 1970), to the political thought of his time as well. His intelligent diplomacy won him the cooperation of even such reluctant African neighbors as Senegal. In regard to the Sino-Soviet quarrel, he managed to remain nonaligned in the best sense of the term. "Before we can coexist, we have to exist, and that's what we're fighting for," is what he would say in substance, never letting himself be diverted to enhance or advance the foreign policy of any great power. By virtue of his political sense, his peculiar blend of intelligence and imagination, flexibility and determination, organizational skill and persuasive power, Amilcar Cabral enjoyed a well-deserved prestige, both within his party and in broad international political circles. And for all those who met him there was also the man himself, with his serene sense of humor, his special poetry. He lived simply, devoted his life to the liberation of his people—a liberation that he wanted to be genuine, without a new corrupt and highly privileged class. I remember a big tree in the middle of a clearing near Olossato, where we arrived, some time back, after a long journey on foot. He said, "You know, after independence, this wouldn't make a bad capital—a tree in a clearing to rest under, after making the rounds of the villages. . . . I can tell you, it will be tough."

The independence of Guinea-Bissau is primarily the work of Amilcar Cabral.

But what precisely is this independence?

For Portugal, the war in Guinea has, for more than ten years, proved to be the most difficult and least profitable of all its colonial wars. The country is poor, and from Portugal's point of view its geopolitical position was weak: it was the only colonialist enclave in a West Africa that has otherwise been independent of European power since 1960. Unlike Angola and Mozambique, Guinea has scarcely benefited from foreign investments. All the conditions were therefore right for the Guineans to try to weaken Portugal's positions diplomatically. Nevertheless, that declaration of independence in 1973, proclaimed not as the culmination of a struggle but as a means of advancing it, raises many questions. Why did the PAIGC resort to such an unusual act? Possibly it was because the Portugal of Caetano offered no better prospect than Salazar's regime for a negotiated peace. The Portuguese were clutching at their possessions harder than ever, and would not give up Guinea for fear of encouraging the nationalist movements in Angola and Mozambique. And possibly it was because the PAIGC knew it could not achieve victory on the battlefield. The impossibility for even the best organized of African liberation movements to reach the point of inflicting a Dien Bien Phu on a colonial power is due to a factor which does not seem to have been given adequate attention: *low population.** A decisive military confrontation requires a massive body of men whose losses can be readily made up out of the population (which is the case in Southeast Asia). In the case of Guinea-Bissau, the PAIGC (going by its own statistics at the time of the People's National Assembly elections), faced with 35,000 men in the Portuguese forces, could not

---

* Algeria did not have to face this problem, since its northern rim is densely populated.

call on potentially more than 20,000 men. The coup d'etat by the Portuguese armed forces under General Spinola, and the prospects it opens up both in Portugal itself and in the African territories, in a way amounts to the victory of the African freedom fighters and the final triumph of Amilcar Cabral.

liberation
struggles
in Asia

1. The Experience of the South Vietnamese NLF

The Vietnamese attitude toward authority, stemming from the concept of the "mandate of Heaven," while not a negligible factor, seems to have been greatly overestimated. As is generally known, the concept of the mandate of Heaven bestowing authority is familiar to the Vietnamese as to all of Sinicized Asia and is related to the idea of virtue. A power which no longer has virtue loses the mandate of Heaven.

Each system has its flaws and all of them degenerate into abuses. People molded by Chinese civilization share a common tendency to put up with these abuses in ordinary times, for lack of anything to do about them, although not without denouncing them: petitions to rulers were customary, which did not prevent a general desire for stability from taking precedence over all the rest. The people thus had a sense of life going on according to a certain momentum, which was what was meant by the "virtue" of the dynasty in power. But these same docile masses behave very differently indeed when the hour of revolution strikes, and the West has yet to get over its amazement. At the moment when a virtue (we would say a system) appears exhausted and another is seen getting ready to take its place, the abuses that people had been putting up with appear in a new light. Then and only then is the moment when, with the help of the new principal, they are to be remedied. Complete patience thus gives way to active intolerance; those who used to put up with everything will no longer stand for anything. The point is just this: that the old values no longer count.

This concept enables Paul Mus in his book [1] to explain how power could suddenly change hands, as in Hanoi in August 1945. It has also been used for more recent periods, by other authors.[2] But in the last twenty years or so, in other colonial or semicolonial situations where that concept does not exist, has not heretofore unquestioned authority also been seen to crumble or collapse because something of greater import had ripened? Of course, in Vietnam as elsewhere, tradition is an essential element in explaining certain aspects of the revolutionary phenomenon, but for this purpose, it seems more sound to refer to the Confucian system of thought as a whole rather than to put sole stress on the single concept of the mandate of Heaven. As the sinologist Etienne Balazs has put it, "All of Chinese philosophy is conspicuously social philosophy, and even when a line of thought tries to cut loose from the temporal world to transcend it toward pure metaphysics, it is impossible to understand it without knowing its starting point to which it will soon return. And since its basic concern is always with relations between human beings, not as individuals but as an integral part of social groups, I would even go so far as to say that Chinese philosophy is primarily *political*." [3]

---

[1] Paul Mus, *Vietnam: Sociologie d'une guerre* (Paris: Seuil, 1952).
[2] Francis Fitzgerald, *Fire in the Lake* (Boston: Atlantic Little Brown, 1972). See our review in the June 1973 *Monde Diplomatique*.
[3] Etienne Balazs, *La Bureaucratie céleste* (Paris: Gallimard, 1968), p. 78. (Author's italics.)

In this regard, the fairly smooth transition from Confucianism to Marxism, gradually accomplished between the two world wars by a part of the Vietnamese elite, has been admirably brought out by Nguyen Khac Vien.[4] A state morality much more than a metaphysics, Confucianism and the mentality it develops are particularly open to that other "rationalist" philosophy which is Marxism, all the more as it has been transformed since Leninism and its metamorphoses into a State dogma.

Confucianism having for centuries accustomed minds not to speculate on the great beyond, Marxism had less trouble being accepted than in Islamic or Christian countries. The Confucians had reacted much more sharply against Christianity, not only because the Catholic missionaries often played the role of scouts for colonialism, but also because the notions of divine grace, of sacraments, of God incarnate, were all strange to Confucian thought.

Marxism did not at all upset Confucians by centering man's reflection on political and social problems; the Confucian school had done the same. When it defined man according to the total of his social relations, Marxism was scarcely shocking to the scholars, who considered that man's highest purpose was to correctly assume his social obligations. From the purely moral definition of social obligations in Confucianism to the scientific definition of social relations in Marxism there is of course all the distance that separates a scientific way of thinking from a purely ethical doctrine, but both move on the same level, within the same order of preoccupations. . . . For their part, Marxist militants readily take up the Confucians' political moralism. The idea that those who have responsibilities should display exemplary moral standards is deeply rooted in Confucian countries and, while giving it a different meaning, the Marxist militants of our countries continue the tradition of the famous scholars of ancient times.

Other traits, brought to full development by a long history, are characteristic of Vietnamese society:

—The village commune with its tradition of relative autonomy in relation to the central power, and its council of notables, not hereditary, to which one could rise by virtue of age—and sometimes wealth. The commune system tends to reject the au-

---

[4] Nguyen Khac Vien, "Tradition and Revolution in Vietnam" (Berkeley: Indochina Resource Center, 1974).

thority of the State if the State practices a policy that goes against the communal tradition. That is what happened, for instance, to the Diem regime.

—The cohesion stemming from the commune, but also forced by the necessity of collectively building and maintaining a vital dike system in the Red River Delta, cradle of the Vietnamese nation. In the contemporary period this shows up, even in the south, both in the ability to carry on a struggle in a coordinated way and when need be, to carry it on even in the flat plains, thanks to a whole system of underground shelters and trenches stretching for miles.

—That cohesion in village society shows up at every step of social life. The success or disgrace of one of its members reflects on the entire village. Thus for instance, the ability to keep secrets, mentioned by many military observers, stems from the fact that a person who betrayed the authority recognized by the village would find himself excluded from the community, which is the worst thing that could happen to a Vietnamese peasant.

—Military traditions, both of resistance and of conquest, are strong and enduring in the Vietnamese nation, used to a patient and sustained effort. Moreover, they are strengthened by an unusually developed and homogeneous *national consciousness*.

—Finally, starting in the late twenties, Vietnam has produced a Marxist revolutionary movement rich in experience which —aside from its social objectives—took leadership of Vietnamese nationalism *all by itself*. This movement—tough and hardy for more than forty years—has managed to produce leaders of extremely high quality, with first-hand knowledge of the national (and international) scene, as well as a great many middle-ranking cadres ready to meet every challenge, and has succeeded in becoming a part of the life of the Vietnamese masses, during both the first and second Indochina wars.

Methods   Even though the NLF set land reform as one of its objectives right from the start, for a long time is was limited to confiscation of fields belonging to rich landowners, while medium landowners were treated with indulgence. It was only in 1965 with the massive intervention of American troops that a campaign was launched against landowners in general, but even that was quickly dropped in order to lay stress on the *national* aspect of the struggle, and the medim owners were once more invited to attend information and explanation meetings organized by the NLF in the villages under its control. On the other hand, the NLF made full use of the villagers' resentment against the abuses committed by Saigon officers. Besides, in violation of commune traditions, the Diem government had imposed its agents to administer and supervise the villages; their abuses went on constantly, and dissatisfaction with the authorities was even greater than the desire for land. It should not be overlooked—and on this point the testimony of NLF prisoners is eloquent—that when it comes to motivation, issues involving dignity are at least as important as aspirations toward economic well-being. According to American reports quoting a large number of interrogations of peasants, Viet Cong, and even NLF deserters, the Front's image is that of an organization that behaves "correctly." Its cadres and militants have "decent" attitudes and live frugally, in contrast to Saigon's soldiers and officials. The cadres, especially, provide a fine example of unselfishness, courage, and simplicity, never taking advantage of the privileges their rank might bestow. The prisoner interrogations consulted by Nathan Leites [5] show a certain number of typical characteristics of NLF militants:

—Hatred for traitors and aggressors.

—Mutual criticism sessions which, under the guidance of cadres, help members of a group to get things off their chests and keep pent-up grudges or resentments from festering.

—The NLF attaches the greatest importance to study in general, to political education in particular and to everything that helps them to know the enemy. (This is also in harmony with Confucianism and the scholars' tradition, and in this respect, the NLF

---

[5] Nathan Leites, *The Viet Cong Style of Politics* (Santa Monica: RAND Corporation, 1969).

is closer to Vietnamese historical models than the Saigon army.)

—Absolute dedication and utmost physical effort are required of militants; whereas being sanctioned for a slight infraction of rules means not being allowed to take part in further operations.

—Constant struggle against waste, of ammunition as well as money.

The NLF attitude toward the population differs sharply from that of the Saigon government's soldiers. The Saigon army treats the population with brutality and contempt, robs, plunders, rapes, damages harvests and in general does not carry on before the eyes of the population as befits the representatives of law and order. By contrast, even to the use of "people's courts," the NLF makes every effort to represent "legality." Also according to Nathan Leites, the NLF strikes at innocents much less often than the government, whose army—when a family is suspected of maintaining relations with the NLF—makes the whole hamlet suffer.

In its contacts with the rural population, the NLF's task is made easier by the fact that in their general bearing and living conditions, the Front's militants are closer to the peasants than the government soldiers. Questioned about the personal qualities of the NLF cadres, many peasants mentioned their concern—so different from that of the Saigon army's officers—to explain things rather than give orders. In the Vietnamese village, where people are used to relating to each other on a communal basis, arrogance (which is a reminder of past humiliations), whether it shows up in one's attitude, dress, or language, is a vice. Dignity is felt to be so important that many deserters from the army changed sides after being humiliated by their superiors.

How did the NLF manage to cause the Diem regime to fall apart and to break down the morale of its troops? And how, after 1965, did it manage to stand up to the growing intervention of the American army, to the point of being able to take the offensive at Tet in 1968? After the Geneva Accords, the Diem government strove to assert its authority; two years later, as American advisors took over from French colonial soldiers, the democratic elections which were supposed to be held to decide the future of South Vietnam were not organized, and from that point on, the question of South Vietnam was wide open. Having set up a police state supported by the United States and resting largely on the 600,000 Catholics transplanted from the North, Diem committed three major errors which led to the formation of the NLF and his own downfall (1963). First of all, he lost no time reclaiming from the peasants the two million hectares of land the Viet Minh distributed during the war against the French. In 1956, he forbade the villages to elect their own representatives, instead sending in his own officials to take over the administration and policing of the village. Finally, he alienated both the religious minorities (Buddhists, Cao Dai, Hoa Hao) and the ethnic minorities of the mountainous areas, while at the same time his fierce repression of the old Viet Minh militants who had stayed in the South (since they were southerners) forced them into armed struggle simply to survive. For—and the fact deserves to be recalled—it was not at all Hanoi's encouragements (in the period 1957 to 1959, "peaceful coexistence" was the prevailing line in what was called the "international working-class movement"), but on the contrary, local initiatives that set off what the Vietnamese call the "second resistance." Despite a repression that took a toll of 170,000 South Vietnamese, between 1957 and 1959, the political cadres clung for life to their villages,[6] hiding in underground shelters during the day, coming out at night to give political explanations and arouse the people, making use of the mistakes of the Diem regime. Their first operations were a matter of loosening the Diem regime's stranglehold by liquidating its agents who were running the villages. Never did the Front move in and take over a village without the political base first having been prepared. The villagers were called on to elect their own administration and to confiscate the land belonging to Diemists and absentee landlords in order to dis-

---

[6] Nguyen Van Tien, "Notre stratégie de la guerrilla" (interview recorded by G. Chaliand), *Partisans* 40, Paris, Jan.-Feb. 1968.

tribute it to the peasants, starting with the poorest. Taxes and debts were abolished. But the families of Diemist agents were always spared.

The Front did not restrict its propaganda to a few villages where repression would come down easily, but right from the start addressed itself to whole regions at a time, in order to confront the adversary with a large zone of insecurity. In 1961, the uprising began to spread, and guerrilla forces were formed in the Mekong Delta, with instructors stressing class consciousness (by getting the peasants to recall instances of personal suffering) and patriotism, which grew in importance as more and more American troops kept arriving. At the same time, the Front continued a policy initiated earlier by the Viet Minh, which was to make every effort to win over the ethnic minorities inhabiting the mountainous regions that the Americans were attempting to control for strategic reasons. To accomplish this, the Front trained cadres to speak the *Montagnard* languages and sent them to share the daily life of the minority peoples. For years these political organizers would live in the mountains, in turn training cadres from within the minority groups who, in some cases, subsequently managed to play a leadership role in their communities. Similar persuasive work was aimed at religious minorities (stepped up after the collapse of the Buddhist movement in 1966). The course of the struggle gradually tended to incorporate the peasants into combat, starting with passive self-defense (traps against intruders in the villages) which became increasingly active (traps set on roads and paths, harassment of army columns), covering villages over entire regions, coordinated with revolutionary forces within an overall strategy. This very conception implies, of course, that the struggle is carried on on a large scale and with broad popular support.

The Front is organized around three types of armed forces: self-defense units made up of local guerrillas; regional troops operating in a well-defined geographical sector; the liberation army properly speaking. All three forces are combined in some operations. Political education is carried on constantly in the liberation army. What characterizes the leadership and cadres of the NLF (and here the contrast with Latin America is striking) is their *solid, detailed knowledge of their society,* their ability to blend into the population, the close combination of political and armed struggle, and the ability to keep secrets (so rare in Latin America —or in Arab societies).

The Front combines three forms of struggle: first, political struggle within the population; second, armed struggle, always both political and military; and third, "persuasion" work within the enemy ranks. Thus, an official American estimate put the number of Saigon army soldiers who deserted in 1966 at 132,000. From the time the first Marines landed in Danang in 1965, and the Americans took over offensive operations from the Saigon army, the military character of the war changed and became more bitter, but the NLF managed to adapt, while at this point, North Vietnamese troops came in to lend a hand. In political terms, the patriotic aspect of the war became more obvious to many segments of the population. Meanwhile, in order to cut the NLF off from the people, the Americans proceeded to "regroup" more than a quarter of the population, or, in military jargon, to "generate refugees." Despite all that, the Front was able to maintain close contacts with the regrouped population, angered by the brutal "regroupment" methods. It was such "refugees," parked in the vicinity of the towns, who made it possible for the Front's forces to penetrate more than forty towns and urban centers during the 1968 Tet offensive.

Patient organizational work to set up a nationwide clandestine support structure, care in figuring out the "favorable moment" and the weak points of the adversary in order to act boldly when objective conditions are ripe, constant linkup of political and armed struggle—these are the reasons for the success of the NLF.

Despite the military power brought to bear against it, the NLF never collapsed, managing to maintain its political infrastructure until the American troops finally left. For the first time in its short history, the United States experienced a "nonvictory." Yet it is certain that the blows to the Front between 1965 and 1973 were terribly hard, and on the whole, the damage caused both to the people and the country was without precedent in modern warfare.

Deprived of the support of U.S. troops, the Thieu regime collapsed in April 1975, after a few weeks of offensive led by the North Vietnamese divisions and the NLF forces. Thirty years of struggle for independence had come to an end in Vietnam.

PART TWO:
THE METAMORPHOSIS OF SOCIALISM

4 anti-imperialist national revolutions

The essential factor that makes a national revolution differ from a neocolonial regime is the government's determination to control the country's resources, and this determination is revealed in nationalization of industry. On the other hand, it differs from a revolution with a Socialist dimension by its care to avoid any profound domestic social upheaval, and this is revealed in its rejection of any sort of class struggle. However, with only a few exceptions the regimes that have proclaimed themselves revolutionary in the last decade have also claimed to be Socialist. Yet, apart from Cuba, when it comes to radical social change, none of them has gone beyond a Socialist-sounding rhetoric. The term *socialism* has been widely abused—especially where the notion of socialism had only recently penetrated countries where the demands, or at least the yearnings, for social justice were widespread. There, proclaiming their intention to create a more egalitarian society was simply one way for the new ruling team to gain popular support.

The ideology of these regimes crystallized around anti-colonialism and a usually rather emotional anti-imperialism, with nationalism as the supreme value. This nationalism, promoted by the State in a more or less abstract form, served as a myth to mobilize the masses, notwithstanding the cases (frequent in Africa) where the nation had no real historic existence as such. Regimes in this category were Egypt under Nasser; Guinea, especially during the early years of its independence; Mali under Modibo Keita; Ghana under Kwame Nkrumah, Sukarno's Indonesia (a particularly complex case); Burma and Ceylon during the 1960s; Algeria under both Ben Bella and Boumedienne; Ba'athist Syria and Iraq; Tanzania; Peru under General Velasco; and, in recent years, Congo, Somalia, South Yemen and Libya (this last taking very special forms). While neocolonial or semicolonial regimes prevail in most Third World countries, these national revolutionary regimes account for—or have accounted for—less than a score of governments, some of which have collapsed, while others, after starting off boldly on what seemed a radical course, have gradually bent their policies in a more and more conservative direction. They are characterized, as we have seen, by the rise of a social stratum, originally petty bourgeois, which uses its possession of modern knowledge, and its control of the State and the nationalized sector of the economy, to turn itself into an administrative bourgeoisie.

These regimes differ markedly from the three or four really radical revolutions that have occurred in the Third World since the end of World War II: in China, North Korea, Vietnam, and Cuba. (The Chilean experience under Allende was in a class by itself; its ambiguous and fundamentally transitory nature put it somewhere in between a national revolution Peruvian style, and a national and social revolution Cuban style.) While the regimes labeled Communist became involved in processes that might or do bring about basic changes in the relationship of forces within so-

ciety, national revolutions make only minor changes. They eliminate the most blatant agents of foreign interests, they pay compensation for land expropriated from big landlords (whom they
often co-opt into the State apparatus or encourage to invest in
industry and trade), and they help to build up a new rural middle
class which becomes one of the pillars of the new order. National
revolutions usually grow out of disgust with the politics of the
traditional ruling classes, with their obedience to foreign interests
and scandalous corruption. Run by nationalists with a petty-
bourgeois—and often military—background, they set out to restore national dignity and promote development. And lastly, they
exalt the cultural values of the past (real or imagined). This can
be seen in the attitude taken by the Arab revolutionary regimes
toward Islam, as well as the Peruvian regime's attitude toward the
family and other values traditionally promoted by the Catholic
church, or the Burmese military leaders' attitude toward Buddhism
in its "Socialist" version. What they have in common with Communist states is mainly the size of the State-controlled sector of the
economy. But however similar their terminology may sometimes
appear, they have rejected the essence of Marxism-Leninism: the
class struggle.

It should be noted that Marxism, essentially in its Leninist version, made its influence felt in China and Vietnam soon after
World War I, as well as in Turkey, Persia, India, Indonesia—
with varying degrees of impact. But except in an ephemeral way
in Egypt, it did not penetrate the national-revolution countries we
have mentioned, until after World War II. Whatever headway
Marxism-Leninism made in the Middle East was mainly among
non-Muslim minorities, more receptive to revolutionary ideas advanced in the Western languages they knew, and culturally more
open than the usual local petty bourgeoisie. In Africa, Marxist
penetration was limited to the French and Portuguese colonies and
took place only through the intermediary of the Communist parties
of the mother countries and the trade unions. In the words of Maxime Rodinson, the Marxist version that gained ground following
World War II was a "Stalinism for the underdeveloped"; for

better or for worse it offered a modern world view, Manichean no doubt, but fairly effective in a practical way, with an explanation for the phenomenon of imperialism, concern for economic development, a sound organizational structure and optimistic voluntarism. That particular caricature of Marxism (there are others) has, up to a point, been mimicked by the national revolutions, but their rejection of "scientific socialism" as an ideology expresses the petty bourgeois interests that govern them.

1. Nasser's Egypt

Nasser's Egypt is the classic example of a national revolution, with all the successes and limitations that implies. Carrying out a revolution from the top, nationalizing broad sectors of the economy,[1] while asserting leadership primarily through opposition to foreign control and corrupt native governing classes, Nasser's "free officers" repeated a process that had been carried out some thirty years earlier by Kemal Ataturk, in Turkey (1923–36). The moralistic free officers were hostile to King Farouk's regime and its corrupt politicians, to liberalism, to letting the country fall to the West or to communism. With no doctrine beyond nationalism, their project was to restore Egypt's national dignity and pride—humiliated as it had been by the Farouk regime, the British protectorate and the Palestine defeat—and to modernize it. But to them modernism was basically a matter of *technology,* for unlike their Chinese or North Vietnamese counterparts, the free officers were socially and culturally conservative. Through each and every metamorphosis and volte-face of the Nasser years, the fundamental message was a *return* to Islamic tradition—badly defined and, in any case, not taken in any spiritual sense, but felt to be an essential component of the Egyptian nation. (The totalitarian aspect of the Koran in any case makes it hard to tell what the strictly

---

[1] See B. Hansen and G. A. Marzouk, *Development and Economic Policy in the U.A.R.* (Amsterdam: North Holland, 1965).

religious part of the Muslim heritage is, as distinct from the less religious or not religious at all.) And when the Nasser group, which started out on the right wing of the nationalist movement, began in 1961 to talk about socialism, they continued to see Islam as the cement holding Egypt together. Within that community, they claimed, there was no place for any sort of class struggle; this was completely rejected—or disguised—throughout the life of the regime, and no social class was ever condemned *as a class,* but only on moral grounds. This is not to deny that awareness of injustice and inequality cannot often grow out of moral motivations. But in Egypt, as later in a number of other revolutionary Arab countries, such as Algeria, the emphasis was on returning to a past that had expressed something special, something unique, outside the range of general laws; this took precedence over any attempt to analyze the society historically and rationally.[2]

This constant recourse to the past is easy to understand in the case of peoples under foreign rule. But with leaders who call themselves revolutionary, it looks like an excuse and an evasion, if not an admission of powerlessness. Perhaps it is due to the low cultural level attained by local elites in decultured societies, who fear that they will lose their "identity" if they accept modern thought. Be that as it may, in the name of a community which was both real (inasmuch as it struck a responsive chord among the people) and fictional (inasmuch as it derived from a mythified past) the Nasserians condemned communism and liberalism. In

---

[2] It is worth mentioning what has happened to the Egyptian Marxists. Marxism-Leninism was first taken up in Egypt in the years 1940–56 by members of minorities, and only in the cities. After the war, so long as the Marxist Left kept the "democratic movement" going, with its anti-imperialist and social platform, the various groups (Hadeto, Dalshin, the Communist party) were fairly popular because of their nationalist image. But as soon as the nationalist campaign was taken over by the Nasserians, and especially after 1956, they found themselves isolated, all the more so because the Egyptian Left, in general, tended to be recruited almost entirely from the privileged classes, more at ease relating to the Western intelligentsia than to the largely peasant minority of their own people. That generation of Egyptians has, for the most part, been sacrificed Egyptian-style—that is, left alive but crippled—and has been kept on the sidelines of every major decision affecting Egypt since 1952. The support offered by scholarly and intellectual Marxists to the Nasser government served both to cover the regime on its Left (especially in its relations with the Soviet Union) and to introduce a certain number of ideas that added a tinge of "scientific socialism" to the Nasser regime's facade.

Libya, nearly twenty years later, a very different place indeed, that same attitude was to be pushed to its logical conclusion by Colonel Qaddafi, condemning both capitalism and socialism and setting Islam as the sole standard.

At the outset, the main task of the free officers was to Egyptianize the civil service and tackle the problem of economic development. An initial agrarian reform was undertaken out of obvious necessity: in 1952, 70 percent of the Egyptian peasantry was landless, while 10,000 landlords owned about one-third of the country's arable land. This first reform limited individual land holdings to 200 *feddans* (a feddan is slightly more than an acre) plus 100 feddans for two minor sons—some 2,000 landlords, owning about one-fifth of the arable land, were affected—and allowed owners to sell land by 5-feddan lots to peasants who owned no more than 5 feddans already. This reform was meant to channel the rural bourgeoisie's capital toward investment in industry and to redistribute the largest estates among at least part of the peasantry. But it failed: the rural bourgeoisie preferred to invest in real estate, while in purely agrarian terms, the reform did not go far enough. This "capitalist way of development" was further hampered by the Suez crisis of 1956 and the Egyptian reaction to it: foreign property was nationalized; the administrative bourgeoisie expropriated the most crucial sectors of Egyptian private enterprise and gave former Egyptian capitalists a place in the administration (this was in 1961); the Nasser regime turned to state planning and to "socialism." A second agrarian reform brought the limitation on individual holdings down to 100 feddans (plus 100 feddans for two minor sons). On the eve of the second agrarian reform 430,000 feddans had been distributed to 162,000 families; in the second reform 267,000 families received 780,000 feddans.

Three major facts stand out: Egypt's huge estates were broken up; a new class of medium landowners was formed; but half of the rural population was still landless. The new class of landowners now controls Egypt's agricultural cooperatives, through both the government and the reigning party. The land reform did not alter the rural social order in the countryside in any profound way, the old hierarchies were scarcely disturbed, and what struggles did take place (as in Kamsheesh in 1966) flared up spontaneously, in opposition to the ruling-party machine. The Nasserian national revolution went from being anti-Communist to being Socialist (in its statements at least), without any major grass-roots social struggles and under the influence of successive models, each of which, in turn, raised hopes of solving the crisis of Egyptian society. In this respect, the policy changes accomplished by Premier Sadat's regime demonstrate the failure of Nasser's formulas. In social terms, a small segment of the peasantry, merging with part of the old bourgeoisie, has formed a new rural petty bourgeoisie, while the landless peasants are still left outside the process of change. The proletariat (not at all numerous) benefits from stable employment but is kept from any real decision-making by the trade-union bureaucracy. The most significant phenomenon is the rise of a "new class," an administrative bourgeoisie that is partly replacing and assimilating the old ruling classes, inheriting their life-style and their standards. This transmutation can be observed right in the very places that were the favored playgrounds of the old ruling class—the Gezireh Sporting Club, Muntazah and Mamoura beaches, among others—and it shows how alluring the old bourgeoisie was, itself under the powerful influence of the Western bourgeoisie. This explains why the urban middle classes continue to look down on the countryside as a realm without status (this is very different from China or Vietnam). In underdeveloped countries in general, city people turn their backs on rural life out of a feeling of cultural and physical repulsion. Even the wish to get to know the countryside is foreign to the ruling party's cadres, whether or not they claim to be revolutionaries.

The Egyptian ruling party, laboriously built from the top down, carefully excluding ex-Marxists who came around to the nationalist revolution, has never been anything but an instrument for regimenting the people, rather than mobilizing them. To the people, the Arab Socialist Union looks like a branch of the government or, to be more precise, of the police. No doubt there are deep roots far back in Egyptian history for this administrative approach to social transformation, but the same could be said for China, where recent changes have nevertheless been *qualitatively* different. The Nasser regime managed to reach the masses on the verbal level with more or less religious appeals on such themes as the nation's dignity, but in managing the country's business it came across only as ponderously administrative and bureaucratic. The refusal to mobilize the people was particularly striking in the case of the peasants, in a country where the agrarian problem is still fundamental.

On the world scene the Nasser regime, between 1956 and 1967, capitalized on the prestige it had gained, but without managing to solve either the crisis of Egyptian society—by which I mean the extreme poverty and underemployment of most of the people—or the consequent problem of development. It is not surprising that resting on such a fragile base, the regime's prestige evaporated when it was defeated by the Israelis in June 1967.

The type of system initiated by Nasser has inspired a number of copies, notably in other Arab countries, and when the conditions are favorable the model has made it possible to build a state in both the administrative and centralizing sense of the term. But the overall crisis of these societies is too profound to be resolved with superficial technical remedies. Unlike China and Vietnam—societies whose national life is of ancient formation and has proved hardy and enduring, whose peasantry is strongly attached to the land (in this Egypt alone can compare to them), and which, thanks to their dense populations and/or their distance from Europe, did not undergo any profound deculturization during the period of colonial expansion (witness for instance the continued use of the national language in the Democratic Republic of Vietnam)—the Arab societies suffered a grave identity crisis. Never in China or Vietnam did people worry about losing their identity if they embraced Marxism-Leninism. Yet who could seriously maintain that China and Vietnam are less themselves than they were at the end of the last century? On the contrary, have they not indeed restored their national dignity, risen to the challenge of modernization, and laid the foundations of a true national rebirth? Their attitude is a far cry from the clutching at the past of the Arab regimes.

2. Independent Algeria

Algeria offers another, and characteristic, example of a national revolution.[3] The Algerian government has made a point of taking direct control of the nation's resources—in agriculture, mining, and industry, as well as its valuable petroleum deposits. In economic terms, for investment purposes and for balancing the budget, Algeria has had the advantage of its petroleum and has also benefited from emigration (800,000 Algerians had left the country in 1974), which has somewhat made up for the regime's inability to provide jobs for its people or to overcome the agricultural crisis. The basic political direction chosen by the Boumedienne regime shows up in the type of development undertaken in the late 1960s, an industrialization creating a limited sector of heavy industry, but not jobs; while postponing land reform for half a dozen years for political and social reasons. It is, in any case, no secret that the agrarian reform was finally undertaken against the will of most of the civil service and thanks only to direct pressure from Colonel Boumedienne, and that it was in practice sabotaged in every way possible by both the FNL and the landlords.

Algeria's "agrarian revolution"—undertaken ten years after independence—was presented, despite its label, as "an act of solidarity between the well-to-do and the poor." It was a revolution from above, without any broad mobilization or changes in the social hierarchy, with the FNL playing its usual postindependence role of keeping the population in check rather than leading it forward. And the nationalist ideology promoted by both the party and the government was, and is, all the more conservative in that it tries to conjure away all social antagonisms by appeals to the

---

[3] G. Chaliand, J. Minces, *L'Algérie indépendante* (Paris: Maspero, 1972).

nation's supposed solidarity. The four-year plan of 1969–73 cost nearly half again as much as it was supposed to, and was only half carried out. Employment continues to be the crucial problem in Algeria, with every adult male jobless or underemployed, while each year more than 200,000 persons of working age come onto a job market where only 25,000 permanent new jobs are created annually.

Basically, only two major developments can be observed in Algeria: the building of a state, and the formation of an administrative bourgeoisie to run it. There is no doubt that the Algerian regime has turned out to be much more dynamic than that of most other Third World countries, but its economic successes are more apparent than real. And, when it comes to broad social and cultural matters, the regime, despite its efforts to expand public education and the like, is bogged down in conservatism. The status of women has hardly been improved at all: the minimum age for marriage has been raised and a law passed against forced marriages; but as of 1975 the family laws which leave a repudiated wife destitute have not yet been amended. And for all the talk of "cultural revolution," the Kabyles and other Berber-speaking peoples are denied the right to learn their language in school.

So the Algerian Revolution has remained a national revolution; it has not overturned the structures of society. This state of affairs has its roots in Algeria's history and in the nature of its nationalist movement. As we have seen from 1920 to 1954 the petty bourgeoisie which initiated the nationalist movement had virtually no perspective beyond its legal opposition to Algeria's status as a colony. Never once during the seven years of the war for national liberation did an ideologically revolutionary leadership form, capable of preparing the social content of independence. It is true that the peasants, especially those in the mountains, played an important role, but they were never mobilized to fight for social objectives concerning themselves, in particular, as well as the national cause. Thus in social and cultural matters, independence did not bring about any major changes. The weight of traditions—traditions distorted by colonialism and disrupted by war—was not balanced by any new ideology, the FLN having none of its own other than a nationalism perceived as a return to an ill-defined Arab-Muslim identity. This was not enough to keep even moderately well-off city-dwellers from adhering to European values and patterns of consumption. The army was the country's only organized force (the FLN was still reorganizing twelve years after independence), and it succeeded in imposing a sharply structured government on the civilian petty bourgeoisie on the country as a whole (its excessive centralization is reminiscent in many ways of the ponderous French bureaucracy): this was essential in a country whose structures had been broken up by a century and a half of settler colonization, whose people had had part of their land and even mastery of their native language taken away from them. But the contrast between revolutionary rhetoric and conservative ideology is nonetheless striking.

3. Revolutionary Experiments in Black Africa

Revolutionary experiments in Black Africa have several points in common, but what primarily sets them apart is that they occur in societies which historically never took shape as nations. In each case a sort of act is put on in imitation of a nation, with the state improvising until its institutions can induce the development of a real nation. Between 1958 and 1969, three such experiences left their mark on West Africa—in Guinea, Mali, and Ghana.

In 1958, Guinea became independent when it refused to become part of the "Community" of ex-French areas proposed by General de Gaulle. Its independence was made possible by a centralized and disciplined mass party, the Democratic party of Guinea (DPG), with branches throughout the country, which had to its credit the organization of several important strikes in the cities and various struggles against colonial administrators in the rural areas. So the DPG played a decisive role both before and after the referendum on independence. It quickly became clear that despite certain appearances, the party's secretary general,

Sékou Touré, had no wish to set the country on a radical course. What he mainly set out to do was with whatever aid was available from whatever source, to soften the effects of Guinea's abrupt break with France and to exercise control over public affairs instead of leaving everything in the hands of senior French administrators. At first Guinea stood out as an example, at least by the boldness of its refusal to cooperate with France, and it won over a number of educated French West Africans.

Before long, having nationalized a major part of its economy, Guinea found itself with a sizable public sector, including a monopoly of foreign trade, a newly created agency for domestic commerce, banks, a government mint, and an economic-planning bureau complete with a Three-Year Plan, at least on paper. Almost all the outward signs of Soviet-style socialism were visible, including mass mobilization—an aspect of human investment aimed at putting the country's idle energy to work. But the country's basic resources, its mineral wealth, either remained in the hands of or was entrusted to foreign capital: Fria bauxite belonged to Pechiney-France and Mont Nimba aluminum to the Harvey Aluminum Company of the United States. When in 1963 it became obvious that Guinea was having trouble with the Soviet Union, new legislation on investments was passed.

According to the now-classic pattern, there grew up with this public sector a new class of civil servants, usually springing from the lower ranks of the old colonial administration, who for all the revolutionary jargon rapidly turned into an administrative bourgeoisie. Its corruption was greatly facilitated by the scope of the public sector they were supposed to be supervising. The situation in the nationalized sector and Guinea's economic life in general ended up stagnating and in some areas declining. Government control over internal trade turned out to be little more than a formality; speculation and smuggling caused the Guinean economy serious losses. The failure of state stores in 1963 was followed by liquidation of much of the state-controlled domestic trade; price controls were a failure; and the currency crisis was accompanied by stagnation in farm production and only mediocre industrial progress. And, as the years went by, the administrative bourgeoisie helped itself to more and more privileges.

Despite all these traits—and the additional one of being a very repressive state (no more so, however, than any number of "Francophone" nations which, because they continue to be tied to France, are treated with special kindness by the French press)—the fact remains that Guinea is the only country in the whole of sub-Sahara Africa to have cut the umbilical cord with France. It has taken ten years for any of the other ex-colonies to make the slightest move in that direction. Given the general level of West Africa, this still seems a fundamental, perhaps even decisive, matter. But it does not change the fact that Guinea is still within the orbit of neocolonialism, with a ruling party almost exclusively devoted to serving itself and above all its leader.

Mali, headed by Modibo Keita, started out three years after Guinea to try economic planning. At the time, when only Albania supported China in the Sino-Soviet quarrel, the Soviet Union's prestige as a model was not in question; Soviet-style state planning seemed to the Malians like a cure-all. But Keita's achievements during his first Five Year Plan (1961–65) were slight (although no poorer than those of neighboring countries). Mali had been excessively optimistic in its ambition to achieve an annual GNP growth rate of 8.4 percent; in fact, the growth rate never exceeded 1.7 percent. Yet government did succeed in getting out from under the wing of the old colonial power, and among other things, it became Africanized fairly quickly. At any rate, for all its importance, the "Socialist sector" should be looked at in the context of the Malian economy: in 1967, the labor employed in modern enterprises amounted to about 25,000 wage earners, out of a population of nearly four and a half million. The rural economy of Mali was and remains essentially a matter of subsistence farming. Moreover, the private trading sector enjoyed a privileged situation with little interference from Somiex, the Malian export firm. Any small increase in production was swallowed up by the consumption of the privileged classes. It may be said that the Malian or

Guinean-style system of state control displayed all the drawbacks of collectivisim, with none of the advantages—inasmuch as the State served as a dead weight at the same time it was being defrauded. In fact, in 1962, two years after independence, a process roughly similar to what had taken place in Guinea began to show up in Mali. Despite the adoption of "scientific socialism" as the Party's official ideology, the creation of a school for party organizers and ideological training courses, the Sudanese Union was harshly criticized during its Sixth Congress by its secretary general, Idrissa Diarra, whose report, one year after the choice of a Socialist orientation, acknowledged a "decline in militant spirit" and "a tendency to become bourgeois." "Militant activity has often turned into a routine considered indispensable not in order to persuade, convince, recruit, and build, but merely to safeguard one's own position."

The material comfort which has been given to those who hold positions of responsibility tends to be looked on by them as their due, whereas it is plainly meant to make it easier for them to do a good job, which is not always the way it turns out. For some time we have been treated to the sight of a race toward superfluous riches, a scramble for outward signs of wealth whose display brings out differences in standards of living in an offensive manner and perverts the role of the party. At a number of levels, militant activity is twisted into a purely tactical means of strengthening or achieving a material position, and if we do not watch out, the party within a few years may have turned into a vulgar combine for the promotion of selfish interests.

It is unusual to hear such straightforward talk, although the situation it describes is quite ordinary. A few years later, however, Idrissa Diarra was driven from office—on charges of embezzlement.

The 1969 military coup d'etat put an end to Mali's attempt at socialism. But it is hard to see how Mali, given its particular situation—landlocked, poor in resources, underpopulated, and furthermore, without a really revolutionary party—could ever have carried the Socialist project of Modibo Keita's regime through to a successful conclusion.

These facts raise the problem of regimes whose proclaimed

programs and voluntarism are quite beyond their means, both because the necessary political conditions are lacking—a scrupulously self-denying leadership, grassroots mobilization and participation, neutralization of political opponents—and because the society as a whole is not ripe for it.

In Ghana—which unlike Mali and Guinea is a rich country—a sizable bourgeoisie already existed prior to independence (1957). The economic power of this bourgeoisie was derived either from plantations or from the export-import trade. Ghana's administrative bourgeoisie was drawn mainly from this class, even though Africanization in the senior ranks of government took place only gradually; British colonial officers remained in charge of the army until 1961 and of the ministries until 1962.

In strictly economic terms, the accomplishments of Kwame Nkrumah's regime during Ghana's first nine years were far from negligible. Cocoa and coffee exports increased at a faster rate than those of the Ivory Coast, which were considered remarkable. The construction of important basic economic installations were financed, such as the Volta dam, the industrial center in Tema, a communications network, and a massive public-school program. But these efforts were made at the price of a huge foreign debt, and depended on a trade balance hinging essentially on cocoa, whose price on the world trade market dropped steadily between 1963 and 1966. (In fact, two-thirds of Ghanaian exports depended on cocoa, sold mainly to three countries: Britain, the United States, and West Germany.) The especially sharp drop in cocoa prices in 1965 threatened to make it impossible to achieve the Seven Year Plan (1963–70). Thanks to a considerable increase in production, Ghana earned about as much from its chocolate as it had the year before, but found itself with a deficit in its balance of payments of 70 million Ghanaian pounds. In order to achieve the Plan's goals despite everything, Nkrumah chose to let the financial deficit continue and to lower the prices paid to cocoa producers. This caused grave discontent among the Ghanaian bourgeoisie, and the result was a fresh outbreak of black-market activity, speculation, and rapid inflation. The National Trade Office, responsible for controlling imports of a considerable number of goods, simply failed to enforce the quotas that the government tried to impose. The network of interests between the trader bourgeoisie, the rural bourgeoisie, and the administrative bourgeoisie was a fact. (It is interesting to note that in January 1966, before Nkrumah's fall, the price of cocoa on the New York market fell suddenly from 22.15 cents to 20 cents per pound—a similar drop occurred in London—while in March, after his fall, it rose to 23.65 cents.)

As could be expected, there was no lack of ready aid, direct and indirect, for the military regime which overthrew the nationalist leader. The decisive factor in the fall of Nkrumah was that the Ghanaian bourgeoisie had not been politically eliminated or neutralized. Within the framework of his single party, the Ghanaian bourgeoisie built up its economic power while strengthening its political power—a power Nkrumah sought to check without ever making up his mind to eliminate it. Several assassination attempts against the head of state failed, but this only persuaded him to venture less and less frequently outside his palace. For all his having opted for "scientific socialism," Nkrumah cherished the notion that socialism could emerge without social conflict and without a vanguard party.

In all examples of this type of regime, and especially in Ghana, the role of the trade unions, as copied from the Socialist countries of Eastern Europe and elsewhere, deserves attention. The task of the trade unions is defined as education and propaganda: vocational training, campaigns for production. "Workerist" tendencies—or whatever is labeled as such—are eliminated and strikes are denounced as counterrevolutionary. The trade union is deprived of any function in the struggle for redistribution of income or the simple maintenance of employment, but one task assigned to it is to explain wage freezes to the workers. In fact, workers take no part whatsoever in working out any choices of any kind. Everything is decided by the leadership group, if not by the top leader himself.

In the final analysis, the limits of these revolutionary experiments depend largely on the ideological firmness of the leadership, which either does or does not decide to do what is required to make a revolution: fight against foreign and domestic enemies, involve and organize the masses, train cadres and so on. This is what Nkrumah did not manage to do, and what caused his downfall. Contrary to what the whole of the Western press claimed at the time, Nkrumah was not overthrown for having deprived Ghana of freedom, but for having left too much economic and political power in the hands of the Ghanaian bourgeoisie. The party's left wing, the revolutionary intellectuals grouped around the weekly *Spark,* were a very small minority and lacked organizational links with the population. If Nkrumah's paranoia led him to surround himself with people ready to carry out his orders rather than with real collaborators, the fact remains that as African leaders go, he was in a class by himself. He tried to put into practice two guiding ideas: a revolutionary process to achieve the necessary development rapidly, and a Pan-Africanism which could enable Africa to get together to strengthen its independence. The aid that Ghana provided in that period to other national liberation movements was genuine. But in the absence of any purge of the state apparatus, of any revolutionary party, of dynamic trade unions, the Ghanaian bourgeoisie was the class in power, despite Nkrumah's wishes to the contrary. It was inevitable that it would try to get rid of him, inasmuch as he stood in the way of free enterprise. Having failed to prepare the political and social conditions required for the realization of his program, Nkrumah found himself in the end with only his praetorian guard to defend him—the only segment of the population with everything to lose from a change in regime.

4. Peru: Populism from the Top

On October 3, 1968, the Peruvian Army deposed a civilian president it had helped to put in office five years earlier. This coup d'état was soon followed by confiscation of the International Petroleum

Company (IPC) refineries. The new regime demanded one million dollars in indemnities from the company for "illegal profits and unpaid taxes." From this point on, the army, which up to then had acted mainly on behalf of the Peruvian oligarchy, as an instrument of repression against the reformist and populist program of the American People's Revolutionary Alliance (APRA), no longer sought to enforce the oligarchy's traditional "order." Rather, it got to work carrying out the reforms long promised but never kept by the populist parties. How did it ever get to such a point?

In 1952, a Center for Advanced Military Studies (CAEM) was set up to deal with Peru's national defense problems. Little by little, courses started being given by civilians on questions of economic development and social problems. At the CAEM, and later at the National Planning Institute (INP), the military officers' *desarrollismo*—developmentism—was born. The Peruvian officer corps gradually discovered that Peru's economic and social structure was archaic and had to be changed, both in order to develop the country and to assure domestic tranquility.

By 1966–67, Peru seemed to have reached a dead end. Belaúnde's experiment was a patent failure, while the guerrillas who in 1965 had attempted revolution from the bottom were in a state of collapse. Certain members of the Progressive Social Movement (MSP, which had won less than 1 percent of the votes in the 1962 elections), joined forces with the army, by way of the CAEM, spreading the idea that what Peru needed was an elitist and authoritarian revolution. This concept fit in with the paternalistic views and taste for discipline held by the army's senior officers —especially since the army, as it became more and more politicized, was losing its sense of solidarity with an oligarchy to which, in fact, it had never belonged. Many officers (civilian intellectuals in contact with them) had begun to show marked hostility toward the oligarchy, which they considered unpatriotic and tied to foreign interests. These officers opposed the parliament, with its tiresome debates over trivia; and, although anti-Communist, harbored anti-American sentiments (especially when the United States refused to provide the Peruvian Air Force with modern equipment, which had to be bought in France).

The political awakening among senior officers being fostered by the CAEM had been hastened considerably by the repression of the peasant movement in the years 1959–64—which had forced the army to become involved in combined civic and military tasks—and was most of all hastened by the repression of the guerrilla movement in 1965.[4] The government's war with the guerrillas made the military men realize just how urgent it was to carry out reforms. It took no less than six months and five thousand men to wipe out three groups, each of only a handful of men.

After the capture in 1963 of Hugo Blanco, who had made a serious attempt to organize the Indian peasantry in the valleys of La Convencion and Lares through a campaign of land occupation —which in the final analysis was the most important mass movement in Peru during the 1960s—a guerrilla movement close to the Castroist model had cropped up in 1965. Its leaders were the late Luis de la Puente Uceda, son of an aristocratic family; the late Guillermo Lobaton, from an upper-class Peruvian bourgeois background; and Hector Bejar. De la Puente and Lobaton were members of the MIR (Movement of the Revolutionary Left), while Bejar [5] belonged in the ELN (National Liberation Army). To tell the truth, this movement made more of a splash abroad than at home and never amounted to a real threat to the Peruvian government, which wiped it out within six months. But in mid-1965, there were still three fronts: the Cuzco region (Mesa Pelada), under the command of Luis de la Puente Uceda; the Ayacucho region (La Mar province), under the command of Hector Bejar; and the Junin region (Jauja and Concepcion provinces), under the command of Guillermo Lobaton and Maximo Velardo.

---

[4] Cf. *Las Guerrillas en el Peru y su represion* (Lima: Ministerio de Guerra, 1966). See also: A. Pumaruna. "Pérou, Révolution Insurrection, Guérilla," in *Partisans* (Paris: Maspero, 1965).
[5] Hector Bejar, Peru 1955: *Notes on a Guerrilla Experience* (New York: Monthly Review Press, 1970).

The army, after having discovered the Mesa Pelada group, forced the MIR to go into action. But there was a complete lack of coordination between the various fronts and with any city organizations, and when Lobaton fired the first shots in June 1965, de la Puente was not yet ready, not to mention the northern front, which never did go into action. The only group that was up to doing useful agitational work was the one located in the zone that had previously been politicized by Hugo Blanco. Inspired by the traces of Blanco's political and organizational work, this group undertook to carry on with the aim of building a clandestine party which could provide guerrillas with support, supplies, and information. In this way, they seemed to be fulfilling one of the conditions of successful guerrilla warfare, namely to have roots in the population. But the guerrillas, absorbed in politics, neglected their military preparation. The repeated failure in Latin America to work out an overall guerrilla strategy combining political and military action in a coherent way is really rather astonishing.

The guerrilla leaders' unfamiliarity with Peruvian peasant life meant that they did not find out until they were already involved in armed struggle to what extent the Peruvian peasants (like peasants the world over) were historically respectful and submissive in their attitude toward long-established authorities. "It is true," as Hector Bejar wrote, "that what with the inadequacy and lack of continuity of its theoretical work, the Peruvian left as a whole is unable to come up with an interpretation of Peruvian reality based on serious study. It has always approached reality on the basis of its own abstractions."

But what would happen if another and better structured sort of organization with broader peasant support managed to become established? The example of Vietnam, where even the United States could not manage to crush the insurrection, gave the Peruvian armed forces something to think about. And this is how the army officers were led to look into the causes of the insurrection and to get at the roots of the trouble. They concluded that dependence, underdevelopment, precarious national sovereignty and internal security were interrelated factors which could not be altered without structural change. In other words, Peru's latent state of insurrection convinced its armed forces of the need for agrarian reform combined with industrialization.

In taking power, they set out to modernize Peru's capitalist system, while neutralizing the masses and defusing the sharpest contradictions between classes which gave rise to social unrest that was bound to be exploited by revolutionary groups. Development ensures social peace: this was the message clearly conveyed to the United Nations in September 1969 by the Peruvian foreign minister: "Independence and transformation of structures are the basic foundations of revolutionary thought. . . . Development thus becomes the most accurate synonym for social peace. . . . The concepts of welfare, development, and security are closely linked, whereas the poverty and exploitation which are the expression of the underdeveloped countries bring on an explosive situation."

But, it was quickly obvious that the officers had neither a preestablished program nor any real cohesiveness. Belaúnde had been promising since 1963 that he would solve the petroleum problem—without doing so; the first thing the officers did was to tackle this problem, moved by a desire to win prestige and authority and an urge to get even with the United States. But then what? To get things going, various groups of nationalist intellectuals, especially from the National Planning Institute, came up with concrete proposals for change. From October 1968 to February 1969, there was no telling how things would turn out. Then a crisis arose within the General Staff, along with a power struggle. General Velasco strengthened his position. The conservative army officers, backed by the American-trained technocrats at the Central Bank, lost ground, while the more daring proposals put forward by the NPI technocrats gained acceptance.

It soon became clear that the modernization which the military had in mind would strengthen the government, which was trying to get rid of archaic structures and sectors (in a word, the oligarchy), and give it a bigger share in the profits of foreign companies exploiting Peruvian mineral rights. In June 1969 the army issued a land-reform decree for the sugar plantations of the north, the hard core of its economic strength, and next for the *haciendas* in Central Peru, where the great peasant mobilizations and guerrilla failures had taken place. Parallel to this land reform, the law on bodies of water, which had favored the accumulation of huge coastal properties, was amended; cooperatives were set up in place of plantations; attempts were made to set up cooperatives in the Indian zones of the *minifundios* and, above all, to promote development of a class of medium-sized landowners.[6]

Meanwhile, the attitude of the United States remained hesitant. In late 1969, a $250 million contract involving the Cuajone mines was proposed by an American firm. The timing was just right. The Peruvian government, caught between the fear of going too far and the need to renegotiate for 1972 the deadlines for settling the country's very large foreign debt, was led to accept the out-and-out neocolonialist terms of that contract for fear of being isolated. The war minister wanted to conclude the contract and the minister of mines turned down the terms and handed in his resignation, but the agreement was signed. In scarcely more than a year the new Peruvian regime had marked out both the scope and limitations of its intended "revolution."

"This agrarian reform is not political but technical, and the government is more interested in seeing the *comunero* work than walk." [7] This statement by M. J. L. Gamboa Pierola, the information director—who on August 21, 1969, refused to authorize a march which the *comuneros* of Cerro de Pasco wanted to make to Lima to thank the head of state in person for promulgating the law —sums up the spirit in which the land reform was undertaken. In reality—and this does not diminish its importance—the law was aimed both at transforming the bourgeoisie connected to the land into an industrial bourgeoisie, and at creating a rural petty bourgeoisie which was to be one of the social props of the regime. At

---

[6] Cf. Luis Soberon, *Reforma Agraria en el Peru* (Lima: Instituto de Estudios Peruanos, 1969).
[7] *Reforma agraria Paruana: un balance a los 120 dias,* Direccion de Promocion.

the same time, it was intended to get rid of the archaic structures that obstructed any broadening of the domestic market and thus to lay the groundwork for a capitalist development of the Peruvian economy.

The agrarian reform law of June 24, 1969, abolished "latifundism"; private holdings are limited to 50 hectares along the coast and from 15 to 55 hectares in the sierra and selva, depending on the quality of the land. The law also fixes a maximum of 5,000 head of sheep. Owners receive cash compensation up to 100,000 soles (100 soles equals $2.3), with the rest paid in twenty-year bonds at 5 percent interest. The law empowered the government to issue 15 million soles' worth of agrarian reform bonds to pay for the expropriations. To get a bond reimbursed, its holder must first invest an equivalent sum in industry; the state will then pay out the exchange value of the bond, on the understanding that the money will be invested in the same industry. This provision creates an organic link between land reform and the industrialization process. But the agrarian debt is a heavy burden on the Peruvian treasury.

This agrarian reform is far more significant than the partial reforms undertaken in Venezuela, Colombia, and Chile prior to Allende. It provides for expropriation of eleven and a half million hectares, all of which were seized on June 30, 1971. More than three million hectares have already been distributed and all should be before the June 1975 deadline.

Cooperatives have been set up on the big sugar plantations, now parceled out, along the northern coast. In the sierra, the land reform has also affected the haciendas, but in practice has scarcely touched the *minifundios,* invited to join in cooperatives. The government is unable to provide anything beyond the most modest technical aid, equipment. On the coastal lands, the strictly technical problems are not very serious. Since it is the same workers who, on the whole, are continuing to work on the same land, broken up into cooperatives, it does seem that in technical terms the land reform—at least along the coast, which is where it really matters—will help develop the domestic market.

On the other hand, its political and social significance is far more modest. There is not a trace of self-management: directors of cooperatives are not elected by the peasants but named by the minister of agriculture. Most of the old landlords may have left, but the administrative and technical personnel [8] are still the same. The cooperative includes administrative and supervisory councils of six members each and a delegates' assembly of 120 members. Workers are denied the right of assembly, and their representatives are hand-picked to exclude union militants. Furthermore, each big farm has its military team—usually junior officers—representing the Central Executive Command headed by a colonel in charge of seeing to it that the sugar industry is run properly.

The *latifundios* were divided into farms of less than 150 hectares, on the principle of constituting more profitable units. The farm workers in these new enterprises have a right to 10 percent of the profits if the farm is run by a single boss, or, if it is run by a company, to 50 percent of the net profits, as well as to a voice—unequal, to be sure—on the managing committee, by way of delegates.

Finally, in the big stock-raising haciendas of the sierra, another type of cooperative (called the SAIS) has been formed, in which the peasants' participation is limited to sending a representative to the managing body and receiving a cut of the profits.

An impressive list of measures were simultaneously decreed by the military in other sectors of the economy. So far, the two most important are the mine laws of April 1970 and the laws concerning industry issued later in the same year. (In another area, the University Law of February 1969 abolished student participation in university administration and in general aimed at breaking the radical student movement.) Also, the Andean Pact signed in Lima in May 1969 with Bolivia, Ecuador, Colombia, and Chile aims at creating a market of more than fifty million consumers, by removing customs barriers. They have this in common: they all stay within the limits to be expected from a reformist regime. For

---

[8] Cf. Pumaruna-Letts, Pérou: *Révolution socialiste ou caricature de révolution?* (Paris: Maspero, 1971).

while they may call themselves revolutionary, the Peruvian military rulers do not in the slightest claim to be inspired by socialism or Marxism-Leninism. As we have seen, the agrarian reform has nothing revolutionary about it: the landlords were all paid in one form or another, and the peasants have been kept outside the decision-making process. The International Petroleum Company (IPC), which had long since become the symbol of Peru's subservient status, has been taken over, but oil has not been nationalized. Other monopolies, such as Belco Petroleum—which provides nearly 40 percent of domestic production—continues to make substantial profits. The military government has obtained only $150 million from IPC in payment of a dept estimated at $690 million.

According to a contract signed on December 20, 1969, with the Southern Peru Copper Corporation concerning the Cuajone copper deposits, the American firm committed itself to investing $138 million (at that date, American investment already amounted to $600 million), and mine operations were to allow national copper production to increase by about 60 percent, while additional currency receipts were expected to run to $100 million. But the currency exchange system left Southern perfectly free to recover its capital investment.

In April 1970, the Peruvian government nationalized ore-refining and sales. But in order to attract foreign investment, the government required foreign firms set up in Peru to sell only 25 percent of their stock to the state.

In May, the state took over the Central Reserve Bank. Its management was taken away from the delegates of the private banks and turned over to civil servants. The job of this state bank is to provide investments and loans aimed at encouraging industry. The state took over two other banks as well: the Foreign Bank, which handles transactions abroad, and the National Bank, which handles domestic transactions. Currency-exchange controls were instituted, especially over bank transfers, and liquid assets were frozen in the banks and confiscated. Three hundred million dollars was recovered in this way.

In late July, the government issued the Industries Law,

aimed at stimulating industrialization by granting low-interest long-term credits and major exemptions, as well as lowering taxes in order to increase accumulation of money available for reinvestment. The state reserved control of basic industries for itself, while granting concessions under contract. Other industries remained in the hands of private enterprise. In early November 1970, the Industries Law was completed by a law on "industrial communities," using a labor-capital concept. The "industrial community" comprises all workers in industrial concerns with more than six employees and an annual business turnover of over one million soles (about $23,000). Ten percent of profits is shared among the workers. Each firm is obliged to allot 15 percent of its net profits to the "community," which by reinvestment is able (in theory) to buy up to 50 percent of the firm's stock. The law also provides for at least one member of the community to take part in the firm's management—on condition he is not a trade-union leader.

In practice, the law incites industrialists to reinvest their share of the profits in order to hang onto control of their enterprise, by seeing to it that there is no increase in the number of stocks held by the workers; this further defers the unlikely day when the workers would possess half the capital. On the other hand, the firm's capital increases and its stocks rise in value. As to the concessions granted under contract, the state offers the following deal to a foreign investor: recovery of his initial investment along with profits and, at the end of a stipulated time period, repurchase of his enterprise at a mutually agreed-upon price.

All these measures show that the Peruvian military rulers want to develop and modernize the country by applying a consistent reformist program, eliminating archaic structures by forcing the classes that are attached to them to transfer their interests into the industrial sector and increasing the nation's independence by trying to get a greater share of the profits out of the monopolies, but not going so far as to break with the monopoly-dominated world market. By structural reforms strengthening the state's role in the development of capitalism, the new regime was doing all it could to transform the country from the top down, with minimal popular participation, to the advantage of the modernist bourgeoisie.

In doing so it could count on the support of those modernist sectors of the bourgeoisie which were delighted to have a *gobierno desarrollista*. Broadly speaking, the reforms enacted by the military government were favorably received by the Peruvian church, which nevertheless had reservations about the regime's authoritarianism and advocated greater popular participation. The new rural petty bourgeoisie is a solid pillar of the new regime, while the various Far-Left groups are having a hard time explaining to the masses—if and when they have the opportunity—just why the regime only *appears* to be revolutionary when it has been recognized as such by Fidel Castro and the (pro-Soviet) Peruvian Communist party.

For the military rulers, the risk is that their "revolution from above" might fail for reasons similar to those that brought about the failure of the guerrillas, who for their part, were aiming at a revolution from below.[9] Forty percent of the Peruvian people do not speak Spanish. Twice the population of Cuba is scattered over a territory twelve times more vast, with a per capita income two or three times lower. The shortage of administrative personnel capable of taking charge of the various tasks stemming from the reforms undertaken has led the government to call on retired officers and priests. But there are fewer than 2500 priests in Peru, and retired officers are even less numerous.

Without questioning the importance and necessity of the reforms enacted, one may doubt that Peru can successfully be transformed into a modern country within the framework of a state-controlled capitalism—for reasons which have almost as much to do with Peruvian society itself as with the nature of the military regime. Without a revolution in depth to get the masses moving, without a party, without an external threat forcing people to close ranks, without a charismatic leader, it seems out of the question

---

[9] Luigi Einaudi, *Peruvian Military Relations with the United States* (Santa Monica: RAND Corporation, 1970).

for the regime to reach the masses with an ideology capable of consolidating its efforts.

As time goes by, the military government's self-proclaimed role as a mediator between classes is less and less credible. But one cannot overlook the importance of the changes undertaken by the military rulers: agrarian reform, industrial reform and the reforms now underway affecting education and the state. In economic terms, the modernization program has enabled Peru to replace the semicolonial relations that prevailed in the mining enclaves with an associative system between the monopolies and the state. This system obviously promotes expansion of modern forms of capitalism and extension of the state-controlled sector. Meanwhile, the regime has shown itself to be actively repressive against trade unions, students, and teachers (in Cobriza in 1971, in Puno in 1972, for example). Its economic difficulties worsened and Peru's isolation has become more marked since the fall of Allende.

5. Chile: Too Many Reforms or Not Enough Revolution

The Chilean experiment, under Allende, was an exceptional case which in various respects fell somewhat between a nationalist revolution—which it surpassed—and a social revolution, from which it differed primarily by the fact that state power did not devolve into the hands of the revolutionaries. If the Peruvian experiment was at first tolerated and then accepted by the United States, the Chilian experiment was regarded as unacceptable in a hemisphere where Brazil represents the type of regime to be encouraged. Leaving aside American interventions, direct or indirect,[10] the Allende experiment failed because it fell victim to a dynamic that it did not control (neither on the Right nor on the Left), and because it was either too timid or too extreme. Given

---

[10] Urribe, *Le livre noir de l'intervention américaine au Chile* (Paris: Seuil, 1974). James Petras, Morris H. Morley, *U.S.-Chilean Relations and the Overthrow of the Allende Government* (Mimeo, 1974).

the objectives and methods that Allende had in mind, the second hypothesis appears more serious.

To some people, notably Communists faithful to the Soviet approach, Allende's election in 1970 raised the possibility of a peaceful and legal transition to "socialism," a transformation of structures with existing institutions. The conditions for such a change looked favorable in Chile, thanks to its democratic traditions—unique in Latin America—which extended even to the armed forces. In practice, all possibilities of legal—and thus peaceful—transition had been forbidden by the opposition, which blocked the institutional paths by a series of measures, legal whenever possible, illegal whenever necessary.

Of course the outside factors that brought on Allende's fall cannot be overlooked. During the six years preceding the Allende experiment, Chile received $1 billion in economic aid through various international bodies: the World Bank, the Agency for Inter-American Development (AID), the U.S. Export-Import Bank, the Inter-American Development Bank. During Allende's term, these agencies, under American control, accorded practically no aid, but demanded payment of the debts accumulated by previous governments. After Allende's fall, the Pinochet regime, in its first six months, collected about $470 million in credits. At the same time, the CIA intervened directly in the financial backing of strikes designed to paralyze the Chilean economy. But these facts should not lead to an underestimation of the errors and intrinsic weakness of the Allende experiment in terms of the relationship of forces within Chilean society.

During the first eight months of his government, Allende proceeded (legally) to make some important changes: nationalizing the mines, expropriating the latifundists, establishing state control of the banks. As this was going on, working-class pressure was building up (with more than two-thirds of Chilean working people in urban areas) to extend the process to industry, trade, and services. The petty bourgeoisie was bound to look askance at such a dynamic, even if to begin with, its living standard was only slightly affected.

Chile began to be seriously affected by the combined efforts of outside and inside pressures in the summer of 1972, which saw a drop in industrial production; and before long, the Allende government, in trouble politically, found itself less and less in control of the situation and more and more reduced to mere efforts to survive. In October, two years after Allende came to power, the Chilean Right launched its first offensive: tradesmen and doctors went on strike, highways were blocked by truckers, protest marchers. To this challenge, hundreds of thousands of workers responded by taking over the factories and running them themselves, organizing their own distribution networks. The Chilean Right gave in, hoping to carry the day in the March 1973 elections, which, however, were won by the Allende government. In June 1973, an attempted right-wing military coup was stopped by loyalists in the armed forces. The middle-class offensive—which sought to paralyze the country at a time when the economy had deteriorated badly (galloping inflation, shortages)—was answered by the workers who, outflanking the government on its Left, called for all power to the people. Management of the means of production was taken over as a matter of course by the workers (with varying degrees of initiative and determination), and they set up new distribution networks, as well as *cordones industriales, comandos comunales* for self-defense, and so on, all of which left the traditional working-class leadership far behind. The most active worker sectors called for nationalizing transportation. Hundreds of violent attacks were organized in July and August 1973, by the extreme right-wing group, Patria y Libertad, while the legal parties were sending the army into the factories to disarm the workers. Within the army, the future leaders of the putsch succeeded in squeezing out officers favorable to the government, such as Prats and Sepulveda—which Allende let happen in the name of conciliation and compromise at all costs. Not long before his fall, Allende had formed a cabinet including all the military commanders hostile to his government.

There was no way to straighten out the economy in a situation in which the question of who held political power was still up in the air; the material means of improving the economic situation were in the hands of an opposition determined to overthrow the government. In fact, Allende was paralyzed by his loyalty to the system and by the dynamics of a situation he had helped create, no doubt without grasping all its implications. The only radical transformations in the course of his last year were undertaken by the workers, without the government or even in spite of government directives. With the government unable to solve the economic crisis, politically outflanked on the Right and vainly trying to put a brake on the Left, the Chilean road could only lead to a putsch, unless the military chieftains—sure to win in the end—had consented to let Allende ride out the rest of his term.

5

national and social revolutions

1. The Case of North Vietnam

American bombing raids did not bring about the collapse of the Democratic Republic of Vietnam. How did a little farming country manage to stand up to the technologically most advanced power in the world? It has often been suggested that the DRV was able to hold out because the country had not yet been industrialized and had few needs, in terms of both its infrastructure and its population. That is only partly accurate, and scarcely explains why North Vietnam hung on while so many other Third World countries have collapsed when subjected to infinitely less difficult ordeals.

The answers to that question can only be found by looking at the historical, political, and social realities of Vietnam. The historical reasons are largely related to the structures of rural Vietnamese society; as for the politics and sociology, they too relate to the ideology and organization of the regime. Thanks to a major decentralization which favored the countryside and was facilitated by village commune traditions and a remarkable level of technical competence, North Vietnam was able to stick it out. What other underdeveloped country can pride itself on having a school and a public-health station in every village? Or on having secondary schools and properly equipped clinics in every district? Or on having institutions of higher education and major hospitals equipped for complex surgery in every province?

In reponse to the U.S. bombing escalation, factories that were not destroyed were evacuated from the cities to the provinces, where they were reconverted into workshops; with production reoriented so far as their essential food, health, and educational needs were concerned. Economic life was obviously very hard hit by the bombing, especially industry and the road network, but resistance was stimulated by the sense of defending the homeland in danger, and productive effort, especially in agriculture, was intense—communications, roads, and bridges were continually repaired or replaced. In fact, the bombing cemented North Vietnam's cohesion and increased its social dynamism. (National sentiment can be at its most heartfelt and yet not provide the material and moral wherewithal to stand up to the enemy. The Saigon regime could not have stuck it out if it had been subjected to the air raids inflicted on the north. Aside from problems of infrastructure, it lacked social cohesion, achievements which the people considered worth defending and making sacrifices for—and which in the light of Vietnam's traditional social patterns, have nothing to do with the ideology of free enterprise.)

If the social gap between party cadres and the masses is not wide, and it never has been in Vietnam, and if achievements that the masses can appraise in their daily lives are credited to the regime, then the morality dispensed by the party—part discipline, part civic pride, part austerity, adding up to a kind of puritanism of primitive accumulation—will give the society cohesion and a capacity for resistance. The experts of *The Pentagon Papers* were wrong to credit nationalism alone. And of course, the bombing futher strengthened the North Vietnamese regime's popularity.

In an air war, people may be wounded at any time in any place. In North Vietnam, where communication and transport had become so difficult, medical care had to be available on the spot, everywhere. But, in fact, the regime had not waited for the escalated bombing to set up a decentralized medical network. In 1954 the country's sanitary and medical situation had been deplorable. Efforts were made then to train large numbers of nurses, midwives, paramedics, and doctors who were sent into the countryside. Stress was laid on preventive medicine. A great number of diseases were spread by water, and the slightest bit of rain drained all sorts of filth into the ponds: thus, double septic tanks simple and ingenious, were built and the result was clean villages and well-fertilized rice fields. Wells were dug. In a few years—after a widespread vaccination program—smallpox, malaria, and poliomyelitis had virtually disappeared; typhoid became sporadic. To save time, the paramedics specialized in illnesses most frequent in the villages, such as trachoma. Treated on the spot, trachoma virtually disappeared. In Hung Yen province, an average province, there were 50 doctors and 800 paramedics for 670,000 inhabitants in 1967; where in 1954 there had been only one doctor and four nurses.

Illiteracy in North Vietnam was eradicated among adults in the mid-1960s, largely because the party decided that the national language would be used at all educational levels. During the years of the bombing, curricula were simplified to concentrate on the essentials, since school hours were cut into by the time spent in air-raid shelters or going to and from school. The Second and Third Cycles (equivalent to junior and senior high school), while providing a cultural and political education, do not neglect questions of agronomy—the study of soils, hydraulics, fertilizers, and seeds—so the students get an education that suits the needs of their society and helps them to raise the technical level of the rural areas. Even during the bombing, evening classes for adults were held nationwide. In Vietnam, the centuries-old prestige enjoyed by scholars created a tradition of study that has been constantly encouraged by the state.

In 1936, the eminent geographer Pierre Gourou concluded his study of peasants in the Tonkin delta with these words:

> There does not seem to be any way to improve the material lot of the Tonkinese peasant very much; the excessive density of the population is an evil beyond remedy. It is difficult to provide any significant amount of additional resources to a population numbering more than 400 inhabitants per square kilometer. The peasants are already getting from their soil almost its maximum possible yield; hydraulic works and improvements in agricultural technique cannot increase production to the point of bringing about an overwhelming change in the material conditions of life. . . . Above all, care must be taken not to impair the peasant's moral and social stability, that set of traditions and customs which enable him to put up with a remarkably wretched material condition. If that balanced and reasonable civilization collapsed, what would happen? The peasant would find himself face to face with his poverty, without the consolations he derives from family and village life—that is to say in certain respects from the religious side of life. What would become of a people who saw their own poverty as clear as day and concentrated their thoughts on it, in the absence of any but material things on the minds; who, considering material comfort the sole possible form of happiness, would contemplate their infernal want; who would, finally, convince themselves of the absolute impossibility of improving their lot, inasmuch as transformation of the political or social system can do nothing to counteract a superabundant population? . . . In this over-populated land whose soil could not provide nourishment much more generously than it does today, there is no room to hope that material well-being may one day prevail. But man's needs are not only material; traditional civilization managed to give the peasant a moral and social balance lacking in many more evolved societies that have been plunged into confusion by exclusively material progress. This traditional civilization, gradually adapted to new necessities, alone can give to an appealing and an irreparably destitute people their rightful share of happiness; outside of it lies only disorder and despair.

Since that time, the population of the delta has doubled. Three-quarters of North Vietnam's population and production is concentrated there. And yet a comparison with Gourou's meticulous description reveals considerable improvement and change.

The landscape has changed. The rice paddies, which up until recently were divided and subdivided into tiny plots, since collectivization, stretch out in long, straight strips within rational boundaries. There are far more dams and dikes than there used to be, and the canal network is more extensive. Hydraulic works, improved irrigation, and drainage have made it possible to go from one to two and even three annual crops in many of the fields. Pumping stations have replaced the old, pathetic, and tedious system of ˙scooping water. Trees line the roads, Japanese lilac and "filaos." Eucalyptus trees grow in the red laterite soil, while in between the rice fields—enriched by green nitrogen fertilizer—high-tension wires link the pumping stations. The yield of unmilled rice per hectare, less than 3000 pounds in 1954, now exceeds 4400 pounds, which with two crops instead of one, makes a yield of more than 4 tons per hectare.

These changes, due to the new regime's organization and ideology, partly explain the causes of North Vietnam's exceptional resistance, but there is still more to it than that.

The basic social structure in Vietnam is the village community, sometimes designated by the term "Vietnamese communalism." [1] This form of social organization has existed since the origins of the Vietnamese nation. The state collected tribute and levied young men for the army, but it was the village community, through its council of prominent citizens, that fixed the amount of taxes for each family and picked the recruits. The state was in charge of, among other things, the organization of hydraulic works, of vital importance in the Tonkin delta, cradle of the Vietnamese nation. The king was surrounded by an aristocracy of dignitaries, members of the royal family or companions of the founder of the realm. These dignitaries received an income from lands allotted to them by the king. These lands were not feudal estates, however, but provisional grants which continued to depend on the king, who was not an overlord but a sovereign. Thus it is not accurate to speak of "feudalism" in Vietnam.

"Royal edicts yield to village rules," according to the old

---

[1] Vy Quoc Thuc, *L'Economie communaliste du Viet-Nam* (Hanoi: PhD, 1951); Nguyen Huu Khang, *La Commune annamite* (Paris: Siney, 1946).

saying. And it is true that communalist democracy gave the Vietnamese village an especially solid social cohesion. But when in a later phase—after the fifteenth century—private appropriation of land tended to predominate, royal centralization had its liberal side, for it partly shielded the peasants from the high-handedness of their local notables. The monarchy, in fact, forbade tampering with the communal lands, which were preserved through the centuries and were partly maintained, even during the colonial period.

The specific factors that make up the Vietnamese national character are determined by the village community, its relative autonomy, and its special solidarity. The constant work of dike-building and irrigation, vitally important for the delta rice fields, developed the ingenuity and patient, meticulous workmanship that characterize the Vietnamese peasant. Finally, the necessity for resistance to perpetual invasions of Chinese, Mongols, and so on forged the military qualities of the Vietnamese people as it also supported their uninterrupted expansion toward the Mekong delta. These traits should be kept in mind, for there are few nations in Asia—or anywhere else—capable of putting up such a tenacious and full-scale resistance to the most powerful nation on earth.

It can readily be seen to what extent the decentralization, dispersion, and local autonomy brought on during the American bombing fit right in with the basic historical structure of Vietnamese society. In a situation which many countries would have been at a loss to deal with, Vietnam organized itself fairly easily. What is more, the struggles it has waged since the 1930s have given it a particularly rich revolutionary experience and toughened their fighting capacity.

But the resistance still cannot be fully explained without an appreciation of the transformations brought by the post-1954 system. From 1956 on, production in North Vietnam exceeded levels reached on the eve of World War II, and this, despite serious errors committed in 1954–56 during the agrarian reform.

These errors were serious enough for a (rapidly repressed) peasant revolt to break out in Nghe-An province—the extent of which was considerably blown up, incidentally, by hostile propaganda.[2] Patterned mechanically after the Chinese model, the North Vietnamese land reform suffered from excesses—the kind of "error" which is apparently inherent to the sectarianism of "vanguard," notably "Stalinist," parties. In every village, a search had been made for a certain percentage of landlords, and as a result well-to-do peasants and even middling peasants had had their land taken away from them; some patriotic landowners were liquidated as collaborators with the old colonial administration. (One might add that these errors were all the easier to make on account of the patterns of ownership in the North, where there were very few big landowners. Anyone who hired labor was considered a landlord, even if he owned only three hectares, usually cut up in tiny plots that the owner redistributed to members of his family.) In 1957, these errors were publicly set right—at least those that could be—village by village, and the men who had been in charge, including the Secretary General of the party, Truong Chinh, were transferred. Nevertheless, about 800,000 hectares of land were distributed to 2,220,000 families, amounting to 72 percent of the rural population. The amount of land in cultivation increased by a quarter, compared to 1939; overall production increased by 68 percent, and individual consumption by more than 13 percent.[3]

The reconstruction phase over, "mutual help teams" were set up. Several families would get together to help each other out at harvest time, with the work assigned according to competence (already no longer the traditional sort of mutual assistance). The next step was a cooperative form of production at the lowest level. Farming was done collectively, with a joint management—but each owner still maintained his property rights over his own land. In 1959, full-fledged cooperatives were instituted—according to the party, this was necessary to raise production. In the cooperative, both land and tools were pooled, while the right to individual prop-

---

[2] D. Gareth Porter, *The Myth of the Bloodbath: North Vietnam's Land Reform Reconsidered*, IREA Project, Cornell University, 1972.
[3] Le Chau, *Le Viet-Nam Socialiste* (Paris: Maspero, 1966).

erty was abolished and each participant was rewarded according to the work he put in. Membership was voluntary, and at first only a few farmers joined. At the end of the first year, the earnings of peasants in cooperatives turned out to be lower than the earnings of individual peasants. This was a tough moment for the village organizers; they had no more experience than anyone else in organizing collective work. Meanwhile, the peasants in the cooperatives were tending to adopt the attitudes they had had in working for landlord boss; naturally their productivity dropped.

The government, mobilizing peasants through the party, reduced, if it did not eliminate, the danger of flood by financing the building of dikes around the main beds of the delta. Dams, canals, and irrigation networks made it possible to grow dry rice in upland fields. Finally, the lowlands were drained, to limit as much as possible the areas hit by rainy-season floods. On a broader stretch of farmland it was soon possible to bring in two, and in places three, rice crops a year.

The party persevered in its collectivization policy, and in the second year, peasants in cooperatives caught up with individual peasants. Before long, cooperative members began to reap the benefits of the hydraulic works, which enabled them to harvest several crops annually, while aid from the state gave more and more advantages to them. Soon everyone was in cooperatives, whether Socialist or semi-Socialist.

The rate of increase in North Vietnam's agricultural production—which, in that period, hovered around the exceptionally high figure of 4 percent—would have been decisive with a lower rate of population growth. Moreover, the regime was also trying to diversify production by developing industrial crops (jute, cotton, sugar cane) and encouraging fish culture. By 1962, the collective structures of the cooperatives were mainly laid out; the hydraulic networks were operating; farming was improved with green fertilizer (*azolla*), the rational use of night soil (with the septic tanks), the better farming tools—ploughshares that worked the soil more deeply, rice-bedding devices, grain threshers, mechanisms to bring water up to the fields, and so on. The DRV launched its first five-year plan (1961–65) to lay the foundations for industrialization, but this could not be fulfilled on account of the air war.

On the eve of the escalation, a significant mutation had occurred in the countryside. The cooperatives were bigger and better, using new, improved farming techniques, and with improved organization and management. Each village cooperative—which included a number of work brigades whose leaders were elected by the workers (among candidates picked by the party)—was headed by a party committee of fifteen elected members and an administrative committee. In theory, the former's job was to explain party directives while the latter's was to carry them out. A People's Council of thirty members, elected by all members of the cooperative, in turn elected the nine members of the administrative committee—five men and four women. This committee saw to tax collection, sales of farm products, and everything concerning agriculture and hydraulics. The local political officer was paid by the state at a salary set at three-quarters of the cooperative's highest income; to earn more, he must take part in production. In principle, he was supposed to win his fellow villagers over, but in practice authoritarianism cropped up repeatedly. Still, when a consensus was reached, the villagers themselves exercised control, just as the group enforced the rules and prohibitions that regulated traditional rural societies. And corruption, so widespread in so much of Asia and Africa, was rare and modest in North Vietnam.

This is the leadership structure of the North Vietnamese village. In fact, the regime did not destroy the village structure but purged it of its most flagrant inner contradictions. The old village commune served as a starting point for the cooperatives; the party was clear-sighted enough not to try to form giant cooperatives made up of dozens of villages; this would have wrecked the village structures and shaken their group security. The old notables are gone, the landlords have had their land taken away from them, and the communal lands have become cooperatives. But the autonomous management of the village cooperative survives, and indeed was reinforced by the conditions imposed by the escalated air war. Indeed it may well be that the village is economically and culturally more unified than it used to be in the past. Yet the DRV's leaders have never claimed to establish a special Vietnamese socialism on the basis of the traditional commune. Socialism is, in fact, a modern factor that differs in spirit and organizational form from the traditional commune, and profound changes must be wrought in the peasants' habits and mentality to reach a modern level of work organization.

In the old days, the state took its cut without giving anything back. "One could travel across the delta without encountering a single motor or machine tool," Gourou observed. Today there is an economic exchange. The peasants sell their surplus rice to the state, which pays for pumping stations and the like, and they buy manufactured articles such as thermos bottles and mosquito nets. There was no nationwide market in prewar Vietnam, but the national market is now evident in even the most remote village, which is also connected to the rest of the country by radio, the press, and the party's activities.

Like all regimes that claim to practice scientific socialism, North Vietnam made an effort to introduce a certain kind of women's liberation. "A hundred little girls are not worth even one testicle," a Vietnamese proverb used to say. The regime has led the struggle against forced marriage and polygamy, and for equal rights to education and so on. But the war years perhaps did more to better women's status than the years of peace. With many men in the army, the women, encouraged by the party, played a more important role in production and above all took on more responsible duties. Young women often served in the militia and learned how to handle weapons. Certainly North Vietnam's young women *seem* liberated and different from their mothers: they often assert themselves fearlessly, want to take part in things, look forward to having fewer children and more responsibilities. And this undoubtedly does represent a profound qualitative change compared to the past. But this emancipation stops short of real sexual freedom. What could be called the puritanism of primitive accumulation has been grafted onto a society that is still only slightly urbanized, and this produces an outlook that could usefully be compared to the sexual ethic of the Victorians. A couple caught unaware on the banks of the Red River in Hanoi is publicly admonished by their neighborhood committee. Repression of sexuality is probably an area in which bureaucratic rigor can be exercised with utmost good conscience, bolstered by the prohibitions and moralism of rural societies, at least so far as women are concerned.

One thing that struck some foreign visitors to the DRV during the period of the American bombing was how stiff and stereotyped so many of the cadres seemed. This kind of thing is obviously related to the particular bureaucratic nature of the regime. In this respect the war brought with it a certain amount of democratization, which was encouraged from the top, starting in April 1967. Local plans, which had previously been imposed by the party, from then on were worked out after consultations and with more cooperative members participating. The party stopped presenting candidates for the People's Council elections; outstanding workers were chosen, without prior designation, by the cooperative members, and members of the administrative committees lost the right to the hectare of land that had previously been reserved for them. But the fact still remains that party cadres continue to impose party directives, and things are a far cry from Marx's "free collectivity of producers."

Still, whether one likes it or not, the party did lead the Vietnamese peasantry in the national liberation struggle, and it was the party which mobilized the masses to build up the country and defend national independence simultaneously. This leads to the problem of ideology, perhaps the aspect least clearly perceived by American observers in Vietnam. Frances Fitzgerald's best-selling book [4] on the war in Vietnam, despite obvious merits, does not escape this defect, for the author, in effect, tries to explain the

---

[4] *Fire in the Lake* (Boston: Atlantic Monthly Press, 1972).

present essentially—if not solely—in terms of the historical and cultural traditions of Vietnamese society, and underestimates the importance of ideology. Thus Americans tend to reduce the social and economic causes of the war to more or less accidental, secondary factors. But if traditions alone really provided the basic explanation for the Vietnamese ability to fight, it would be hard to see why, before the massive intervention of American troops and the participation of North Vietnamese troops in the fighting, the NLF was defeating the South Vietnamese army.

It is no simple matter to explain the role of ideology, especially if one starts out believing that one's own thought—and consequently the thinking of one's own society—is "rational," whereas only the adversary is "ideologized." This problem is more common in the United States than in other Western countries, notably since the cold war. (For instance, in that period, the United States did not produce any political thinker who, like Raymond Aron, was capable of combatting Communists on Marxist grounds and able to make the distinction between what Maxime Rodinson calls "Marxist sociology" and "Marxist ideology." [5]) Thus the American approach to North Vietnamese political realities was misdirected by a priori ideological assumptions that distorted and falsified the view of the adversary. (This can be seen in all but a few of the documents in *The Pentagon Papers*.) This is what I mean by "anti-Communist ideology," whether conscious or unconscious, fed by ignorance and misunderstanding of what motivates the adversary. In Vietnam, the ideology dispensed by the cadres of what was then the Viet Minh not only made it possible to forge a victory over colonialism that solved the crisis of Vietnamese society as a whole, but also enabled the North Vietnamese to strengthen their newly won independence and lay the foundations of industry and commerce. In North Vietnam that voluntarist ideology—characteristic, by the way, of the Leninist conception of the party—worked to mobilize the masses around a few central ideas:

---

[5] Maxime Rodinson, "Sociologie Marxiste et Idéologie Marxiste," *Diogène* 64 (Oct.-Dec. 1968), 70–104.

- First of all, national independence—an independence moreover, maintained equally vis-à-vis China and the Soviet Union.
- Next, economic construction to modernize the country. This transformation is aimed at changing the lives of the whole population and not just at bringing advantages exclusively to a particular stratum of society. To hasten the process, the ideology spread among the masses by the cadres was based on notions of national *dignity* and social justice; it tended to change the traditional relationhips of work and time, making them more rational in the modern sense of more efficient. By constant pressure—not police coercion, but a social pressure based on rural traditions in which the individual's interests count far less than those of the group (it is a travesty to mistake this for violent coercion, as if North Vietnam were the U.S.S.R. at the height of Stalinism)—the cadres nudged the peasantry into changing their traditional behavior so as to make up for lost time, for that historic retardation which characterizes so-called developing countries. This mobilizing ideology could obviously get results only if life as the masses experienced it did not noticeably contradict the slogans. And only when the masses shared in this ideology did it become possible to accomplish things that only a short time before, the stagnant, submissive traditional society had seemed—in its own eyes as well as in the eyes of Western observers—unable even to muster the force to engender.[6]

The important fact is that starting in the 1920s and especially the 1930s, the political organization that was successively the Indochinese Communist party and the Viet Minh was the only

[6] Nguyen Khac Vien is surely right to mention the favorable ground for this ideology prepared by the state morality which Confucianism used to be. "Marxism did not at all upset Confucians in its concentration on political and social problems. The Confucian school had done just that. By defining man as the totality of his social relationships, Marxism hardly came as a shock to the Confucian scholar who had always considered the highest aim of man to be the fulfillment of his social obligations. . . . For their part, Marxist militants readily drew Confucian political moralism. The notion that leaders should exemplify high moral standards is deeply engrained in Confucian countries. Today, Marxist militants, while giving it a new meaning, carry on the tradition of famous scholars of old." (*Tradition and Revolution in Vietnam,* David Marr and Jayne Werner, eds. [Washington, D.C.: The Indochina Resource Center, 1974].)

party to take up not only the people's aspirations for social justice, but also, and especially, the national independence movement. After the French wiped out the Vietnam Quoc Dan Dang, modeled on the Chinese Kuomintang, in 1930, no other party in Vietnam existed to lead the nationalist movement.

The qualitative difference on the social level as well as in national construction and independence is striking when one looks at the Vietnamese experience, compared to the previously mentioned nationalist revolutions. But its limitations, referred to in passing (especially when it comes to democratic freedoms) call for a general examination of the "Socialist" project both in theory and in practice, as it relates to the phenomenon of bureaucracy.

6
*the theory
and practices of
Marxism-Leninism*

1. A Retrospective Glance at the Bolsheviks and the Marxist Project

No evaluation of socialism in the Third World is possible without a reminder of both the historical experience of the Russian revolution and the principles of its founding fathers. It is necessary to go over this ground, however elementary it may be to those familiar with Marxism, because grotesque lies and distortions have—deliberately or unwittingly—spread a great deal of confusion.

The Russian revolution stemmed both from social contradictions and clashes and from severe hardships caused by World War I. Despite Russia's recent burst of industrialization, the country was still backward, and for all its 3 million industrial workers, more than 80 percent of the populace were still rural peasants. Within the Russian Marxist movement, the need for a bourgeois democratic revolution was taken for granted, just as the poor peasantry was recognized as one of the forces whose mobilization could help overthrow Czarism. In contrast to the Mensheviks, the Bolsheviks considered the Russian bourgeoisie too weak to lead the revolution. Thus Lenin foresaw an alliance between the proletariat and the peasantry culminating in a "democratic dictatorship of workers and peasants" that would rid Russia of its archaic social institutions and spur the development of a capitalist type of economy, as the first step toward socialism. Trotsky also thought that only the proletariat was able to lead the revolutionary process, and that, far from stopping short at the bourgeois democratic stage, it ought to forge right ahead from one thing to the next, undertaking its own proletarian revolution—a "permanent revolution."

While the February 1917 revolution brought to power a provisional government of bourgeois liberals grouped around Kerensky, the soviets that had been set up in the early stages of the revolution—councils of workers' delegates, elected in the factories and sometimes in neighborhoods, some by soldiers in the army and still others by peasants—played an increasingly important role.

Until April, the Bolshevik party was in a state of confusion, with most of its leaders supporting the provisional government and continuation of the war. But in April, at Lenin's instigation, the party sharpened its stand, arguing that only the proletariat was able to assume leadership of the revolution (thereby aligning with Trotsky's position). What the worker and peasant masses wanted—"bread, peace and land"—was unattainable within the framework of Kerensky's bourgeois republic. Only the proletariat was up to guiding the revolution, and the soviets were parallel governing bodies destined to replace the existing government. At the time, however, there was no thought of expropriating the capitalists. Rather, the idea was first to develop capitalism under the political leadership of the proletariat, in order to create conditions that would eventually make it possible to proceed to socialism. With this in mind, Lenin called for "revolutionary democratic" measures (nationalizing banks and monopolies, grouping industrialists into cartels, and so on). There was no notion of abolishing private property. The idea was to set up a system of state capitalism in which the government's role would be limited to supervising the economy. But that objective could not be attained without destroying the old state apparatus and replacing it by the state of workers and peasants based on the soviets.

The October uprising desired by Lenin brought the soviets to power. But at first the Bolsheviks—along with other strains of Russian social democracy—were left behind by the workers, who took full control of the factories. Not until June 1918 did the Soviet government somewhat reluctantly take the first measures nationalizing basic industries. Meanwhile, land was redistributed, becoming the property of the nation, with its fruits to those who work it. Wage labor was banned; only family and cooperative management were allowed. In towns and villages, the soviets organized production, food supplies, defense. (Although the war was ended by the Treaty of Brest-Litovsk which, signed after considerable internal debate, formally recognized the loss of large stretches of Russia's nations' territory, the White counterrevolution supported by the Allies was threatening.) The economic situation was steadily worsening. In order to deal simultaneously with the Whites, the problems of getting production going again, shortages, the growing discontent of the peasants (who were loath to trade their farm products for devalued rubles), and the hostility of the old parties, the new rulers centralized decision-making. This meant de facto suppression of the workers' democracy that had developed in the early months. To meet military and economic needs, the Bolsheviks, who henceforth ruled alone, reconstituted a conventional state apparatus and a conventional type of army. The masses of workers and peasants rapidly vanished from the scene as an organized force.

By the end of the civil war, in 1920, the situation was catastrophic. Industrial production had dropped to less than a quarter of what it was before the war; agricultural production had fallen off considerably. Famine stalked the cities: Petrograd and Moscow lost nearly half their populations, and the number of workers dropped to 1.5 million. The "proletarian revolution" had triumphed, but the working class itself had virtually melted away. The life had gone out of the soviets, which were scarcely more than transmission belts for orders from the party. During the civil war, the party had ended up depending completely on the state and the army (both of which absorbed a goodly share of Bolshevik militants, many of them workers). What with the urgent need to raise production, the way was open for the emergence of a new hierarchy of highly paid experts and political officers beyond their control. This was unpopular among those segments of the working class who enjoyed a high level of political consciousness, and among some political groupings—especially outside the Bolshevik party. In 1921, the Worker Opposition, whose main spokesmen were Alexandra Kollontai and Shliapnikov, demanded that factory and workshop committees take charge of production and the producers themselves to choose the country's top economic decision makers. The Worker Opposition was defeated at the Tenth Party Congress and condemned for "trade-union deviationism." Not only was the gap widening between some of the most politicized workers and the state, run by the Bolshevik party; but, in fact, the party had substituted itself for the class that was theoretically supposed to lead the revolution.

But is not the seed of the Bolshevik party's bureaucratization contained in the very concept of such a party—a vanguard of professional revolutionaries acting as the conscience of a class considered incapable of carrying through its own revolution by and for itself? The party's intervention as an instrument of agitation and propaganda to get everything ready for the seizure of power is bound to lead to a more or less exclusive arrogation of decision-making power. True, the debate is strictly theoretical so long as one views the "dictatorship of the proletariat"—that is, a situation in which the workers themselves take charge of economic, social, and political life as a whole—as utopian. In any case, if the proletariat itself does not create the necessary conditions for a Socialist organization of work and society, nobody can go ahead and do the job for it.

At the Tenth Congress, which was held just when the Russian revolutionary government was putting down the Kronstadt rebellion, the Bolshevik party, now exercising a dictatorship "in the name of the proletariat," officially admitted the failure of the proletarian revolution to spread (as was theoretically indispensable) to Central and Western Europe. The Russian revolution found itself isolated in the midst of a hardier capitalist system and a more firmly rooted reformism in Europe than it had reckoned on. A drastic shift in direction was unavoidable; the New Economic Policy (NEP), the Leninist project for developing state capitalism (while waiting for the German revolution) and maintaining proletarian power at the same time, failed. Revolutionary political power was now embodied solely in the Bolshevik party. And the party did not exist independent of the economic and social structures: it virtually controlled the public sector. The growth of a state apparatus more and more cut off from the masses was encouraged by a steadily increasing interpenetration of the party and the economic and governmental bureaucracy. In political terms, the NEP did not amount to a "momentary setback" in the march toward socialism. If it got the economy going again, it in no way enabled the proletariat to gain political strength. Once more reduced to the status of wage-earners and kept out of all important decision-making, the workers had enjoyed power for only a brief period of crisis. Within a few years, the bureaucracy totally dominated both the party and the state, in an ever more authoritarian manner. This amply confirmed the fears expressed in 1918 by Rosa Luxembourg when she protested against oppression of opposition parties and newspapers. "Freedom reserved solely for supporters of the government and party members, no matter how numerous they may be, is not freedom. Freedom is always freedom for the one who thinks differently." Since all that mattered anymore was to develop the economy—never mind abolishing exploitation—the bureaucracy no longer had to link the fate of the regime to that of the world revolution. Before long, Stalin decreed that "socialism in one country" was possible. A Socialist system could be built in the U.S.S.R. by pushing exploitation of the labor force to the utmost. All that was left was to smash the opposition within the party. When Trotsky and the Left Opposition, who until 1927 had called for restoration of party democracy (but not for a multiparty system), decided to appear to the workers, they found themselves talking to the air.[1]

Under Stalin's rule, the obedient bureaucracy went ahead with purges, with forced collectivization, with the Five-Year Plans; these turned the U.S.S.R. into a great power and established government dictatorship. With hindsight it can be said that Stalinism was merely a prolongation of the Lenin era, some aspects of which it consolidated or erected into theoretical principles. That is both true and false. False, because the spirit was different, and under Lenin the antidemocratic measures were considered "temporary" and not presented as the very epitome of "socialism." True, because the objective situation led to the taking of antidemocratic measures, and these were consistent with the very essence of bolshevism, even if Stalin's personality added a special ferocity to the proceedings.

Let us go back to the founding fathers, mainly Marx. The proletariat, according to Marxist theory, represents the only social force capable of achieving the transition to a higher state of civilization. The proletarian revolution will abolish all classes, the proletariat included, as the culmination of a process. The state, which has always served as the instrument of the dictatorship of one class or another, will wither away, and a community of free men will

---

[1] Trotsky criticized the growth of the bureaucracy, the notion of "socialism in one country," the transformation of the Bolshevik party into a guardian of the status quo and exclusive defender of Soviet policy. Nevertheless, when it comes to analyzing our own era, the core of Trotsky's thought appears to be inoperative. On the eve of World War II, Trotsky had no doubt as to the collapse of capitalism, and was even further from imagining that it is capable of yet another boom; he thought the war would necessarily lead to either worldwide proletarian revolution or a return to barbarism. He continued to view the U.S.S.R. as a workers' state, no doubt deformed, but the workers' nevertheless. Consequently, the bureaucracy was not a class. It is obviously impossible to start from such premises and successfully analyze the phenomena of the postwar world.

take shape so as to bring out the full potential of each individual. "Between capitalist society and Communist society lies the period of revolutionary transformation from the first to the second. To which corresponds a period of political transition in which the state cannot be anything other than the revolutionary dictatorship of the proletariat." According to Marx, this dictatorship is the most democratic of dictatorships, since it is exercised by the majority over the minority who used to own the means of production. When he spoke of the dictatorship of the proletariat, Marx got his ideas from the Paris Commune. (Lenin, in *The State and Revolution*, argued that the working class would exercise its dictatorship by way of councils whose members would be directly elected by the workers and subject to recall. The councils would run the economy and the state, building from the bottom. Simplified administrative tasks would be performed by everyone in rotation, with no salaries higher than that of a skilled worker.)

The transition from capitalism to socialism is preconditioned by a high level of productive forces and by the reign of freedom. Socialism itself is the stage below communism. Socialist society, in Marx's terms, would be a gathering of free men; productive forces would be in the hands of the associated producers, with free and equal association among producers. (For Marx, as for all Marxists including Lenin, no coercive state body would be placed above the associated workers, who would themselves constitute the Socialist state.) However, free development and free satisfaction of individual wants would remain subordinate to a fresh development of productive forces, especially labor productivity. The worker would still be bound to his specialization and individuals would be subordinated to the division of labor.

"In a higher phase of Communist society," Marx wrote, in *Critique of the Gotha Program,*

when the enslaving subordination of individuals to the division of labor will have disappeared, and with it the antagonism between intellectual and manual labor, when work will have become not just a way to make a living but the primary need in life, when with the multi-sided development of individual faculties productive forces will be increasing and all the sources of collective wealth will be pouring forth abundantly, only then can the narrow horizon of bourgeois law be completely left behind, and society will be able to inscribe upon its banners: "From each according to his abilities, to each according to his needs!"

Judging by these standards, it goes without saying that never in the course of contemporary history has any dictatorship been exercised by the proletariat long enough to count. Still less has there ever been any socialism in the original transitional sense of the term: a state run by workers in free association, with a high level of productive forces, under the reign of freedom. Aside from the fact that this could only be a matter of a planet-wide phenomenon, is not socialism (in the eyes of those who have sought to define it) the end of the social division of labor between those who produce and those who accumulate, as well as of the hierarchy between those who lead and those who are led?

After going over this ground, familiar to all who have a smattering of Marxism, one can only remark to what extent Marx's thought, judged nonideologically, appears in its "prophetic" aspect (only a tiny part of his work, in any case) seems utopian if not downright "nonscientific." In this respect, Marx, like the other Socialists of his time, was an heir to the rationalists of seventeenth- and eighteenth-century Europe, as well as to the optimists of the enlightenment, whose faith in scientific progress carried on into the nineteenth century. But now, especially after Nazism and then Stalinism, one is moved to take a critical view of the confidence displayed by Marx and Marxists in history's conformity to reason, and in a science capable of discerning the meaning and direction of the historical process.

As of the early twentieth century, capitalism's capacity for survival—unexpected from a Marxist standpoint—had the effect of strengthening reformist tendencies within working-class movements in industrialized countries. In his theoretical effort to adapt to this state of affairs, Lenin, for one, tried to redefine the prospects for both revolution and capitalism's development in its "imperialist" stage, and to integrate the peasantry into Marxist theory and strategy as a revolutionary ally. But without doubt, his major contribution was his theory of a vanguard party: a party made up of professional revolutionaries, intellectuals, and semi-intellectuals.

The workers, we have said, *could not yet have* [2] social democratic consciousness. That could come only from outside. The history of all countries shows that through its own efforts, the working class can arrive only at trade-union consciousness, that is, at the conviction of the need to get together in unions, fight the bosses, demand that the government pass such and such laws required by the workers, and so on. . . . As for Socialist doctrine, it is the product of philosophical, historical, and economic theories elaborated by the educated representatives of the propertied classes, that is, by intellectuals. The very founders of scientific socialism themselves, Marx and Engels, were by their social position bourgeois intellectuals.

From this, Lenin concluded that what was needed to get the working class going was a vanguard party, distinct from the majority of the proletariat and embodying its real class consciousness.

One might be tempted to blame all the bureaucratic evils that have afflicted Socialist revolutions on this Leninist concept of the party, but it is only fair to say that no Marxist-inspired revolution of any duration has been accomplished without recourse to it. There has been little sign of the supposed revolutionary potential of the working class in the industrialized countries during the past half-century. More or less sharing in the dominant ideology and economic advantages that flow from Western imperialism's commanding world position, Western proletarians have in their various ways all been essentially reformist. Their attitude can no more be satisfactorily explained away by "betrayal" on the part of the "Stalinist" parties than it could be explained away during World War I by betrayal on the part of the Social Democratic parties. It is self-evident that the theorists who developed proletarian ideology were bourgeois, and that the proletariat has never had a world view of its own to oppose to that of the bourgeoisie.

---

[2] Lenin's emphasis in *What Is to Be Done?*

On the other hand, whenever a revolutionary upsurge comes along, drawing its strength from the bottom, without guidance from the top, the proletariat—or at least its most active segment—tends each time in differing ways and circumstances to spontaneously set up more or less identical democratic institutions. Councils are by no means peculiarly Soviet. Representatives democratically elected by the working people in a given locality or on a larger scale, and tending to take on legislative and executive powers, can be seen in the shop-steward committees in Britain, as well as in councils formed in Bavaria, Turin, Hungary, Catalonia, and elsewhere. The mere existence of councils does not automatically solve the problem of political power, of course. They can go on being "parallel" bodies right up until they are repressed. And historically, councils and committees set up spontaneously by workers seem to follow the initial burst of energy, with a subsequent rapid loss of momentum, due to lack of cohesion and an accelerated process of delegating responsibility.

As to what is called the proletarian party, in countries where it has managed to triumph during the past twenty-five years, its troops have been peasants and its leaders intellectuals, usually of petty bourgeois origin, whose nationalism was exasperated by the humiliation stemming from Western expansionism and the corruption and servility of the traditional ruling classes. If Marxism-Leninism—despite being codified into elementary dogmas during the Stalinist years—has still managed to be operationally effective, this is because, starting from Marx's conception of class contradictions, it provides three of Lenin's contributions which follow from the concept of "imperialism"—the vanguard party; incorporation of the poor peasantry into revolutionary strategy; and the priority of industrialization over Socialist liberation. To the extent that he thought the Russian revolution was only a prefiguration of the imminent proletarian revolution, Lenin was led to develop concepts foreshadowing Stalin's policy on economic development. For socialism presupposes a high degree of industrialization and productivity of labor, which means that in a backward country, industrialization and development take priority over socialization in the sense of sharing.

It is important here to be precise. Given the revolutionary nature of the proletariat historically speaking, Lenin's concept of the vanguard party is either at the very root of the confiscation of power from the workers, who have been deprived of the chance to exercise their dictatorship, or else the proletariat, as a class, is historically incapable of running society. If the latter is so, then the mediation of the party as conceived by Lenin—with all its consequences, not just those related to Soviet history, since the Chinese experience stems from the same theoretical kernel—is the only strategic conception that has yet brought about any radical social change in backward countries. This is true even if the changes involved the growth of a ruling bureaucracy.

In the U.S.S.R., the Bolshevik party apparatus turned out to be the unconscious instrument by which a new layer of society took power. Integrated into the state apparatus and identified with it, the party was in no position to combat a development in which it played a leading part. The Soviet experience gave rise to a number of features that today are considered classic aspects of the heritage of the "international working-class movement": suppression of other political parties; the dismissal of the free play of contending opinions as a bourgeois luxury, if not a mystification; a centralized dictatorship by the party (or its leader) reaching into all areas of social life and eliminating whatever fails to conform to the standards of the moment; a revolutionary rhetoric used to conceal the practice of traditional power politics in order to safeguard the interests of the state. The policy of national interest practiced by the Soviet Union with particular cynicism during the Stalin period has been just as thoroughly adopted, although on its own scale, by China (which need come as a shock only to those who view China as Utopia incarnate). The idea, introduced by Stalin in 1936 when promulgating the new Soviet constitution, and still current, that the U.S.S.R. has achieved socialism (although still behind the advanced industrial countries when it comes to the level of productive forces, for example), is a parody of Marxism—just as the Stalinist dictatorship is a ghastly parody of what the dictatorship of the proletariat was intended to be. When Khrushchev promised that communism would be achieved in the U.S.S.R. by

1980 (four years ahead of George Orwell and with more butter), it is hardly likely that he meant to suggest the forthcoming withering away of the state.

The facts show that productive relationships do not change simply because the state takes over management from the private boss and his agents. They change only if the workers get a grip on running their enterprises and on the country's political life. This does not seem to have happened anywhere, even though the extent of nonparticipation varies considerably.

2. Self-Management in Yugoslavia

In the early 1950s, shortly after Yugoslavia broke with the U.S.S.R. in 1948—a break made possible by the fact that Yugoslavia had waged a large-scale resistance against fascism and the Yugoslav leaders were the home-grown product of such struggles —the country adopted self-management. At first the idea was to provide a model of socialism other than that of the U.S.S.R. and the "people's democracies." It was a system meant to combat what the Yugoslav leaders called "bureaucratic socialism." The idea was to fight bureaucratization by having the workers run their enterprises themselves.

The following basic rights were granted by the Yugoslav Constitution to Management Committees, to which all employees of an enterprise were eligible for election by universal and secret ballot:

● To determine the volume of production and price of goods produced.

● To take charge of all transactions required by production.

● To split the earnings left over after meeting collective social needs.

● To use and distribute investment funds.

● To make decisions concerning enlargement or modernization of the enterprise.

● To hire or fire workers according to the conditions laid down by the law in labor relations.

- To work out the internal organization and work plans of the enterprise.
- To make decisions regarding the merger of the enterprise with others, or to shut it down.

The institutions of self-management within an enterprise were:

- The Workers' Council, elected so as to allow equal representation to engineers, skilled workers, and unskilled workers; it makes the firm's decisions on the basis of proposals presented by the Management Committee, and approves the annual report.
- The Management Committee, elected by the Workers' Council to carry out its orders and run the enterprise.
- The director, named by the Workers' Council with the approval of the local community.

Aside from workers' self-management which deals with industrial and agricultural enterprises, there is also social self-management which runs apartment houses, schools, hospitals and so on. The institutions of self-management outside beyond the scope of a single enterprise were:

- The Community People's Committee, the local political governing body, the basic administrative and social unit. Elected by direct ballot, the People's Committee supervises the self-managed enterprises, works out local plans and adjusts them to suit the industrial plans, and administers the community territory.
- The trade union, which mediates disputes and strives to increase productivity.
- The federal government, which sets the general rules that the enterprise must follow.
- The Communist League—the party, which stimulates, supervises, and arbitrates the self-management process.

People usually tend to praise or criticize Yugoslav self-management as if it were all of a piece. But the Yugoslav economy is far from being simply a matter of self-management. (Algeria provides an interesting example of how self-management, isolated within a free market economy, fails to make any difference in the way the country is run economically and politically.) First of all, the free market was restored and foreign trade is only loosely controlled by the state. Thanks to this economic liberalism, new privileged classes had sprung up in Yugoslavia by the early 1960s—a process denounced by Marshal Tito in an important speech in Split in 1962. Ten years later, shortly after a "purge" of the party to "restore the health" of the economy, a major campaign was launched in the course of which he denounced the existence of a considerable number of billionaires (counting in old dinars). These nouveaux riches were mainly executives of firms engaging in foreign trade. Meanwhile, in the countryside, 80 percent of the peasants work on privately owned farms. In the richest farming areas of Slovenia, Croatia, and Voivodina, a peasant owning ten hectares can quickly get rich by selling his produce directly at the town markets, price controls being fairly loose. On the other hand, the poorer regions of Kosmet, Montenegro, and Macedonia are stagnating—their populace the source of a rural exodus that is swelling the ranks of the urban unemployed (the many workers who emigrate temporarily to Western Europe are usually Serbs or Croats). It is obviously in the cities that the sharpest social distinctions have arisen, especially thanks to the import-export trade, banking, administration, handicrafts, and the tourist trade. By the early 1960s, the psychological groundwork had been laid for a Western-style consumer society. It must also be said that daily life in Yugoslavia, in the towns as in the countryside, is on the whole more relaxed and less monotonous than in most of the "people's democracies," for hierarchic relationships carry much less weight.

Within the self-managed enterprises, the same work may earn very different wages depending on the region and branch of activity. There is tough competition between firms to win a place in the market, and those in the most developed of Yugoslavia's six federated republics are obviously the ones that come out on top. All of this contributes to the fragmentation of the working class, whose immediate interests are increasingly divergent, a state of affairs exacerbated also by the gaps among the republics, a source of ever-recurring and highly delicate nationality problems. At the community level, competition is also quite lively, and a group spirit develops that is focused on local development to the detriment of the Federation—and of the poorest republics within it. Each of Yugoslavia's six hundred communities does its best to get the most it can of federal investment. This tends to hold back heavy industry, since the communities would rather invest in sectors that are profitable in the short range. Having to operate within the context of a competitive economy, self-management means primarily trying to involve the workers in caring about their enterprise through their own direct interest in its profits—leaving real power in the hands of the state and party bureaucracy. Bestowed on the workers by the bureaucracy, self-management has turned out to be a way of keeping the workers' perspective limited to the horizons of their own enterprise, which they only partially control, since the functioning of an enterprise is subordinate to the functioning of the state and the economy as a whole. Within their enterprise, the workers remain subordinate to the party. In fact, self-management disperses and divides the workers and makes their lives depend solely on the prosperity of the organization they work for. Decentralization involves only minor decisions on the local level. Major decisions are made at the federal level, under the control of the Communist League. The existence of self-management hardly conceals the fact that the system in Yugoslavia—as in the other people's democracies, although more flexible—is based on the political monopoly of a party that is run from the top by a small group centered around an unquestioned leader.

3. The Leninist Bureaucracy and Foreign Policy: China Since the Cultural Revolution

The Leninist concept of revolution has provided the model for virtually all of Asia's modern revolutions. Everywhere, the phenomenon of bureaucracy has apparently been seen as inevitable. It is no simple matter to block the omnipotence of a party that controls the state, as China's Red Guards found out. In their country, even a fight against bureaucrats is waged via more or less large sections of the ruling bureaucracy, both political and military. When the masses come on the scene, they are there usually to be manipulated or else are quickly taken in hand if they get out of control. Yet as far as domestic policy is concerned, the Soviet model—where an all-powerful bureaucracy is the price paid for development and pressure on the peasantry is the price paid for industrialization—is in principle rejected. Great emphasis is put on the "human factor" in development. The cadres mix with the masses; students and intellectuals are involved in production; efforts are made to keep new privileged classes from emerging—but bureaucracy keeps cropping up again and again, as robust as ever.

It is true that the theory put forth by Mao Tse-tung in 1957 with the "rectification" of the Chinese Communist party line, and his reference to "new" antagonisms coming to the fore after China's victory over capitalism, had a new ring. Inter-class antagonisms, according to Mao, should be dealt with not by violence and repression, but rather, in principle, by persuasion and education. This idea of "contradictions" arising between the people and leaders who run the risk of succumbing to bureaucratization, is an expression of the Chinese attempt to build up both "socialism" and state power at the same time. To combat currents that appeared to him to be bureaucratic and overly "economistic," Mao called on youth and the army—inasmuch as the party and the administration were the two main strongholds of the entrenched bureaucracy. At the start of this Cultural Revolution of 1966, the masses were not easy to mobilize, which is not surprising considering that ever since 1949 they had been ever more strictly regimented by the party and the government. But the Red Guards movement was eventually tumultuously successful, and when the army judged it to be excessively antibureaucratic, it stopped it. However original and exemplary the Chinese Cultural Revolution may have been, the root cause for the bureaucracy's development was not eradicated and privileged classes, particularly at the decision-making level, tend to hang on or regroup without disturbing the continuity of the power structure. The little that can be said about China without fear of error shows at least a few points which make short work of the pious image cherished by a goodly number of Mao's unconditional admirers. The personality cult of Mao Tse-tung; absurd, Stalinist-style accusations against political opponents after their fall (Liu Shao-shi, Lin Piao); a limitation of criticism of Russia to the post-Stalin era; extremely sharp and clearly defined hierarchies within the leadership, suggesting that China's presumed grass-roots democracy has very narrow limits; and last but not least, a foreign policy and official diplomacy attentive not to the development of revolution but to the interests of the state.[3]

China's quarrel with Russia has altered the course of Chinese foreign policy, and in the years 1960–65 that policy had as one of its aims to weaken Soviet hegemony over the Socialist camp by seeking support there for its own ideas, while making what alliances it could among the nationalist governments of Africa and Asia. Previously, the Peking government had had no choice but alliance with the U.S.S.R. (to which the Chinese revolution, incidentally, owed nothing) in the bipolar postwar world. After the Twentieth Party Congress in 1956, it had made a brief stab at challenging Soviet control over the Socialist countries, but it needed Soviet technical aid and kept up its alliance with Russia. It was Khrushchev's policy, hinging primarily on détente, and meaning above all the stabilization of the status quo in central

---

[3] Compare and contrast the situation in a very different country. In Cuba, even though the party did not exist before Castro's group took power and was laboriously built up only afterward, Fidel's leadership group nevertheless engendered a bureaucracy. Sketchily criticized in a party organ *Granma* in 1967, the critics suggested remedies which presumed some kind of growth in awareness of Socialist morality, an unselfishness about material things, the emergence of a "new man." In practice, centralization was extreme in both politics and production, which resulted in considerable waste of energy. If supplies were inadequate in Cuba between 1966 and 1972, this was not only due to the American blockade, but also the Cuban leadership's conceptions of organization. By concentrating more and more on sugar production, the government deepened Cuba's dependence on Russia (which explains its publicly voiced approval of the 1968 invasion of Czechoslovakia). After the not unforeseen failure of the *zafra* in 1970, Fidel Castro was obliged to speak several times on the need to democratize Cuban life by setting up production assemblies in which production workers could offer criticisms and suggestions. But there has been no reorganization of economic policy and no effective decentralization.

Europe, that sacrificed the Sino-Soviet alliance. All the Soviet experts in China were called home in 1960. In the course of the early 1960s Chinese foreign policy then met with a number of failures. Within the Socialist camp and Communist parties around the world, the Chinese line, exalting the revolution and preaching solidarity and "fraternal" obligations between Communist parties, aroused little interest outside Albania. Even the Korean and Japanese parties, which had been friendly at one time, took their distance. Alliances with nationalist governments fell flat, mainly because China's Indonesia policy failed. (Sukarno's foreign policy had suited Peking, and he further endeared himself by calling on the powerful Indonesian Communist party [PKI] to cooperate with the "national bourgeoisie" in the framework of an anti-imperialist front. However, this left the PKI defenseless when the Right undertook to wipe it out. The fall of Sukarno and the resulting disaster for the PKI put an end to China's hope of creating a new Third World U.N.) The other allied governments—General Ne Win's Burma, Ben Bella's Algeria, Sihanouk's Cambodia, and Nkrumah's Ghana—turned out to be fragile. The fall of Ben Bella ended the Chinese project of a second Bandung conference, and Nkrumah was overthrown by a putsch while he was visiting China. As for Pakistan, it scarcely met the minimal standards to be considered "progressive," although in geopolitical terms it was an adversary of India and thus the enemy of an enemy. Before long, however, the U.S.S.R. strengthened its position in the Indian subcontinent, and the war in Vietnam, with massive American intervention, managed to isolate China even more. Then came the Cultural Revolution.

The political course mapped out for Chinese foreign policy during the Cultural Revolution, known as the "Lin Piao line," amounted first of all to a turn inward. Cooperation with either revisionism or imperialism was ruled out, and the United States was seen as Enemy Number One. Self-sufficiency was preached. But in practical terms, moral support was the only kind given to revolutionary struggles elsewhere around the globe. Regimes that only a short time before had been looked on kindly, such as the one in Burma, were now harshly criticized.

Then, at the end of the 1950s,[4] as Chou En-lai's authority began to make itself felt, Chinese foreign policy became active and flexible. The point was to break out of isolation by no longer settling for a diplomacy limited to some small Asian countries. The United States was perceived as the only counterbalance to Soviet power, the main threat to Chinese security, and as the only key to the Taiwan problem and United Nations recognition. From then on, the Chinese—who in the past had supported national liberation movements simply because they were rivals to other movements supported by the Soviet Union—began to support whatever regime appeared politically or geographically opposed to the U.S.S.R. Chinese foreign policy became more closely wedded than ever to its own national interests and security; and this development was bolstered by the shift in United States policy toward China in 1971. There was not the slightest Chinese denunciation of the massacres of the population of Bangladesh, and left-wing opposition in that country was discouraged, since the weakening of Pakistan obviously strengthened India. The Ceylon (Sri Lanka) government's liquidation of the Trotskyist-Guevarist "ultra-Left" was endorsed: what mattered was for Mrs. Bandaranaike's government to remain uncommitted, especially in regard to Russia. In the Sudan, China supported and applauded the regime of General Nimeiry when it crushed the (pro-Soviet) Sudanese Communist party and had its members hanged.[5] After the September 1973 putsch in Chile, which overthrew the Popular Unity coalition in which the pro-Soviet Chilean Communist party had taken part, the first country to expel the ambassador of Allende's fallen government was China.

---

[4] J. K. Fairbanks, "The New China and the American Connection," *Foreign Affairs* (September 1972).
[5] North Vietnam supported the people of Bangladesh; Hanoi and New Delhi have diplomatic relations; and Hanoi condemned the repression in Sudan.

**CONCLUSION:
toward
what futures?**

1. The Third World and the Present Crisis

The outcome of the colonial process has been an ambiguous one. Colonialism upset traditional economic, social, political, and cultural balances, introduced new forms of exploitation, strengthened racism. But by the same token, capitalism created a world market and exported many kinds of progress, about which opinions may vary, but whose impact is undeniable: political modernization, with parties and republics; changes in social patterns, with formation of new classes; a soaring population increase; and new ideas such as nationalism, social revolution (notably in its Marxist-Leninist version), and individualism. At the same time, it sowed the seeds of new forms of servitude and of demands for national independence and lessened inequality.

In fact, new ideas have for at least the last two or three centuries burst forth regularly from the West—in philosophy as in technology. And it is also the West that has come up with the most radical modern challenges to status-quo values—whether involving relations between citizens and the state, among social classes, or between generations and sexes. In this regard, Western culture's major contribution to the world may well be its freedom to search for knowledge and to criticize, a freedom gradually won by limited state power and separating secular and spiritual powers.

By assimilating and making the most of these elements of progress, while at the same time drawing from their national traditions, a few countries have managed in the past century to escape from Western hegemony: Japan (which has since become a major capitalist power), China, Vietnam, Korea (in the North). Is it mere coincidence that four of the most important revolutions from 1868 to this day have taken place in Sinized Asia? The question is worth asking.

At least part of the answer to this is surely to be found in a series of factors: the distance from Europe and the United States; the strong Asian traditions of a national state, and an indelible national consciousness on the part of populations more homogeneous than elsewhere; in most cases, Confucianism, as a secular morality, singularly attuned to interests of state; and dense populations. Once these societies, with their robust traditions still intact, figured out how to adopt whatever contemporary efforts of the Western world struck them as useful, they went ahead without fear of losing their identity.

Yet the Third World, as we have seen, is still economically and culturally dominated by the industrial capitalist nations. For the past quarter-century, this phenomenon has shown up mainly in a relative decline in the prices of raw materials to the considerable profit of the industrialized world, which thanks to flagrantly unequal exchanges, has managed to enjoy a fantastic economic growth while most of the Third World countries stagnated. A few nations have indeed been developed—Taiwan, South Korea, Singapore; more recently Iran, and Brazil. Even unbalanced growth dictated in no way by the country's own needs and very unevenly distributed, ends up being a sort of development if it is vigorous and prolonged. However, considering the Third World as a whole, the remedies proposed by capitalism—assuming they were ever really intended to overcome underdevelopment—have proved inoperative: integration into the capitalist market (on unequal terms); export of raw materials (with the producers being paid less and less, at least until about 1971); recourse to foreign capital in the form of investments more profitable to the industrial countries than to the Third World; and, finally, foreign aid, which, aside from the dependence it entails, has steadily decreased. The list of countries that in absolute terms are getting poorer gets longer all the time: India, Pakistan, Bangladesh, Sri Lanka, Bolivia, Ethiopia, Kenya, Mali, Sudan, Tanzania, Uganda. . . .

At a time when people are talking of nothing but the current economic crisis, the basic fact that emerges is that from 1945 until 1968 the industrial capitalist countries enjoyed a period of extremely high living, thanks to the very low prices they paid for raw materials from the Third World. The United States, along with Western Europe and Japan, reaped the benefits of a state of affairs they had created and vied with each other to maintain. An initial price increase in 1968, followed by another in 1973, enabled the energy-producing countries (which are not numerous) to benefit more than in the past from their natural resources, but the world is still a long way from any real reorganization of economic relationships between nations. At any rate, it is interesting to note that even the United States, although much less dependent than Europe when it comes to energy, imports huge amounts of the dozen basic minerals considered of primary importance: including 53 percent of its zinc, 56 percent of its tungsten, 83 percent of its tin, 89 percent of its nickel, 97 percent of its bauxite and manganese, 100 percent of its chrome, and about 50 percent of its iron and lead. (The countries producing certain commodities are so few in number that it would seem they might be able to get together some day to defend their interests in a systematic way. Eighty percent of the world's copper comes from Chile, Peru,

Zaire, and Zambia; 70 percent of the world's tin from Malaysia and Bolivia; 95 percent of all bauxite from Guinea, Guyana, Surinam, and Jamaica.)

For the moment, however, the overall picture is gloomy. The deterioration, in the terms of trade, has weighed too heavily and too long on the Third World, piling up and deepening all the ills of underdevelopment, not the least of which is hunger. As ever, the fundamental need for far-reaching social reforms is blocked for primarily political reasons. In the second place, the future depends on an improvement in the terms of trade—assuming one has something valuable to trade—and this is one of the main things at stake in the current crisis.

But what is this crisis really all about? For the moment, one cannot blame the crisis on a slump in industrial production in the West, where growth rates are positive everywhere except in Great Britain. In terms of joblessness, the present crisis cannot be compared to the Great Depression of the 1930s, when in the United States production virtually ground to a halt (in 1932 a quarter of the active population was out of work). The current crisis—which is a crisis of the capitalist system—is due not to rising petroleum prices, which only hastened the process, but to an inflation in turn produced by, among other things, a completely disrupted world monetary system. (The importance of petroleum in overall energy consumption had increased considerably, from about one-third of U.S. energy consumption in 1950 to 60 percent in 1970. Of course, this happened when petroleum was singularly cheap.)

Endemic since the mid-1960s, the monetary crisis reached an acute stage in 1971 with the devaluation of the dollar (no longer officially convertible into gold). This turns out to have been one of the first signs of the overall crisis now under way. Inflation hit and rose to 10 to 20 percent in most of the industrialized countries (with the exception of West Germany and the Netherlands) and over 20 percent in Japan and Italy. The shift in the rhythm of price rises accelerated inflation, then picked up speed when commodity prices rose at the end of 1972, and again when oil prices quadrupled at the end of 1973.

The dollar is no longer convertible, and all the major currencies are floating, each in terms of the rest, which explains the rising price of gold and major raw materials since the end of 1972. The need to restore some sort of international balance obliges the industrialized countries to slow down their energy consumption, and with it their growth—while making more or less coherent efforts to strike a new world balance, especially in the distribution of earnings.

The crisis comes on the heels of an unprecedented period of economic development within the industrialized countries, which have benefited from cheap natural resources ever since World War II. This development took place thanks to the hegemony of the United States, which guaranteed their security and provided them with a currency. The gradual erosion of American economic power (due to the war in Vietnam, among other things) and the rise of Western Europe and Japan upset the balance. In 1950, the United States GNP was twice that of the Common Market countries and Japan combined. Twenty years later, the total Common Market and Japanese GNP had outstripped that of the United States, and America could no longer go on guaranteeing convertibility of the dollar into gold. In that same period of time, the underdeveloped countries' share in world trade halved, despite rising production. The prices of the goods exported by industrialized countries rose constantly in relation to the prices of the basic commodities they imported.

But the growing awareness that world supplies of natural resources were dwindling was bound to make prices go up sooner or later. High production profits, for the most part, had been divided up within industrialized nations—quite unequally, to be sure—between major corporations *and* wage earners. The crisis means that from now on a share must also go to certain commodity producers. Those destined to pay for the crisis within the industrialized countries are people living on savings, and unskilled workers. In the rest of the world, the main victims will be Third World countries which do not possess any natural resources generally in demand. It is in these countries that the problem of famine—which, in the last analysis, is caused not by overpopulation but by inequitable distribution—will have the gravest effects.

The crisis is seriously weakening the competitive position of industry in Western Europe and Japan and unbalancing their foreign trade. On the other hand, the United States, like the U.S.S.R., a major producer of basic commodities, is only slightly hurt by the energy crisis and will easily restore the hegemony it seemed only a few years ago to be losing. The day seems to have passed when American industry saw itself being more and more outclassed, even on the domestic American market, by its European and Japanese rivals. It is less probable that the crisis will bring to question the myth of growth per se.

The crisis ought to serve to call attention to the problem of a new distribution system and a new definition of the terms of trade. No doubt the only Third World countries to benefit from this will be those in possession of important natural resources. Still, after years of unbridled plunder, the time may not be so far off when the economic organization of the world that has prevailed from the postwar period to the present will appear as barbarous as the slavery of long ago or the colonialism of the recent past.

The future of the Third World is as diverse as its composition. What is likely is increasing misery, want and famine, especially in the Indian subcontinent with its seven hundred million human beings; likely, also, is the extinction of the pastoral societies of the African Sahel. Another likelihood is that in the long run the combination of endemic diseases and malnutrition over large areas will weaken and impoverish the physical and mental faculties of a significant proportion of the human race. Ever so many nations will go on being dependent, whether because they lack the human and material wherewithal to start a development process up—at least without some sort of regional cooperative setup that might change the situation—or because they are located on the fringes of an industrial zone, where it is easy for their ruling classes to cash in on the expansionism of powerful neighbors. Only in a few very rare cases will a society and its elite, drawing strength from their socio-cultural heritage and determined to overcome all difficulties, meet their needs by their own efforts. The inability displayed, up to now, by most Third World societies to develop independently raises questions both about their elites, who have been deculturized, and about their political and cultural traditions, which are rarely solid and coherent. In such conditions, the admonition to "rely on one's own forces" more often than not is devoid of meaning. In this connection, all the more credit must go to Amilcar Cabral, who managed to come up with an original and creative approach to the whole range of problems facing the peoples of Guinea-Bissau and the Cape Verde Islands at a time when their overall conditions were particularly unpromising.

Throughout the Third World, the obviously desirable thing would be a degree of political, economic, and cultural independence. The way to attain this would be to mobilize all productive forces to meet the most basic needs—food, health, housing, jobs, education (adapted to local needs)—within the framework of an economic development based on agriculture and a certain amount of industrialization, and to do this with as little waste and as much fairness as possible. The obstacles here are not technical but, rather, political, and thus not easily overcome. Instead of this sort of development (the sort which has been undertaken by North Vietnam, a small country with limited resources) we have mainly been treated to the spectacle of nostalgic returns to the fountainhead, and assertions of authenticity that amount to so many mystifications, the restoration of the most backward aspects found in all traditional cultures—magical-religious obscurantism, caste system, the domination of women by men, youth by age, country by city. Behind all the diatribes that forever shift the blame elsewhere, the gap of inequality between social classes grows wider. Pathetic stabs at development, bloody if not downright grotesque dictatorships, pretentious bombast: how many living caricatures are awaiting their satirist?

A few states with the necessary material and human resources (unlike the oil-rich Emirates of the Persian Gulf, which between them count only about 12 million inhabitants) are no doubt going to manage within the next few decades to become regional powers to be reckoned with: Iran, Nigeria, Brazil, Algeria, Venezuela, Ivory Coast, Mexico, and a few others. (It must not be forgotten, however, that the most important transformation which has taken place in the Third World—and one that will make itself felt more and more in the future—dates back a quarter of a century: the Chinese revolution.) Without shaking up the planet to the extent of the exceptional upheavals of 1945–49, the current crisis will bring about considerable changes. Its ironies are already apparent: less than sixty years after it subjugated the Arab East, England—only yesterday the world's foremost empire—has seen Saudi Arabia refuse to accept its currency in payment for Arabian oil.

Further trade bargaining can be expected to be tight, and it is also foreseeable that more and more Third World countries will be taken over by leadership teams that strengthen government control of the economy in order to derive greater profit from their resources—mainly, if not exclusively, for the benefit of the ruling and privileged classes.

2. The Contemporary World and U.S. Diplomacy

In today's world, and probably for some time to come, the United States will remain the dominant power. Confronted at the end of the 1960s with a many-sided crisis due to the war in Vietnam, monetary problems, and a relative commercial decline in relation to Western Europe and Japan, as well as with a substantial movement of internal dissent, the United States in the 1970s has taken a new lease on life, thanks largely to initiatives in a revived foreign policy conducted by Henry Kissinger. But what is so original about Kissinger's foreign policy?

Until recently, the United States had scarcely any contact with the facts of life that emerge from a constant struggle for national self-preservation. As a prosperous merchant society with an empirical outlook on life, it was hardly disposed to develop any awareness of the world of nation-states that characterized Europe. While using force whenever seemed necessary, just like any other nation, the United States never conceptualized relations among nation-states. Engrossed in contemplating its own history and virtues (no colonies, no rival nations, a Protestant moralism, and a democracy with a high degree of social mobility), the United States had not advanced beyond a distorted and simplistic view of contemporary history. This special context enabled it to carry on in what Stanley Hoffman has called a state of "perpetual historical virginity." Finally a moralizing rhetoric with universalist pretentions, employed throughout American history, so conditioned public opinion that its support had to be sought in such terms.

Right after World War II, everything changed. The U.S., now the dominant world power, saw itself faced with the task of containing communism, but its ruling elites seemed unaware that it was thus getting involved in a whole new process of international relations.

Kissinger's primary originality lies in setting the United States before the mirror of history, where it can see itself in perspective. His strength comes from being a cultural outsider; his view of the world is not American in the traditional sense. His analyses, which reflect his study of classical political thinkers (Machiavelli, Clausewitz, et al.), seize the U.S. in its singularity only to bring it back into a world of inter-state relationships, in which war or peace are only aspects of the pursuit of a single aim.

What Kissinger is actually saying is that the most important challenge facing American foreign policy is a philosophical one, and that for those who are a product of the American tradition in foreign policy, this challenge is not easy to accept. The American attitude in foreign relations is shaped by the fact that the United States has never experienced a national disaster. The natural tendency is to believe that if things don't work out, it is always possible to start all over again. Indeed, to a pragmatic mind the facts show that until Vietnam, the United States always succeeded in whatever it undertook. The fatal, irrevocable error (which has become possible now that the U.S. no longer has sole possession of nuclear weapons) was not yet part of America's national experience.

Neither the training nor the usual outside pressures felt by

American leaders have been conducive to thinking in political or strategic terms. For over a century these leaders have developed their skills through concentrating on building up the nation internally. Most of the men that fill the top government posts in the administration come either from the major corporations or are lawyers. Big business produces competent administrators, while the law trains men to settle one individual case after the other. No wonder, then, that these men—often remarkably able within the scope of the free enterprise system—were apt to busy themselves with technical and economic problems, while overlooking conceptual and political ones. Throughout their history, Americans have always judged a presidency by its vigor in tackling problems and its success in solving them once and for all. Faced with apparently insoluble problems, the impatience to be done with it has made American foreign policy fluctuate between rigidity and the urge to try something new just in case. Decisions tend to be made during periods of crisis, limiting policymakers to a defensive posture, since long-range questions are neglected when they do not come up in connection with current business. While the United States scored major successes in Western Europe after World War II, this did not prevent Russia from managing to set up a buffer zone in Eastern Europe at a time when the United States still held a monopoly in atomic weapons. Moreover, China had gone Communist, and the Korean war ended in compromise rather than in victory.

The new United States diplomacy takes into account the military power of the Soviet Union, the economic dynamism of Japan and Western Europe, and the rivalry between Russia and China. While the world is still bipolar militarily, a certain political multipolarity has developed. A new international stability is thus called for. Implicitly, the new diplomacy accepts the fact that the Communist countries have vital interests that the U.S. must take into account. Still, if everyone's interests are to be safeguarded, arrangements promise to be particularly tricky in the Far East, where the Soviet Union, China, Japan, and the U.S. all are involved. The most urgent item on the agenda was obviously disengagement from Indochina.

The parameter of a new détente with the Soviet Union, based on curtailment of the arms race, began to be worked out at the Strategic Arms Limitations Talks,[1] which attempted to freeze the number of nuclear warheads at parity, both sides tending to seek greater security as the risks converge. Regarding alliances, associations with Western Europe and Japan as regional partners, and maintenance of stability through a system of bilateral and multilateral commitments, with key nations in a given zone undertaking to maintain stability (for instance, Iran in the Persian Gulf)—these, essentially, are the new parameters of American diplomacy.

As for the world crisis stemming from or aggravated by oil-price adjustments and a shortage of petroleum, this is outside the scope of a purely diplomatic approach. But it is safe to say that the United States has succeeded in exporting its crisis. Europe and Japan have had occasion to take the measure of their own fragility and to think some hard thoughts about their alliances with America, which has shown bitterness toward them.

The ultimate aim of Kissinger's foreign policy was to establish a stable world order dominated by U.S. hegemony. This implies keeping changes in the world relationship of forces down to the bare minimum. Policy toward Latin America may take on a new style, but basically, any government that dares threaten what the U.S. considers the security of the hemisphere will find itself thwarted and fought every step of the way. If military intervention proves necessary, the task will fall first of all to regional allies, such as Brazil. Africa poses no great potential threat; it is the Middle East and the Far East that for nearly thirty years have been the areas of greatest instability. The loss of Indochina was a serious defeat, even if the consequences were essentially regional. Nevertheless, throughout the Third World a vast range of possibilities remains between radical revolution and the useless preservation of outdated social structures, offering the United States plenty of room to maneuver. Europe lacks the political

---

[1] For the unfolding of these negotiations and their spirit, based on first-hand sources, see John Newhouse, *Cold Dawn, the Story of SALT* (New York: Holt, Rinehart and Winston, 1973).

will to be independent; subjected like Japan to the hard facts of military bipolarity, it will remain a competitor within the American domain.

Obstacles to this policy are not lacking, however. In the past ten years, the Soviet diplomatic offensive has picked up considerably, especially in the direction of the Indian Ocean, the Persian Gulf, and the Mediterranean. What is more, the U.S.S.R. has perhaps surpassed the United States in nuclear weapons. Are the SALT agreements an American success? The U.S. is now trying to catch up. It remains to be seen whose political interests will actually be best served by the general Soviet-American exchanges stemming from détente.

The world order in its present balance of power between nations would appear to be threatened only by an increase in Chinese military power over the next ten to twenty years; there are obvious dangers in military tripolarity. Meanwhile, Chinese-American relations will surely tend to develop substantially. Until then, Kissinger's adjustments will contribute, not to peace (the awarding of the Nobel Peace Prize to the secretary of state would be an irony of history if it were not an absurdity on the part of the jury), but to a sort of stability which partly consists in maintaining the status quo. On a global level, the setback of the United States in the last decade has been limited. Resources of energy, and above all, technological advancement, guarantees its supremacy in the coming decades.

3. On Armed Struggle

Whichever guerrilla war is examined, whether of anticolonials, as in Algeria, or during the first Indochina war, or of partisans against a foreign invader as in Yugoslavia, or of guerrillas who are not nominally fighting for national independence—such as the Huks in the Philippines or the NLF in South Vietnam—the common denominator turns out to be *nationalism*. In each case, the masses oppose the aggressor, the colonizer, or the particular regime, because in their eyes revolutionary forces stand for *authentic national values.* The more the uprising manages to convey its nationalist character to the masses—whether or not the nationalism is joined to social objectives—the harder it is to defeat.

In Latin America, as we have seen, the fundamental cause for the failure of the various urban and rural guerrilla movements in the last fifteen years, is that they could not get the population to recognize the struggle as both national and social. In this regard, the Chinese and Vietnamese revolutionary movements were helped considerably by Japanese aggression, French colonialism and American military intervention. But in Latin America, even the failures are on a more modest scale—no movement of any real strength has managed to develop. The reasons for this are many, as I have already brought out, but the most important is the conceptual weakness, the lack of any strategy adapted to the social and political terrain. This weakness is also characteristic of the leadership of Latin American armed movements. How else could Guevara's focoism and "Revolution in the revolution" ever have been taken seriously? Against this, the geopolitical determination of the United States to limit revolutionary experience in the Western hemisphere to the Cuban "accident"—as illustrated in the Dominican Republic in 1965 and Chile in 1973 —is only one negative factor.

In fact, in the case of national liberation movements worthy of the name, what seems to be decisive is the conjunction of national objectives with a tradition on the whole favorable to change and to the prolonged effort required and, last but not least, a modernizing revolutionary ideology; up to now this has always been an ideology inspired by Marxism-Leninism. To be realistic, there is no getting around the fact that in Vietnam, as in China, revolution was made possible only thanks to the interpretation provided by the Leninist version of Marxism, adapted, to be sure, to local conditions and national traditions; some sort of Confucian or Buddhist socialism would have amounted to no more than a Far Eastern equivalent of the ineffectual "Islamic" or "African" versions of socialism we know so well.

On the other hand, contemporary history provides virtually no instance of a class struggle in a backward country managing by itself, without recourse to nationalism, to mobilize the population to achieve the proclaimed goals of socialism. On the contrary, patriotic exaltation in circumstances of foreign aggression, occupation, or general domination proved to be decisive. Tradition goes deep and has many ramifications; to underestimate it for fear of falling into determinism, if not racism is to underestimate the weight of history. In sociological terms, the conditions of the Arab East around the Fertile Crescent are far removed from those of Vietnam, with its village solidarity, communal institutions, strong national cohesion, thousands of years of collective labor—the careful, patient labor of hard-working and ingenious rice-growers strongly attached to the land. Iraq, Syria, Lebanon, and Jordan also lack anything like Vietnam's enduring and resilient military traditions of conquest and resistance. In the Middle East, only Egypt has a peasantry so strongly attached to the land, but it lacks the communal tradition and the work habits born of having to fight for a living against a river's depredations (on the contrary, until very recently, the Nile floods fertilized the valley all by themselves). Another difference lies in the Near East's merchant traditions, a geo-historic heritage that creates a propensity for compromise at all costs. The deculturization of the Arab East is no doubt largely due to proximity to Europe. But in any case, the Vietnamese and Chinese societies, not having been so profoundly decultured as the Arabs, with the help of the Confucian tradition have found it much easier to break with past religious and cultural traditions, precisely because they have not been afraid of losing themselves.

Many of these remarks can be applied to certain Latin American nations, which have more than a few things in common with Arab societies, sociologically speaking. None of this implies that a radical revolutionary process is impossible in the Near East or anywhere else, but it does explain some of the obstacles that many political analysts, in the name of universalism or other abstract conceptions, usually fail to emphasize.

In Africa, the weaknesses of the liberation movements, observable over the past fifteen years, stem from a series of factors of uneven importance.

● Revolution by exile. Quite a number of revolutionary movements have largely exhausted their meager forces in factional quarrels waged in exile. Cut off from real life back home, their already slight representativity has, in time, vanished. The leaders then inevitably turn into a miniature bureaucracy whose essential activity is verbal and whose raison d'être eventually is revealed as self-perpetuation for its own sake. Erroneous strategy is another hallmark of exile revolutionism, as in commando operations directed from outside the country, setting out from bases in neighboring countries. Whenever an action has been undertaken on this basis, it has led to failure and to a revision in strategy after a useless bleeding of troops.

● Revolution in theory. Oblivious to local realities, the revolutionary leaders seem unable to formulate a coherent strategy suited to local conditions. The ignorance that many African leaders, educated entirely abroad, display about their own societies is often blatant, and the lowliest local street vendor will be better informed than many students.

So long as no political infrastructure has been created in the population, the identity between revolutionary goals and popular aspirations is a matter of abstract rationality. And in Africa, there are especially serious obstacles in the way of mobilizing the people in the national modern way required by a guerrilla movement. This means that the guerrilla leaders must constantly remobilize, both to make the war effective and to change people's way of thinking.

● Lack of a real nation, even if only in its formative stages. Tribalism is another fundamental handicap that facilitates the perpetuation of colonial domination.

● Finally, sparse population, which characterizes almost all of black Africa. (Nearly half the African states count fewer than ten inhabitants per square kilometer.) With the exception of Nigeria—whose population is larger than all the other West African countries put together (this partially explains the intensity of the Biafra war)—no country has the human wherewithal for a large-scale guerrilla war. No guerrilla force, which by definition depends on only a part of the population for support, can face losing more than a few thousand men.

All these problems are fairly well summed up in the case of Angola. The division among revolutionary movements is seen in the active rivalry between the Union of Angolan Populations, which has become the Angola National Liberation Front, led by Holden Roberto, for a long time recognized by the OAU as the Provisional Government of Angola in exile; and the People's Movement for the Liberation of Angola (MPLA), led by Agostinho Neto. The basis of this division, at least in the case of the former, was tribal (the Bakongo of the northeastern part of the country). The latter's leaders were in exile from 1961 to 1966, in Rabat, Conakry, Algiers, and Leopoldville (Kinshasa); its ignorance of local conditions was all too clearly revealed in a serious crisis in 1963, when its former secretary general, Viriato Da Cruz, went off to join Holden Roberto. (The problem of tribalism is not limited to the case of the Bakongo: it shows up in the third Angolan movement, UNITA, led by J. Savimbi, basically Ovimbundu.) In addition, the sparseness of the population in a huge country (5.5 million inhabitants spread over 1.25 square kilometers) creates grave problems of communication, transportation, and clandestine political infrastructure, which it is not easy for fighting groups to solve. After more than a dozen years of fighting, the nationalist movements still had not reached the central plateau (occupied by part of the 400,000 white settlers), nor the areas with the densest African population, notably Ovimbundu country—one of the keys to Angola—nor yet the mining regions, where the territory's mineral wealth is concentrated. According to its own communiques, the MPLA in 1974 controlled a territory of 400,000 square kilometers and about 500,000 inhabitants, with some 20,000 guerrillas. It is easy to see just how loose their hold must have been.

After more than a decade of colonial wars, the fascist dictatorship in Portugal collapsed as a result of the hopeless contradictions created by the African liberation movements. The Armed Forces Movement's seizure of power in April 1974 brought a radical change in the colonial situation in Guinea-Bissau, Mozambique, and Angola. Portugal recognized Guinea-Bissau's independence and Portuguese troops were evacuated from the country; the Cape Verde Islands were promised independence in 1975, along with Mozambique and (in more difficult conditions) Angola. These sudden shifts in the situation in southern Africa led the Rhodesian government to agree to discussions with African nationalist organizations—a dialogue undertaken in time to allow the white racists of Rhodesia to hope they might maintain economic and political hegemony over the mass of Africans, even if it meant having to share it with a fraction of the black elites. In South Africa, the relationship of forces being what it is, there is as yet little sign of change, and since the small armed groups of blacks were decimated in the early 1960s, white control is stricter than ever.

As for minorities, whether ethnic, religious or both (in southern Sudan, Eritrea, or Biafra), they run into infinitely greater difficulty in furthering their cause. Primarily, and most obviously, they are up against a central government that enjoys at least the benevolent neutrality of most of the country. Secondly, throughout the Third World, to raise the question of autonomy for minorities, much less the right to secession, is absolutely inadmissible and contrary to the very notion of state power. Champions of minorities are always said to be "manipulated from abroad" or "agents" of some imperialism.

Struggles against neocolonialist setups such as prevail in the formally independent African states run into special problems. Various military coups have shown just how little is propping up some of those governments, which could conceivably be swept away by an uprising—like the one in Brazzaville in 1963—as easily as the Congo government was. But there are very real difficulties. One result of the generally low level of African development is that social cleavages and clashes are not so sharp as in other parts of the world. Still they may cause trouble when the expansion of education produces more trained youth than the job markets can absorb, although the petty bourgeoisie as a class is, for the most part, integrated into the government power structure. With its monopoly of modern knowledge, it has held power ever since independence. Opposition figures or movements have encountered scarcely any support within it, while other parts of the world provide most of the revolutionary cadres. The number of opposition figures who, sooner or later, have come around to supporting regimes in neocolonial countries is too great, proportionally, for the matter to be stated in terms of "betrayal" but, rather, raises the question of precisely what the social base for political opposition is in those countries. The land-reform problem scarcely exists for the peasants of Africa, where there is plenty of land; in a subsistence economy with very few work days, this means that efforts to mobilize the countryside are apt to fall flat. Frantz Fanon was apparently not aware of these features when, in *The Wretched of the Earth,* he painted a mythical portrait of a revolutionary African peasantry.

In short, the myth of the invincibility of guerrilla warfare led people to overestimate the importance of most of the armed struggles taking place in the world—with the exception of those waged by the Indochinese revolutionary movements. In the past thirty years, only Sinized Asia (Vietnam, Korea) and its most immediate margins (Laos, Cambodia) have produced victorious armed struggles. But there the struggles have long since gone beyond the stage of guerrilla warfare, by definition a limited and temporary method, and developed into full-scale warfare—a people's war to be sure, but *classical,* if not conventional.

4. Perspectives on an Era

Third Worldism was a phenomenon born of the crisis of Stalinism and fed by the policy of peaceful coexistence. It prospered in the 1960s because of the new hopes in the spread of socialist revolution in and by the Third World. But it has turned out to be a myth.[2] The last colonies (Portuguese) have become virtually independent, a dozen years after Algeria and the rest of Africa. Except for Cuba, the only victorious people's war—this one of heroic proportions—has been that in Indochina, Vietnam in particular. A few conservative regimes have collapsed, but not as many as might have been expected (King Hassan II of Morocco, King Hussein of Jordan, Ferdinand Marcos in the Philippines, and General Park Chung Hee in South Korea are all still in power). More "progressive" governments have been overthrown than reactionary ones. Other regimes, including that of the Shah of Iran and the Brazilian military rulers, have defied expectations by achieving spectacular economic growth and attaining the status of regional powers.

Third Worldism saw the revolutionary potential of the Third World as deriving from two main factors: on the one hand, the grinding, humiliating poverty of the masses, and the contradictions that produced it, and on the other hand, the crisis that could not fail to erupt in industrial countries, once revolutionary regimes put a stop to their pillage of the Third World's materials. Ironically, that change is now partly under way through the action—and to the profit—of the Shah, the Emirs, and their hangers-on, and a few other more or less conservative regimes. Meanwhile, political immobilism has been perpetuated as the urban middle classes are integrated into the system; the workers still lack class consciousness, and most of the people in most Third World countries are seen as marginal. The revolutionary potential of the Third World had been overestimated, and too much importance was assigned to the possible role of revolutionary ideology, without always evaluating just what sort of society the ideology was to be grafted onto and under what circumstances. The ideology spread by an active minority is of prime importance, but it is wrong to shrink from acknowledging the importance of

---

[2] A myth in which I believed and which I helped to spread in the early sixties in some of my journalistic articles.

the historical and cultural texture of a society, which conditions much of its behavior and attitudes.

In national revolutions, the leader's role is often ambiguous. On the one hand, he vouches for a certain line—an anti-imperialist foreign policy, let us say, and statements or even measures in favor of the lower classes; on the other hand he is head of a state that is primarily the instrument of the privileged classes. The forms vary from country to country, but the phenomenon is always the same. Sometimes the social class seeking to secure political domination right after a national-liberation struggle cannot do so openly, in full accord with its interests, on account of the hopes and demands of the mobilized masses. In such a case, the leader is the *deus ex machina* who appears on the scene to solve the dilemma; he is the more or less temporary agent of the future ruling class, whose role is to "mystify" the masses while their mobilization peters out. (Not so long ago, the British used to play a similar game of their own, putting moderate anticolonialist leaders in prison so as to make them into symbols of the struggle for independence.) Sometimes the contradictions within the petty bourgeoisie are sharp enough to allow the leader to set himself up as an arbiter, while seeking to reinforce his own power with reforms that win the support of other parts of society. Earlier class relationships may be somewhat modified by all this, but national revolutions never produce any radical social upheavals, even when the leader—a convinced nationalist eager to strengthen his country's independence—really wants to radicalize his regime's social orientation. These are usually transitional regimes that enjoy a certain amount of social autonomy and that, while safeguarding existing class relationships, politically dominate the very class which, according to those relationships, should logically be in power. In this respect, there is nothing surprising in the turns taken in Egypt after Nasser. The ambiguous nature of the leader becomes secondary once the social class of which he is the expression or instrument is clearly discerned behind the facade of national unity which he embodies. One thing all these leaders— Nasser, Nkrumah, Boumedienne and the rest—have in common is that they deny, as far as their own national life is concerned, the existence of social antagonisms and do not go beyond denouncing the corruption of the privileged in strictly moral terms. Behind the screen provided by even the best of them—whatever their sincerity or good will—a social class is rapidly constituted, then strengthened, for which the social ambiguities created by the leader have become useless or inhibiting. At this point the social class can start to think of running the show itself, solely in its own interests, taking over a society demobilized by unkept promises and modeled in the image of its own corruption. Many coups d'etat that finish off this kind of regime have no other cause.

During the 1960s the type of regime just described was called a national democracy, using the nomenclature spelled out in the *Statement of the 81 Communist Parties* (Moscow, 1960). This theoretical innovation (neither a bourgeois democracy nor a people's democracy) was soon to fall into disuse, for the governments in question were so transitory that very few of them stayed in power or within the definitions that had just been laboriously devised for them by the theoreticians of national democracy:

The specific and transitory character of the National Democratic State is due to the fact that it is not a single-class state, or even a two-class (workers and peasants) state; nor is it the dictatorship of one or two classes. It is a state embodying the interests of the entire patriotic part of the nation which has to repress the overthrown reactionary classes. . . . The relationships established between the democratic classes in power, victorious over reaction and gathered together in a national front, will mean both a lasting alliance of these classes and a struggle between them with a view of furthering national prosperity.[3]

In reality, relationships between classes cannot remain static after independence; the privileged classes tend to use their position to shift relationships constantly to their own advantage. Whenever revolutionaries get the idea they can get along for any length of time with the local bourgeoisie and need not prepare to defend themselves in a confrontation, on the pretext that the leader is tolerating or encouraging them, then they have entrusted

---

[3] A. Sobolev, in the *Nouvelle Revue internationale* (February 1965).

their freedoms and their very lives to the chance fact of one man remaining in power.

Political independence for former colonial countries has meant, in social terms, the emergence of the petty bourgeoisie. In an exceptional case like Cuba, a limited fraction of the petty bourgeoisie may, with the support of the proletariat and the poor peasants, throw out the bourgeoisie and try to develop the country in a hurry. Whether such a process can eventually succeed depends on certain factors: a radical ideology that refuses to compromise with imperialism, whatever the cost; a genuine alliance with the masses of the people. In short, if a fraction of the petty bourgeoisie wants to go all the way with revolution, it must consent to a class struggle within its own society. The tougher the fight, the more it tends to radicalize the leadership team, which has no choice—if it wants to stay in power—but to go further. In its fight against imperialism and social forces hostile to change in the status quo, the revolutionary fraction has no allies other than the masses of poor people and some remnants of other classes (usually intellectuals). This support obliges those in responsible positions to accept at least a relative degree of austerity, if they are to go beyond Socialist-sounding slogans, and give concrete proof of their alliance with the masses. If this process is carried out rigorously, it is inevitable that broad sectors of the petty bourgeoisie will opt for defection or counterrevolution, which has the effect, at least at first, of bringing the leadership group and the masses closer together.

What must be stressed is how *voluntarist* this whole process is. This is what Amilcar Cabral was talking about when he said that in underdeveloped countries the petty bourgeoisie had no alternative in regard to revolution other than "betrayal or suicide as a class." As a rule, of course, it "betrays"—that is, it serves its own interests—which makes sense, after having served the nation during the fight for liberation. Besides, everything pushes it in that direction: material advantages, the line of least resistance, the carrot-and-stick wielded by imperialists. However, even if a fraction of the petty bourgeoisie, under the leadership of a revolutionary hard core, turns radical (as in Cuba or Guinea-Bissau), it is no less the leadership class for all that: it commits "suicide" only to be reborn as a bureaucracy. This process, at least in underdeveloped countries, seems to be inevitable. The leadership, if it so desires, can then grapple with the problem of how and how much to check the power of that bureaucracy—through mass organizations, militia, unions, youth, or appeals to spontaneity.

It should not surprise us that radical groups of that mettle have been so few and far between. They have usually amounted to no more than small, hard-core opposition groups, often imprisoned or otherwise rendered ineffectual. The fingers of one hand are too many to count the revolutionary teams or parties that have managed to take power. It is quite natural that the petty bourgeoisie should produce elements concerned more with their own selfish interests than with the welfare of the masses of the people. It is the moralistic voluntarism of the revolutionaries that is remarkable.

Over the past twenty years, then, there have been pathetically few radical national and social revolutions. And the suicide of a segment of the petty bourgeoisie in order to be reborn as a revolutionary bureaucracy calls for a particularly stern voluntarism; the choice of such a course is not to be taken for granted. It follows that national revolutions—which enable administrative bourgeoisies to develop both politically and materially without having to steel themselves excessively to resist outside pressures—have been much more numerous. There will surely be more of them. These revolutions, greatly strengthening the state, while not going very far in transforming society, make it possible to recuperate a country's natural resources and orient investments. In countries rich in natural resources, such regimes achieve an unequally distributed but nevertheless genuine growth, and no growth at all when as in Egypt, the country is poor in resources.

In those countries where a national *and* social revolution has taken place, bureaucracy is the central issue. The poorer and more backward the society, the more all-powerful its bureaucracy turns out to be. Authority can be brutal in societies that have never known bourgeois democracy and its liberalism. (When it comes to freedoms, the bourgeois democratic revolution has so far generally produced the least despotic societies.) Besides, there is the inevitable delegation of power, which occurs all by itself in a very short time, once the burst of early organizational enthusiasm that got things started has died down. The process in which power is delegated by the less qualified to the more qualified—that is, by the amateur to the professional—leads straight to the constitution of bureaucracies, even in countries (such as Cuba) where they did not already exist in embryonic form. They spring up all the more easily where shortages are bound to arise, bringing with them an inegalitarian distribution that shapes and maintains a minority in possession of modern and techological knowledge. The social revolution does indeed demand the development of productive forces; otherwise, as Marx put it, all that is socialized is poverty. But the objective causes of bureaucratic growth are not economic underdevelopment of productive forces or cultural development of the proletariat. They are related not only to the historic immaturity (or inability?) of the workers, but also to the fact that those engaged in productive work are far from being managers interested in the political and technical problems of how to run society and the economy. Bureaucracy is not a politico-administrative phenomenon that can be avoided by political measures emanating from a *truly* revolutionary leadership. The ups and downs of the Cultural Revolution in China give an idea as to just how quickly bureaucracy recovers its forces; even antibureaucratic campaigns themselves are launched and finally controlled by a segment of the bureaucracy. "If collective management of production and social life, as a major undertaking of human history, is not rooted in men's desire and ability to make it a living reality, then it is condemned to exist only as a stimulating Utopia," wrote C. Castoriadis[4] quite cor-

---

[4] Castoriadis: *Le phenomene bureaucratique* (Paris: Plon, 10/18, 1973).

rectly (and perhaps not quite wanting to believe it himself). It may be that the famous "ash cans of history" to which the orthodox Left has repeatedly consigned its adversaries and rivals for more than half a century will turn out to contain, after all, the corpse of a certain Marxism.

If bureaucracy is both a spontaneous social phenomenon—that is, one that arises all by itself in given conditions—and by its very function, a structured one, it easily prevails over workers. Worker organization, spontaneously generated in times of crisis, maintains its own structure only for a very short time. One practical criticism that comes up all too rarely in discussions of workers' councils—or *self-management*, to use the more current term—is the importance of sectors vital to the operation of society and the state that are structurally out of the reach of workers engaged in production—such as currency and foreign trade. Bureaucracy takes its place as an inevitable phenomenon, all the more since its seeds are to be found in the very conception of the vanguard party. But even when the vanguard party is not there first to point the way, it emerges out of the specialization of administrative and political tasks.

If the phenomenon is indeed inevitable, it is time to take a hard look at its function and uses. As a privileged group—even without material privileges, its decision-making power alone makes it privileged—its function is to involve the masses in the process of developing the country. Once the first period of accumulation and industrialization is over, bureaucracy, by definition a centralizing force, with a tendency to bolster its own political and material privileges, in turn obstructs development. If, as in China, the leadership, or part of it, is concerned about the uses of bureaucracy, then the bureaucracy's tendency to set itself up as omnipotent needs constantly to be thwarted in order to keep popular mobilization going as long as possible. Needless to say, even in the best of cases the mere fact that an antibureaucracy campaign is going on bears in itself the seeds of yet more bureaucrats (not always more democratic than their predecessors). Differences between bureaucracies can be considerable, and without suggesting that the Chinese bureaucracy is diametrically opposed to the Soviet one (they in fact show plenty of points in common), it seems likely that Maoist conceptions are much less economist than those of Stalin and grant an important place to the human factor. What is happening in China, for better or for worse, is of prime importance—all the more in that China will probably be one of the major powers in the world of tomorrow. But the Chinese bureaucracy, even if it has its own special approach and methods, appears assured of its historic destiny as a ruling class, just as the bureaucracies of the other Socialist countries do. How is it possible, for instance, to think that proletarian democracy can really function in a system where hierarchic relationships within the bureaucracy are so obvious and strict? If the existing Socialist regimes bear only a scant resemblance to the Marxian model, no one has yet managed to pull off a national and social revolution that was not bureaucratic. The fundamental fact is that the starting point for every system can only be the society that produced it. That puts a considerable damper on the notion of abrupt changes producing a "new man."

After what we have seen or been subjected to, the world over, in the course of the past forty years—German, Japanese, and other varieties of fascism, atrocities committed by the Soviet regime, especially under Stalin, the exactions of colonialism—the faith and hope which the nineteenth century, itself the heir to the enlightenment, placed in human nature and progress are, to put it mildly, open to doubt. Human nature as we know it is not an abstract entity but the product of human history. In view of this, it is hard to dismiss out of hand the circumspect attitude of theologians and Chinese legalists alike, more inclined to trust in laws and institutions than in the impulses of the species.

Rationalism—the belief that history has a purpose, not to mention faith in one's ability to discern where it is heading—has given way to acceptance of the irrational, even of madness itself. How, indeed, can it be denied that beneath the apparent orderliness of laws and codes, today as yesterday the world we live in is cruel and murderous? It is a world where some two-thirds of the human race do not get enough to eat, while a large fraction of the lucky third is glutted with plenty; where for thirty years conflicts have constantly raged at the expense of dispossessed peoples, while a white skin continues to be valued above a "colored" one. (Nor can we overlook the conflicts within a Third World that refuses to grant any real rights to minorities, least of all the right to secede.) It is a world in which the women who enjoy equality with the men of their own social milieu cannot even be counted in percentages, there are so few of them. Everywhere, we are still living in a tribal universe in which nationalism—admirable only when downtrodden—is regarded as the highest value both by states and by the majority of their citizens.

Aggression and destruction, domination and submission are a much greater part of the historic heritage of the species than once it seemed. Sole responsibility should not perhaps be attributed to leaders and systems. It is an illusion to believe, as so many do, that Marxian thought was purely scientific, as opposed to Utopian socialism. Marx was consistent and made sense, but his aims were no different from the Utopian Socialists: the withering away of the state through the disappearance of class distinctions. Be that as it may, it is still true that capitalists are the dominant class, that profit plays a central role, that human labor is the instrument of property (private or state), and that government exists to manage the merchant order. Perhaps it should also be added that capitalism, far more than any other mode of production, represents the great leap forward of the human race. But the growth of productive forces is obviously not everything—which one sees with especial vividness if one compares certain aspects of daily life in West Africa, say, with the human impoverishment, sullenness, and urban tension found in industrial societies (the United States in particular).

Still for the last two centuries, the key ideas of Western society—freedom and equality—have brought important changes. It is generally accepted that men are equal, if not in fact, at least before the law (subjects have been transformed into citizens). Freedoms have been institutionalized. Government rule has—at least somewhat—lost its sacred character. Torture, while still practiced, is no longer usually taken as a matter of course. And the claim to equality goes beyond the political and institutional level to economic and cultural life. However, schemes for ending inequality have failed insofar as they involve canceling out the existing relationship of forces.

It is time to announce the death of Utopia—as embodied for some, a while back, by the Soviet Union, for others, more recently, by China, and also, for a large fraction of the American liberal intelligentsia, by the United States, prior to the Vietnam war. It is essential to debunk sacred cows and break down Manichean simplifications, even though the role of Utopia, like that of ideology, cannot be denied. Dreams can be as stubborn as facts. In this respect, intellectuals all too rarely fulfill their main function, which is to provide criticism. Most of the time, in the Third World, intellectuals are nothing but bootblacks, hack propagandists for whoever is in power. In Western countries, where freedom of expression is very great (and irresponsibility practically complete), snobbishness and fashion all too often prevail over critical analysis. And too often intellectuals make themselves the unconditional spokesmen and promoters of ruling powers and ideologies by actively lending a hand—often in good faith—to the upkeep of mystifications, simplifications, and sectarian dogmas.

If the essence of politics is domination, is the aim of socialism—the abolition of conflicts and the end of history—a dream worth defending? It is still necessary to fight for the people's more active participation in decision-making, as well as for the educational means and institutional forms to make such participation more than an illusion; to extend freedoms; to reduce, and, insofar as possible, eliminate inequalities, especially those affecting women, so that the relationship of forces may be less out of balance at all levels. The task remains to challenge the mythologies of the nation-state, the cult of work, the submission to authority, the imposture of groups and parties who claim to possess the truth—in short, to sift carefully through all established assumptions (for they lie at the root of many consented servitudes) with a view to satisfying all basic needs and eventually attaining the supreme luxury: free time.

The world is no doubt pregnant with change. But nothing indicates that it is possible to alter the course of a history based on the relationship of forces, in which the comfort of the victorious is nourished by the often unwitting bondage of the victims and the grief of the vanquished.

POSTSCRIPT
revolution in the third world
revisited

I

The scientifically inaccurate but convenient term *the Third World* refers to Asia, Africa, and Latin America. The term was invented by the French demographer Alfred Sauvy as analogous to the term *the Third Estate* (a concept dating from the time of the French revolution referring to everybody who did not belong to the nobility or the clergy); it refers to a grouping distinct from both the capitalist industrialized countries and the so-called socialist industrialized countries. Following the 1955 Bandung Conference held in Indonesia, which marked the emergence of the Afro-Asian world, the term spread all over the world. As

Maxime Rodinson pointed out,[1] "The Third World is not a single entity. It is made up of peoples formed by a wide variety of cultures at various levels of technological, economic, and cultural development. But in the last 150 years or so, at different points in the evolution of these peoples, they have been placed in new conditions, those of a situation of humiliation and subjection to a single ruler: the American-European West, and it has suffered one and the same break."

This humiliation, inflicted by the colonial ruler and the often violent break which resulted—using the master's own weapons—represent an experience common to the Third World. Since these countries became independent, other realities to do with cultures, levels of development, and the highly divergent growth rates that emerged show instantly that there is not *one* Third World, if one wants to retain this expression, but several.

To think in the light of what will for us now be the past, present, and immediate future realities of the countries of Asia, Africa, and Latin America is a many-sided and perilous undertaking.

At the beginning of the twentieth century, Europe dominated Asia and Africa, either directly, which was the usual case, or indirectly. The Europeanization of the world, which began at the very end of the fifteenth century with the discovery of America, was completed between the second half of the last century and the First World War. This final expansion was the consequence of the industrial revolution, which provided the material means for the conquest: in communications—steamer and telegraph; in weaponry—the machine gun; in medicine— quinine to treat malaria. Almost everywhere—except for the British disasters in the First Afghan War and Italy's attempted conquest of Ethiopia in 1896—small but better-organized and -armed military forces were victorious in subjugating empires and kingdoms.

---

1. "Marxisme et tiers monde," in *Marxisme et monde musulman* (Paris: Le Seuil, 1972).

This expansion was pursued not only by most of the states of Western Europe, headed by Great Britain and France, but also by Russia. During the second half of the nineteenth century, Russia conquered a large part of Central Asia—with Afghanistan acting as a buffer state between British India and the Russian Empire. The tsars seized some 2.5 million square kilometers from the Chinese Empire through unequal treaties. While the other white powers eventually handed back to China the concessions that they had extorted from it, Russia, and later the USSR, because it was a matter of contiguous territory, held on to what it had acquired.

In 1898, after their victory over Spain, the United States moved into Puerto Rico and the Philippines. Most of the northern Pacific with its hub in Hawaii was already under U.S. control. As for the Caribbean and Central America, they were the imperial republic's backyard—or the American Mediterranean. This white expansion, carried on in the name of civilization, was reinforced pseudoscientifically by Social Darwinism (domination, and survival of the fittest). Faced with this rising tide of perils, only Japan succeeded in finding within itself the means to respond to the challenge, thanks to the fact of its being an island, its cohesion, and the determination of a section of its elites. After 1867, Japan rapidly industrialized itself. In 1905, the naval victory at Tsushima, won by a nation with no maritime tradition against Russia, had an enormous impact, for it gave proof that the whites could be defeated, provided their ways were learned.

Despite attempts at modernization, no change or even reform embarked on during the nineteenth century came to fruition: neither that by Mehmet Ali in Egypt nor that of the "tanzimat" projected by the ever-sickening Ottoman Empire. The Persian (1905–7), Young Turk (1908), and Chinese (1911) revolutions were abortive. The tiny modernizing elites of countries with a state tradition knew what they were rejecting but could not clearly chart out what was to be done. Rejection of the foreigner, rejection of subjugation or foreign control, in short, awareness of humiliation, was strong, although by the eve of the First World War it still affected only a very thin stratum of the populus. It proved hard to work out how to overcome enslavement and resume control of the fate of their countries. Was a modernization limited to military matters enough? Or would it also be necessary to imitate European parliamentary institutions? How could one adapt without abandoning one's traditions? These were some of the questions raised by sections of the elites in countries with a state tradition, and they did not always find an answer. It goes without saying that, out of a mixture of laziness, caste arrogance, and incomprehension, the bulk of the traditional elites—whether in the Manchu Empire or in the Muslim Empire—steeped in self-sufficiency and proud of a glorious past, had no intention of changing or being changed.

In any case, it would take time to base the response to the challenge of the West on the very novel concept of the nation-state and turn against the Europeans their own major ideology: nationalism. Meanwhile, Europe continued its expansion: Morocco became a protectorate (1912); Libya was taken over by the Italians (1912); on all sides, the Ottoman Empire, which had been shrinking continuously since the eighteenth century, was getting smaller at an accelerating rate, which precipitated the crisis of its elites.

Two non-European states took part in the First World War (not counting the United States, which had emerged from the matrix of Europe): the Ottoman Empire and Japan. The former, which had allied with the Central Powers because of its opposition to Russia and in the hope of recreating a great Pan-Turkish empire (a hope that led to the mass deportation and massacre of the Armenians, the first genocide of the twentieth century), collapsed. However, thanks to an outburst of national feeling and the determination of Mustapha Kemal, modern Turkey was built on the nation-state model. With a considerable advance on the other states of Asia and North Africa, Kemal succeeded in forcing acceptance of his country's independence. He was a precursor in many respects, not only in more or less formal Europeanization: he was also the first to have played on East-West rivalries, forming a tactical alliance with Lenin long enough to ensure his position. As for Japan, it was on the winning side and inherited the German colonial possessions in the northern Pacific, which enhanced its strategic presence in an area whose importance at the time was growing. Lord Horatio Kitchener had already confided to the German geopolitician Karl Haushofer in 1909: ". . . War between our two countries would benefit the United States and Japan in the Pacific."

Following a war in which Germany had failed for the first time this century to impose its hegemony, the colonial world underwent few major changes. Wilsonian principles in fact recognized the right of European peoples to self-determination. This right was granted to Central and East Europe and to Armenia (1920). The Arab territories—except for what was later to become Saudi Arabia—came under French or British mandates. At the time of the founding of the League of Nations, Japan, then the sole non–white power, asked that an article be added to the preamble to the Covenant condemning racial discrimination. Their request was rejected by the American delegation.

It was at this time that the first communist parties in Asia were created and that, on the initiative of the Bolsheviks, disappointed not to see the proletarian revolution spread to Europe and particularly to Germany, the Congress of Peoples of the East was held in Baku (1920). This initiative was not followed by much in the way of results. It was in fact premature. The balance of power still weighed heavily in favor of Europe and the West.

The interwar agitation only bore fruit following the Second World War. Until then, all the insurrections and resistance movements in the colonial countries were defeated. This is what happened to the resistance of Sheikh Moukhtar to the Italians in Libya (1922–32) or the remarkably well-organized uprising led by the Abdelkrim in the Rif in Morocco. Imperial and colonial ideology were accepted by a large majority of Europeans. Public opinion supported the colonial expeditions carried out by professional soldiers that were in any case few in number. As for colonialism, except for a narrow sector of urbanized people, it was endured by the populations as a matter of fate. But already these elites were gradually succeeding in mobilizing part of the urbanized masses. Such was the case in India with the Indian National Congress, which found in Gandhi a charismatic personality who was able to use the technique of nonviolence against a democracy. Congress succeeded in becoming a mass movement, and in 1943 launched the "Quit India" campaign which led to British withdrawal after the war. By then, the second German attempt to impose its hegemony had terminally weakened Europe. In Asia, Western defeats—of the Americans, British, French, and Dutch—inflicted by Japan had already been turned into an advantage by the liberation movements, communist and nationalist alike.

European colonization in the imperial age had three characteristics: a concerted effort to impose the civilization of the metropolis on the colonized peoples in terms of religion, culture, and language; subordination of the economic activities of the colony to the interests of the metropolis; and racial discrimination based on the superiority of the white man, his religion, culture, and technology.

Following the Second World War, while the United Nations Charter accepted the right of peoples to self-determination (one should add that the right extended to all peoples with a state), the colonized peoples rejected the values that underpinned the justification of the colonial world.

The end of the Second World War marked the great turning point of the century. It signaled the decline of Europe and the undisputed hegemony of the United States and the system it incarnated, as well as the values and mass culture that it spread all over the world. Nuclear weapons established a decisive breach: qualitatively, the nature of war was transformed, and world peace for decades to come rested on their deterrent power. There was the gradual rise of the USSR, which, having extended its shield, strengthened its military capacities and became a world power in a militarily bipolar world. Colonial countries became independent, often through violent struggles. There was the beginning of the population explosion in the Third World, which continued throughout the half-century and altered the numerical balance between North and South. Between 1945 and 1973 there was a period of exceptional growth of a capitalism that had been said to be moribund, and despite the crisis that followed, the postwar period was one of extraordinary technological advances, especially in the United States and Japan, and to a lesser extent, Western Europe.

Among this great variety of phenomena, some political observers have focused only on the East-West conflict. One such was Raymond Aron, who intervened courageously on the subject of Algeria when the Algerian problem was becoming a threat to France itself, yet whose published works, extensive though they are, hardly refer to the colonial phenomenon or the emergence of the Afro-Asian world. Others, especially from the 1960s onward, saw or pretended to see only the North-South dimension. And yet, very rapidly, the regional dimension of local conflicts, barely perceptible at the beginning, became clearer and clearer with the increase in the number of autonomous conflicts which only indirectly inpinged on the East-West confrontation. The frontier wars in 1959–62 between China and India along their Himalayan border, portrayed at the time as a confrontation between a communist state and an anticommunist one, were above all the expression of regional hostilities between two states with antagonistic geopolitical interests. As for the Algerian war, portrayed by some supporters of French Algeria as a fight by the West against the expansion of communism, it was a colonial war in the strictest sense of the term.

For all intents and purposes, apart from the Portuguese possessions, colonial rule ended between the independence of the Philippines in 1946 and that of Algeria in 1962. Holland held on for a while to Indonesia, then decolonized in 1949. France wanted to resume its position in Indochina but lost the war through the absence of a coherent policy even before the military defeat at Dien Bien Phu in 1954. Meanwhile, China, to the general astonishment of both Stalin and the Americans, fell into the hands of the communist forces led by Mao Zedong. After 1947–48 the cold war made people aware of the military bipolarity of the postwar world. Communist advances in Central Europe and in Asia (China, Korea, Vietnam, threats in the Philippines and Malaya) were compensated for as best as could be by the creation of NATO and containment of the Asian "Rimland," as the geopolitician Nicholas Spykman had advocated: a network of alliances stretching from the Middle East to Pakistan and from Thailand to Japan by way of the Philippines.

In reality, and gradually in people's consciousnesses, the fifteen years between the end of the Second World War and the beginning of the 1960s saw two radical changes occur: the emergence of the Third World, which became the main site of East-West conflict, and the gradual withering away of the imperial mentality.

If the colonial period in the age of imperialism was short— it lasted about eighty years—the phenomenon of Third Worldism lasted even less time, since it barely covered the 1960s and 1970s. For the historian, Third Worldism will be seen above all as an overestimate of the political potential of the Third World.

Looked at over a century, the decisive phenomenon is neither Third Worldism nor its rejection but the change in the spirit of the age, often won through very hard struggles between the imperial mentality based on colonialism and the emergence, today fully accepted, of independent states, some of which manifest a very robust political autonomy.

What lay behind the temporary unity of the Third World, and more precisely of the Asian and African colonial world, was a shared humiliation at being dominated and treated as inferior. The major motivation of the nationalists—or the communists—was not the revolt against economic exploitation but the demand for dignity. But the very concepts of the demands put forward in the struggles were inherited from colonial models: exaltation of modern nationalism with the goal of a nation-state, another Western innovation.

By a remarkable turn of events, it was just when it was most sharply rejected that the West was most imitated. But the model was no longer, as in the time of Mustapha Kemal, demanded as the most advanced. It was adopted as self-evident, while rising up against the West. However, the frontiers inherited from the colonial period were respected not only in Africa but also in the Near East—leaving aside the case of Israel. Wherever the nation does not exist, the state seeks to create one or acts as if one existed. As for the rights of peoples to self-determination, it has essentially if not entirely meant the right of peoples to free themselves from control by the West. The sole exception is the secession of Bangladesh, and that is to be explained by Indian intervention and by geography.

If, with hindsight, we look at the historical period separating the end of the Second World War from the mid-1970s, which marks the end of the period when the Third World was given special treatment by a wide swath of opinion in the West, three major conflicts stand out. They are major in the sense that they helped to produce a radical shift in the way in which the contemporary world is viewed.

These conflicts are, first, the Indochina War, which culminated with Dien Bien Phu, a defeat that was inconceivable before it happened. The second was the Algerian War, a colonial war par excellence in the impact it had worldwide. Militarily, it was lost by the FLN, but it destroyed forever the myth of French Algeria and administered a decisive blow to imperial and colonial ideology. Finally, the Vietnam War, with its major consequences, which put a halt (Would anyone have bet on it with any certainty in 1965?) to a certain type of total imperial commitment on the part of the United States. Psychologically, this defeat plunged America into ten years of military impotence. There is nothing surprising in the fact that these struggles and their consequences should have progressively mobilized a large number of the youth and intelligentsia in the West and, going beyond the framework of activist minorities, altered the appearance of the world today much more profoundly than it might appear. Compared to these decisive conflicts, all the others directed against the West (except for the Korean War) were minor and often of little consequence. Meager balance sheets indeed, between the proclamation of socialism and the taking of power by the Sandinistas in Nicaragua nearly twenty years later, for a continent where the cordillera of the Andes was alleged always to be on the point of becoming a new Sierra Maestra. In Africa, too, the balance sheet was meager, with no more than the belated liquidation of Portuguese colonialism and the disappearance of Ian Smith's Rhodesia, which gave way to Zimbabwe; simultaneously, in South Africa, the clock of change obstinately stopped at the same time, since Sharpeville in 1960 began once again to move slowly with the clashes in Soweto and other urban centers in 1977, and above all with the uninterrupted clashes in the urban centers in 1984–86. But the African front-line states were unable to change anything. And what can be said about the majority of regimes, especially in Africa, that have declared themselves to be "socialist" at one point or another over the last quarter of a century? There is a meager balance sheet in the Near East too, for the Palestinian movement endlessly tearing itself apart and being first manipulated, then hit by Syria, a movement that in 1969–70 saw itself as the "spearhead of the Arab revolution." The Palestinians' most serious advantage lies in the people of the occupied territories, who pose a problem for Israel that is insoluble if it wishes to remain a state that is both a majority Jewish and a democratic state, if mass expulsion is an unacceptable solution and indifinite occupation, in present circumstances, is unlikely.

In short, Third Worldism, which puts its hopes at the beginning of the 1960s (remember Frantz Fanon's *Wretched of the Earth*) and the spread of the "socialist" revolution through-out the Third World, proved to be a myth. But before analyzing this myth today, it is important to recall its historical background.

"It is not so long ago," recalled Jean-Paul Sartre in his preface (which itself is debatable from several points of view) to the *Wretched of the Earth*, that "the globe contained 500 million men and a billion and a half natives." Colonial ideology was profoundly absorbed right from primary school by young Europeans, whether they were British, French, Belgian, or Dutch. In the mass ideology, which was nationalist and imperial, peddled from the beginning of the century, the imperial idea based on overseas colonies was solidly anchored in the con-sciousness of three generations. It is true that, looked at from a historical perspective, the period between the zenith of co-lonial expansion and its end was a short one. But it was enough, from a human perspective, to form, if not a spirit of the age, by definition always changing, than a true world view based on an absolute belief in the superiority of European civilization and its values.

For Europeans—and Americans—of the nineteenth cen-tury, their country incarnated civilization facing barbarism. Moreover, the great anthropologists of the Victorian age who defended the idea of a hierarchy of civilizations served to leg-itimize the colonial enterprise. Even when this certainty was subsequently shaken by the work of science and the appearance of new views, the notions of a variety of civilizations and of cultural relativism did not, for most people, alter the idea of a decisive superiority of whites over natives. Europe was confident of its rightness. Apart from a few isolated voices, no doubt arose as to the legitimacy of the colonizing mission, whether in Great Britain, in France, or elsewhere. At the beginning of the twentieth century, Europe was superior on every level: military, scientific, financial, intellectual. The white man caused his law to reign and his civilization to shine on a powerless multitude.

And yet this apparently quiescent world was moving. The movement was often better-articulated in the old national formations with a long state tradition such as China, Vietnam, and Burma. But the Japanese example remained unique and the Chinese, Vietnamese, and Burmese students who hastened to Japan after 1905 to study how an Asian nation had succeeded in defeating the whites brought back no recipe applicable to their realities. It is too often forgotten that, paradoxically, at the very time when Europe and the United States were dominating the world, one of the major topics in the West was the "yellow peril." What a fantastic reversal, against which Third Worldist projections seem banal and devoid of imagination!

Africa, lagging behind Asia and not having experienced the national state south of the Sahara—except for Ethiopia—gradually absorbed the pan-Africanist ideas that were abroad in the Afro-American diaspora: W. E. B. DuBois, Marcus Garvey, and George Padmore, later taken up by Kwame Nkrumah.

The colonial period, like any period of conquest, had its toll of exactions, repressions, and massacres—terrible ones, such as that of the Hereros in Southwest Africa (Namibia) in 1905–7, at the time of German colonialism, when the rebellion, precisely because of its success, was severely put down by General von Trotha. After the military operations, a total population of eighty thousand fell to about fifteen thousand in two years. But in addition to providing an infrastructure, colonization provided the weapons that made it possible to throw it off. It shaped the new elite, a section of whom rose up to fight colonialism in the name of identity, dignity, and independence. Modern nationalism, a concept born in the West, is the major ideology in the history of the nineteenth and twentieth centuries. It is not by chance that the liberation movements called themselves *national* liberation movements.

But once one has reviewed colonialism and reviewed it again, it is impossible not to recognize its modernizing contributions. History has seen many conquests and many dominations, but few have been so short-lived and few have brought so much. It is a fact that European societies, while destroying the traditional economies and creating underdevelopment—for underdevelopment only exists where the traditional society that existed before the interference of modern capitalism has been distorted—also disseminated the very ideas that were to enable the defeated to overthrow their rulers and yet have a modern infrastructure.

It is impossible to exaggerate the importance of the defeats inflicted by the Japanese on Westerners during the Second World War for the colonized peoples of Asia: the Americans in the Philippines, the French in Indochina, the Dutch in Indonesia, the British in Burma and Malaya. The undisputed rule of the white man was approaching its end. But imperial certainties were erased slowly and painfully: This revolutionary shift in relations between masters and slaves, between rulers imbued with their own superiority and the ruled humiliated to the point where they doubted themselves, took two or three decades to accomplish, from the independence of the Philippines in 1946 to that of the Portuguese colonies in 1975. The high points of this period were Dien Bien Phu, the end of French Algeria, and the American war in Vietnam, which, while it was not a colonial war, had many of the features of one.

The dice were cast by the end of the Second World War. Great Britain successfully decolonized the Indian subcontinent. That did not prevent British troops fighting discreetly for almost three decades: Palestine (1945–47), Malaya (1948–57), Kenya (1952–54), Cyprus (1955–59), Aden (1963–67), and independent Oman (1972–76). These colonial wars, waged with professional soldiers, often bore political fruit: the Chinese communists were put down, and independence was granted to Malayan traditionalists; the Mau-Mau movement was crushed, and power was given to Jomo Kenyatta, transformed by his imprisonment into a nationalist symbol. Independence was not handed to General Grivas, who fought the British troops, but to Archbishop Makarios. In Oman, British officers enabled the sultanate's forces, backed by Iran and Jordan, to overcome the remarkably well-organized Marxist guerrillas in Dhofar. The British managed the crisis of colonialism with more pragmatism and a better appreciation of the relationship of forces. It is true that Great Britain, unlike the continental colonialists—France, Belgium and Holland—had not been defeated and did not experience the obsession with abandonment that was synonymous in the eyes of many people in the home country with irremediable decadence. It enjoyed a very broad national consensus and, unlike France, never saw one part of the nation at loggerheads with the other.

In the Netherlands, as soon as postwar conditions allowed, an operation to reconquer the Dutch East Indies was launched in 1947 and 1948. France had started to do the same in 1946, seeking to reestablish itself everywhere in the empire—the rejection of all but cosmetic changes was patent. During the war, the imperial idea had been exalted both by Vichy and by Free France. The empire was seen as the last bastion of a greatness that was to be restored. After the Second World War, the empire was rechristened the French Union but that in no way changed the colonial mentality embedded in the collective consciousness of the French.

In reality, it took the Indochinese and Algerian wars for colonial and imperial certainties to collapse. It took two decades of rear-guard wars to shake and sweep aside the faith imbibed in school in the absolute and universal superiority of Western civilization and in the legitimacy, not to say the necessity, of colonization. This radical shift—whose consequences were worldwide—was the work of the colonized peoples, but it was also the work of all those in Europe who contributed to this transformation by what they said, what they wrote, or what they did. What is criticized today as Third Worldism started out as anticolonialism. And the triumph of this militant anticolonialism occurred in the years 1954–62, the years of the Algerian War.

It took ten more years and a complex unfolding of events for people to come to accept in their minds the autonomous existence of colonial societies and their fundamental problems. These were the ten years leading up to the American failure in Vietnam and the collapse of the last imperial regime in Europe, Portugal, sustained throughout its thirteen years of colonial warfare by NATO.

Contrary to popular opinion, this change was not the work of a movement of intellectuals addressing themselves to intellectuals, but an extraordinary society-wide reassessment of how it interpreted and viewed the world. It was in part the triumph of those who were on the side of the colonized. But it was chiefly produced by the attention given to the societies of the Afro-Asian world and an interest in other civilizations and respect for their culture—something to which numerous orientalists contributed—combined with more active political movements and, finally, the national liberation struggles.

Imperial certainties and colonial good conscience were only very gradually undermined in Europe. It took the feeling of powerlessness to control mass national movements in a world in which liberation from the colonial yoke was the order of the day and the weariness born of rear-guard actions. But before that point was reached, public opinion remained massively colonialist, probably until about 1960. Vehement though they were, the protests of the colonized, scarcely heard between the wars, began to be heard and relayed following the Second World

War. The intellectuals of the colonized countries found a response in Europe among a section of the left, liberal, or Christian intelligentsia. Sartre's remarkable preface, "Black Orpheus," to Leopold Sedar Senghor's *Anthology of Negro and Malagasy Poetry* (1949) was a striking sign of it. Although the French Communist Party defended anticolonialist positions during the Indochina War, all the more so because the Vietminh was communist, it continued until 1956 to advocate the "true French Union" on the model of the Union of Soviet Socialist Republics. The official Marxism peddled by the French Communist Party was an often sinister caricature. It voted for full power for the government headed by the socialist Guy Mollet in 1956, which gave the government the means to carry on the war in Algeria. The climate in Europe was very hostile to the nationalist demands made by the Afro-Asian world. The almost unanimous reactions of the press and opinion in both Great Britain and France at the time of the nationalization of the Suez Canal and the Anglo-French expedition were in this respect significant. Gamal Abdel Nasser was looked upon as a fascist dictator, recuperation of the Canal by the Egyptians as an act of banditry, and they were accused of being incapable of managing it. Among nationalists in Asia and Africa, as among anticolonists in Europe, the intervention was perceived as a colonial expedition. The failure of the operation due to the combined pressure of the United States and the USSR was seen as an important victory in the Third World and was a visible indication of the decline of the old European imperialism. The modifications or upheavals that had occurred at the end of the war had been geographically far removed from Europe: India, Indochina, Indonesia, Korea, etc. The Algerian War and the nationalization of the Suez Canal brought the scene of conflicts much closer to home. Moreover, after 1956, the increase in the number of French troops in Algeria, made necessary by the policy of close surveillance of the whole country, transformed what had begun as a police operation into an undeclared war in which conscripts were involved. The colonial era was approaching its end. For Great Britain, the independence of India, the evacuation of the military base in the Suez Canal Zone and the nationalization of the Canal markedly weakened the advantages attached to its possessions in East Africa and Southeast Asia. Great Britain watched over the Gulf until the beginning of the 1970s and then passed the baton to the United States.

The settler colonies—Algeria, Kenya, Rhodesia—posed problems that were only settled by violence. Elsewhere, decolonization accelerated while nationalist demands grew shriller and shriller: Morocco and Tunisia left the French Union in 1956; in the same year, Great Britain evacuated the Sudan; the following year, the Gold Coast was the first colony in tropical Africa to win independence, as Ghana. This was an important event. Until then, independence had been granted or seized by Asian or Arab states which had retained a degree of autonomy under a French or British protectorate. The granting of independence to Ghana came shortly before the abolition of the French Union in 1958 and the referendum that offered the choice between independence or sovereignty within the French Community. Only Guinea chose independence. But in 1960, all the states of the former French West Africa and French Equatorial Africa became independent. The speeding-up of their accession to independence was largely due to the Algerian war.

But in 1956, the climate was altogether different. The supporters of French Algeria were able to impose war on a government that was relatively powerless. A war described as a process of "pacification" was stepped up. A generation reared in anti-fascism (the Second World War had ended only a dozen years earlier) and for which resistance to Nazism represented a model discovered both the reality of colonialism and the methods of warfare used to fight against terrorism and clandestine action including how to dismantle an underground political infrastructure and the use of torture. At the time, this practice was wrongly thought of as being used only by dictators. It was a terrible shock for the children of the Republic. Compared to what was said in the United States during the Vietnam War and in Israel about the massacres in the Palestinian camps in Lebanon, official France lived a lie which was only broken by anticolonialist activists or liberal or humanistic circles. This problem of torture was a shock: the French army was torturing Algerians because they were colonized.

This period from 1956 to 1960 saw opposition crystallize. The war waged in the name of the defense of the West by a section of the French army haunted by Indochina made even less sense because the FLN was nationalist and anti-communist. The stalemate in the war in Algeria, a settler colony where settlers represented 10 percent of the population, came from the fact that, faced with the FLN's demand for national identity, France had nothing to offer except the promise of an improvement in the economic situation. With the impossibility of an integration of almost 10 million Muslims, the logical conclusion would have been to agree to independence. But there are precious few examples of logical solutions to conflicts involving the emotions. Passions rose, and the Fourth Republic was overthrown and General Charles de Gaulle returned to power. However, as the years passed, protests and opposition to the Algerian War were making a greater and greater impact. The importance of Jean-Paul Sartre's voice at this time was enormous. Although the FLN was militarily defeated on the ground by 1960, the true outcome of revolutionary war was being played out in the political arena, as the French officers who had reflected on this type of war following Indochina knew. Public opinion soon learned of the existence of FLN support networks organized by young Frenchmen. A manifesto signed by hundreds of the most prestigious names in France including Sartre and André Breton proclaimed: "We respect and deem justified the refusal to take up arms against the Algerian people. We respect and deem justified the behavior of Frenchmen who feel it their duty to give help and protection to the oppressed Algerians in the name of the French people. The cause of the Algerian people who are contributing decisively to ruin the colonial system is the cause of all free men." Gradually, the internal front cracked. General de Gaulle proposed a referendum on self-determination. The Algerian urban masses demonstrated in strength at the end of the year; a corner had been turned which led, after difficult upheavals in 1961 with an attempted coup d'état and then the formation of the Secret Army Organization (OAS), to a dearly won independence in 1962.

Third Worldism took root in this anticolonial context. Briefly, Third Worldism in the West was carried by two trends: the first derived from Leninism; the second, more liberal, from the Judeo-Christian tradition. Perpetrators of the first trend saw in the revolutions of the colonial and semicolonial world a substitute for the proletariat in the industrial countries which had ceased to be revolutionary. Those responsible for the second trend, more concerned with morality, rebelled against injustice, oppression, and poverty and tended to put the victim on a pedestal.

Among the colonized, Third Worldism—which Fanon's thought symbolizes better than anyone else's—had two effects: a therapeutic one because it comforted the humiliated, restored his dignity, exalted his struggle and put the fate of the world on his shoulders; and mystifying because it attributed to colonialism all the ills of the past and to the capitalist system responsibility for the present ills of the Third World.

Third Worldism was basically "anti-imperialist" at a time when American supremacy was total. This was the time when General de Gaulle himself was seeking to free France—and Europe, at least verbally—from American hegemony. Most Third Worldists were Leninists and were looking for an alternative to the sterile and oppressive Marxism of the communist parties. It was in these years that the small Trotskyite groups took a second lease on life and that the first pro-Chinese began to define themselves both as Stalinists and as revolutionaries. Finally, these years also saw trends, which above all were fighting against colonialism for the emancipation of the Third World (including Latin America following the impact of the Cuban revolution in 1960–61), and before long against the American intervention in Vietnam.

The apparent conjunction of the Chinese revolutionary line focused on the Third World following the Sino-Soviet breach, and the radicalization of the Cuban revolution and the Algerian liberation war created the feeling that a second revolutionary wave was emerging. The first, that of the October Revolution, was seen as having gotten lost in bureaucracy and a Stalinism which only the most rigid pro-Chinese continued to admire aloud.

In fact, tricontinentalism, formalized after the 1966 Havana conference, was already in existence by the end of the Algerian War, and defined itself, sharply and often simplistically, as anticolonialist and anti-imperialist. Not since the Twentieth Congress in 1956, at which Khrushchev officially declared that the king was naked, was the USSR considered a political model, though it was still seen as a success of planned and accelerated development. In 1957, Sputnik produced its psychological impact. It ought not to be surprising that France should have been the crucible of Third Worldism, given its heritage of Marxism among a good portion of its intellectuals and a harsh colonialism. Third Worldism spread through Europe during the Algerian War, but only reached the United States later through the experience of Vietnam and the influence of Fanonism among Black Americans. This moral dimension, imbued with a thirst for justice and dignity for the oppressed, made it possible for the radical Third Worldist trend to link up with liberal, Christian and humanist circles.

Such is the political and intellectual context in which what came to be called Third Worldism developed.

This political context was still pervaded with the spirit of the cold war. The Berlin wall was built in 1961. Right-wing conservatives were often still archaic and as Manichaean as the left wing: they peddled racism with all the arrogance and contempt of the well-off.

In any event, it was not a time of nuances. McCarthyism had only recently ended. But the context was not devoid of ambiguities: the USSR, with its totalitarian and bureaucratic regime, where the victims of the Stalinist period were to be counted in their tens of millions and which kept Central Europe under its rule, was also the country which supported numerous liberation movements. Conversely, the liberal democracies led by the United States, which were concerned with the rule of law at home, installed or sustained tyrannies that were both bloody and retrograde, intervened directly or indirectly to maintain an unjust status quo (Iran, 1953, Guatemala, 1954), or practiced racial discrimination at home—the last great civil rights struggles dated from 1961–63. The gap between declared principles and the facts seems to be a constant in history.

The rejection of colonialism often involved violence. Fixed opinions probably cannot be overthrown without a crisis. Crises fulfilled a positive function which societies embedded in the status quo appeared to fear, so pejorative had the term *destabilization* become, as though history had not always been a succession of stabilizations and destabilizations. Algeria was the time of the crisis of the French conscience as Vietnam was that of the American conscience.

The anti-imperialist movement which condemned the wars waged by the West was, apparently paradoxically, fascinated by armed struggle and guerrilla war. This young left absorbed pell-mell into its imagination fragments of the Spanish Civil War, the October Revolution, the resistance to Nazism, the Mexican Revolution, the Long March and Che Guevara.

To the Third World, Third Worldism peddled a mixture of exacerbated nationalism and populist slogans. Nationalism was reflected in the mythical recovery of an exalted past. Religious ideology, especially in Islam, became more than ever a cultural value underpinning identity. As for "Marxist-Leninist" ideology, it provided an explanation of the world that was at once simple, optimistic, and voluntaristic. For many "revolutionary" states, this version of scientific socialism constituted both an ideology of opposition to colonialism and imperialism and a tool of mobilization from which the class struggle was often removed. For others, which rather saw the class struggle as playing a central role, ideology was based on a Stalinism for the underdeveloped. As for the adversary, it was treated as totally evil. This stark, black-and-white contrast is not peculiar to revolutionary movements or those that proclaim themselves as such, as with the recent revolution of the Iranian mullahs. Such Manichaeanism was one of the major weaknesses of Third Worldism. Initially, it had the excuse that it was confronting a colonialist Manichaeanism that was equally obtuse. However, in the name of a universalist justice and egalitarianism, and generally from ignorance of non-Western societies, Third Worldism rarely perceived the specific features on which the quests for identity that are one of the major features of most Third World movements are based. The agent of the struggle, all the dominated peoples together, was perceived as a single whole, and the complexity of particular situations underestimated.

During the 1960s, the impact of the urban revolution made Latin America particularly receptive to this type of trend. There, American imperialism incarnated absolute evil to the exclusion of any other. For reasons to do with geography and history, this continent-wide but provincial view took the place of ideology and analysis for many Latin American militants.

The large-scale commitment of American troops in 1965 to the Vietnam War precipitated the crystallization of more numerous and more structured movements opposed to the

United States for obvious reasons, but also to Western Europe and Japan. The "movement," as it was called in the United States, began in the universities in 1964–67 and became massive and respectable following the Tet offensive of February 1968. With this psychological victory, the NLF, actively supported by North Vietnam, made a mockery of General Westmoreland's claims shortly before that pacification was entering its final phase. It does not matter, as has been many times stressed, that this offensive ended in a military defeat. In this type of warfare, the political dimension is far more important than the military aspects. The 1968 Tet offensive marked the turning point of the Vietnam War. The very logic of the war was called into question. Did an expedition begun with the assumption that the fight was against Chinese expansionism accord with the interests of the United States, and was it important for its security? Was the domino theory well-founded outside the Indochinese peninsula? American opinion underwent a tremendous change, and this was partly responsible for the beginning of negotiations for a withdrawal which would enable the regime in the South to hold out for at least a decent interval. The intervention in Cambodia and the establishment of the Lon Nol regime was a political error that led to the taking of power by the Khmer Rouge without in any way decisively hindering the supply of reinforcements and equipment from North Vietnam to the South. In any event, this intervention antagonized a section of public opinion against the policy being pursued by the American government which had previously not been very active.

No more than was the case with the colonial question can it be claimed that the anti–Vietnam War movement was a movement solely of students and intellectuals. It was a mass movement, made up of very diverse currents, from the churches to the Third Worldists, from liberals to the most extreme radicals. The myths of this movement relate not to the struggle itself but to the presumed moral virtue of the victimized North Vietnamese. This is a common phenomenon in conflicts where morality and politics are mixed up, these being the very stuff of great mobilizations.

More particularly, Third Worldist features can be seen in certain black Americans, among whom the ghetto riots after 1967 fueled the activism of small groups recently marked by Fanon's thought, such as the Black Panthers and others. At this time Eldridge Cleaver went to Algiers, Stokely Carmichael to Havana, Hanoi, and then Guinea. At this time, the linguist Noam Chomsky was playing the role that Sartre had played during the Algerian War. A market with an enormous capacity to adapt was flooded with all sorts of opposition literature. In the opposition to the war, for the vast majority the moral dimension was far more important than the more or less confused and indeed contradictory theories of the more political elements. In the context of a major crisis, the Third Worldists disseminated a new sensitivity, and opened up America to a less insular view of the world. But they were only one of the components of the turbulence of the years of prosperity, which saw the appearance of the feminist movement and the ecology movement, the new hippies and new black elites who often became very well-integrated economically.

Third Worldism was effective in the anticolonialist struggle and against the Vietnam War, because each posed a serious problem of national policy, but it showed the weakness of its worldview in struggles where, without a mass base, it projected its voluntarism and fantasies alone. The Latin American guerrilla movements which raised so much enthusiasm in some student circles at the time of the *foco* theory and Che Guevara, the urban terrorist movements called urban guerrillas in Uruguay and Brazil, the Allende experience in Chile—all were defeated primarily *internally* and not because of indirect interventions by the United States. It was with five hundred thousand men that the United States intervened unsuccessfully in Vietnam.

In France after 1968, Third Worldism, hitherto involving relatively few people, capitalized on the recruits from the May Movement. At the same time, the workers' struggles and the reintegration on the ground of industrial society were on the agenda: factory work, the problem of immigrants, and so on, mobilized the Maoist movements that were the praise-singers of the cultural revolution which, in their eyes, was utopia. Elsewhere, in West Germany and Italy, terrorist-type movements made their appearance modeled on the Tupamaros in Uruguay who had also inspired the Weathermen in the United States. The Red Army fraction (the Baader-Meinhof group) and the Red Brigades thought that they could use a spiral of violence and repression to mobilize the masses by showing them that the democratic state is in fact repressive and antipopular. These brilliant analyses were shared in France by the "Nouvelle Resistance" (France was seen as occupied by the bourgeoisie) but did not lead to violence.

A mishmash of populism and anti-imperialist Third Worldism affected minorities to which great names lent their voices (Sartre, Jean Genêt).

When it went beyond the framework of anticolonialism or mass movements like the one against the Vietnam War, Third Worldism, whether dealing with Latin America, the Cultural Revolution, or the Palestinian problem, was a succession of aberrations. These had their common origin in an ideological dimension whose role is to mask reality—seen as less interesting than the theoretical assumptions. Of course, one cannot lump every Third Worldist trend into a single category, but broadly, it can be said that these trends oscillated between revolutionary messianism and a Judeo-Christianity with a bad conscience and guilt feelings. The Vietnamese, for example, during the American intervention, were wonderfully able to play on this latter. The Chinese Cultural Revolution attracted the Christians less than a section of the Marxists, who thought that in its declared principles they had found a new way of avoiding running onto the bureaucratic reef. For some, the transfer of the utopia being realized from the USSR to China was effected without difficulty. With *Chinese Shadows*,[2] Simon Leys delivered a decisive blow to these reports of visits to China that were strangely reminiscent of reports of visits to the USSR of the 1930s. The Palestinian national movement too, especially in Europe, tapped into ideological simplifications and schemas in an emotionally charged climate. Slogans such as "Vietnam and Palestine—the same struggle" were totally without foundation. Third Worldists long underestimated Israeli nationalism, the State of Israel being exclusively perceived as a pawn of American imperialism. Sensitive to the dispossession of the Palestinians, and conscious that the Palestinians were now a national reality, Third Worldists conversely perceived the Palestinian resistance as the vanguard of revolution in the Middle East.

What is described as Third Worldism took many different forms, from conceptual elaboration to the caricature of wearing combat fatigues as dress in town. It did not prevent people who did not consider the Third World as an exotic utopia or an infatuation of gilded youth in crisis before they got caught up in career problems from pursuing serious surveys or research. Those who closely followed developments on the ground became aware sooner than others that revolutions are relative and that the gap between discourse and reality is almost always rather wide.

The major facts that precipitated the end of the Third Worldist utopia were numerous, but were concentrated in the second half of the 1970s. In a climate of economic crisis that was felt increasingly sharply, they were various in nature, but all contributed in their way to combine and come together to open a new epoch.

The particularly vigorous denunciation by Alexander Solzhenitsyn, coming though it did after many others—from Victor

2. New York: Viking Penguin, 1976.

Serge to Kravchenko, including Anton Ciliga, Boris Souvarine, Arthur Koestler, and others—delivered the last blow in the West to Marxism-Leninism, based on a vanguard party possessed of historical truth, the agent of growth, and the alternative to the capitalist system. Moreover, after Khrushchev's bluster promising the economic supremacy of the socialist countries by 1980, the realities of stagnation under Brezhnev became more and more perceptible. Military power and space programs are not enough to give the status of great economic power.

The "human rights" ideological offensive, which was the first serious ideological counteroffensive by the West for many years against the myth of "socialist" society, bore fruit even though it was highly selective about the countries it chose. Radicals rediscovered the virtues of democracy.

The collapse of the myth maintained about the cultural revolution in 1977–78 was a severe blow to those who had been putting their revolutionary hopes in Maoism. At the same time, the denunciation of the atrocities committed by the Khmer Rouge in 1977, launched by the Frenchman François Ponchaud, the Khmer Rouge being admirers of the cultural revolution, threw into disrepute voluntaristic revolutionaries ready, in the name of an idea, to liquidate part of the population. The Vietnamese—who intervened in Cambodia in 1978 and set up a regime entirely dependent on them—"normalized" the situation in the South in their own way in 1978–79, and provoked the departure of numerous boat people who were not privileged members of the previous regime. Revolutionary Vietnam, yesterday's persecuted victim, revealed itself as the bureaucratic persecutor in a new climate of corruption. Having won the war, Vietnam was unable to win the peace. Finally, the Sino-Vietnamese conflict, in the classic tradition of conflicts between states over regional hegemony, was a timely reminder for some that national interests are stronger than the supposed solidarity of countries sharing a common ideology.

Added to these phenomena, there were in the Third

World, Africa and especially the Middle East, other factors that led to a rejection of the Third World. First and foremost of these has been Islam (incarnated in the Iranian revolution), which violently rejects the West.

What is more, the West experienced the brutal discovery of its own vulnerability with the oil crisis of 1973–1979, while in the United States the Vietnam syndrome reflected a deep psychological malaise. The most spectacular and humiliating American setback was the seizure of hostages in the American embassy in Tehran. Soviet military power was strengthened and won successes while becoming more aggressive: Angola (1976), Ethiopia (1977), and above all the intervention in Afghanistan (1979). This latter can be seen as the event that closed, definitively, both the period of lyrical illusion about the Third World and that of Western guilt feelings. From then on began a period of counteroffensive symbolized by the words and gestures of President Reagan.

Today, infatuation with the Third World belongs to the past. But few independent observers try not to give way to the conformities of the spirit of the age and not to embrace the most dyed-in-the-wool conservatism after having cultivated radicalism. It is just as ideological to scorn all that one fought for yesterday and to defend with the same vehemence that which was formerly seen as the incarnation of evil. One Manichaeanism can precede another.

II

Economically, two questions have often been raised to which very different answers have been given: (1) Was colonialism the cause of what is known as underdevelopment? (2) Did colonialism make a decisive contribution to Western development?

It seems, with all necessary reservations, that one can answer yes to the first question, if what is meant by underdevelopment is distortion of the traditional economy and the breach of a certain equilibrium with various consequences, such as specializing in food, agriculture, and so on. But if India, for example, is underdeveloped, other states such as North Yemen, Afghanistan, and Ethiopia, less touched by the West, are more backward.

To the second question, on the other hand, the response is largely negative. When the changes of the English industrial revolution began in the mid-eighteenth century, Great Britain was far from being a colonial power. The England of 1830 had already carried out its industrial revolution. By that time, without any significant imports of primary commodities, it already had only one-third of its working population in agriculture. During the nineteenth century, countries with colonies, such as Great Britain, France, and the Netherlands, developed more slowly than Germany, Sweden, Switzerland, or the United States. For the period when Europe industrialized, from the second half of the nineteenth century to the First World War, imports of raw materials from the Third World, particularly energy, were very small. Between 1800 and 1938, only 18 percent of Europe's total exports were shipped to the Third World. The most notable exception was Great Britain, where the percentage was nearer 40 percent.

The wealth of the industrial world is not the factor that explains the poverty of the Third World. However, the impact of the industrial world was largely the basis of underdevelopment. It is not possible to do as some economists have done and treat the problem of the underdevelopment of the Third World simply and solely from the economic angle. The approach must be global. Why did not Manchu China, at the end of the last century, successfully carry out an industrial revolution like that of the Meiji in Japan? Does the major responsibility for this lie with the Europeans or with the Manchus? Were not the corruption and passivity of the Manchu dynasty and the obstinate refusal by the overwhelming majority of the Mandarin class to adapt tradition to deal with the challenge the decisive factors? The balance sheet of colonialism is inevitably ambiguous. Apart from conquests, enslavement and exploitation, it is undeniable that the West brought aspects of *modernity*. Not only does India owe Great Britain its territorial unity and communications infrastructure but also its democracy, which makes it, for those social classes able to take advantage of it, one of the least despotic in the Third World.

There are no grounds at all for believing that a "normal" evolution would have led the traditional societies of Asia and Africa to end up with an accumulation of capital that would have led to development. The despotic societies, whether the Moghul Empire, the Manchu Empire, or the Ottoman Empire, Malayan sultanates, or African kingdoms, were not harboring any revolutionary potential. At most, here and there, there was a dream of returning to some real or imagined primitive purity. Thus, making dependency the sole cause of the reproduction of underdevelopment seems altogether mechanistic if the political, sociological and cultural blockages and the problems arising from low productivity and attitudes to work are not taken into account.

In the case of Latin America, for example, holding the penetration of British, and later American, capital exclusively responsible for underdevelopment is a partial explanation that has more than a hint of evasion. The internal political, social, and cultural factors are equally fundamental: survivals of agrarian "feudalism," weakness and corruption of the state, problems of racial and national integration, lack of the entrepreneurial spirit among the local bourgeoisies, unproductive investments, the value system, and attitudes to work. After all, if Argentina and Canada in the 1930s are compared, there is no denying that Canada, peripheral, an exporter of raw materials, economically dominated, has nevertheless made a successful transition as a dynamic industrial society, while Argentina has still not done so, and has continued to be caught up in political crises and economic waste for several decades.

Is it surprising then that the increasingly marked differentiations that are appearing in the Third World seem to be making most of the countries of Black Africa dependent on aid? Conversely, societies in East Asia with strong traditions of work, organization, and economy are emerging in the framework of the market economy. Are we simply to highlight the investment of foreign capital, low salaries, and repressive laws to explain the development of South Korea, Taiwan, Singapore, and Hong Kong, or should we not also recognize that these are societies with undeniable qualities of hard work and initiative? It would be paradoxical to be accused of Western-centeredness when a concern for universalism leads to neglecting the peculiar features of Asia and Africa and with racism if one mentions them when they do not reflect a mythical Third World.

In economics, the major observation is that there has not been any *alternative* to the capitalist system. While state intervention was decisive in the dynamism of capitalism in many countries, from Bismarck's Germany to Meiji Japan and from South Korea to contemporary Brazil, the rigid, bureaucratic, and centralized planning of the USSR and China has proved to be a failure even in the view of those who advocated it. In the Third World, the few "socialist"-type experiences have not lived up to their promises of accelerated growth. Here and there, serious progress has been made in the areas of school enrollment or health, or there have been improvements in the living conditions of disadvantaged groups, but the global balance sheet, whether it be Vietnam, China before the reforms, Cuba or even North Korea—not to mention Ethiopia or Angola—is, compared to the project, disappointing. In most Third World countries, the situation is often grim and the prospects not encouraging. There has been an enormous amount of literature on underdevelopment. Robert McNamara, who was president of the World Bank for ten years, drew attention to the tragic conditions of the majority of Third World countries and, within these countries, of the most disadvantaged sections of the population. Almost one billion men and women experience very serious malnutrition and have no access to any health service. Poverty in most of these countries has increased continuously over the last decade. Perhaps one day the conditions in which the majority of the peoples of the underdeveloped countries currently live and the type of unequal relations between industrialized countries and Third World countries will be seen as barbarous as slavery seems to us in the twentieth century. In practice, and despite the declarations, the famous North-South dialogue never happened. Indeed perhaps, for structural reasons, it cannot happen. The inequalities are inherent in the system and given population growth, they are being reinforced. But are they inherent only in *this* system?

At international conferences, calling attention to Third World poverty has become a ritual. But the crisis is embittering relations. International monetary instability, the recent oil crisis, the growth of balance-of-payments deficits, and the ever-growing debts of some countries are having their effects. However, at least a dozen countries, with the inevitable distortions and marked social imbalances, have recorded spectacular growth. The most striking cases are in East Asia, where growth has been built on the classic model of the market economy plugged into exports: Taiwan, South Korea, Singapore, Hong Kong, and to a lesser extent Thailand and Malaysia. In Latin America, there are Brazil and Venezuela. This type of growth involves the marginalization of part of the population, which in Brazil is happening to both the Northeast and among the (black) populations of the *favellas*. But it is not possible to account for Brazilian growth in the 1970s simply by looking at the Northeast. One needs only to recall Engels' description of the English working class in Manchester when England was reigning over the globe.

The densely populated countries of Asia (China, India, Bangladesh, Pakistan, and Indonesia) all, in varying degrees, pose very serious problems—Bangladesh and Pakistan dramatically. China, after the death of Mao Zedong and the collapse of the imposture of the Cultural Revolution, began, under Deng Xiao Ping, to attack economic problems. Despite a liberalization of the economy in the rural areas and special conditions created in the coastal areas, the scope for bureaucratic foot-dragging is considerable. In India, despite undeniable successes in some sectors, a good third of the population, some 250 million people at least, live in terrible conditions, while 5 percent of the population shares half the national income.

At international conferences, populist diatribes and protests from Third World states do not prevent these latter from being represented by highly privileged and corrupt social strata to whom hunger and poverty are so radically alien that they are indifferent about the welfare of their own peoples. The West in general feels more compassion or more guilt about these problems than the ruling elites in the Third World for whom famines only have consequences if they lead to riots.

Looking at the countries of Asia, Africa, and Latin America during this century, few factors have been more important than demography. At the beginning of the century, Europe was the most densely inhabited continent. During the nineteenth century, it had been able to double its population, helped actively to people the North American continent, and managed at the same time to colonize the whole of the Afro-Asian world. The position of Europe, including Russia, with its 440 million inhabitants, to which should be added over 80 million North Americans, was considerable. In 1900, the white world accounted for 33 percent of the world population. By 2000—in barely ten years' time—the figure will be 18 percent.

Two deadly wars and numerous regional conflicts—between 1945 and 1988 there have been over 15 million victims of war—will have failed to prevent world population from rising from 1.6 billion in 1900 to about 6 billion in 2000. Before the Second World War, the population of the globe was growing at a rate of slightly above 0.8 percent. But by the 1950s and 1960s, the rate was between 1.8 and 1.9 percent, which indicates a doubling of the world population every forty years. The principal cause of this phenomenon lies in the falling mortality rate. This population explosion ended for Europe and the United States in the mid-1960s and, what is more serious, the work force there will begin to fall in the 1990s. Conversely, population growth is continuing in the Third World at an average rate of some 2.5 percent. The demographic revolution in the countries of Asia, Africa, and Latin America is profoundly altering the North-South relationship that existed at the beginning of the century and which accelerated from 1950. Africa, which had a population of 110 million in 1900 and 220 million in 1950, will have about 800 million in 2000. Latin America, which had only 90 million in 1900 and about 160 million in 1950, will have more than 600 million in 2000. As for Asia, which had 925 million in 1900 and 1,380 million in 1950, it will have more than 3.6 billion in 2000. We shall leave aside the numbers of Chinese who will rise from 600 million in 1950 to 1,250 million in 2000, or of India, who will rise from some 380 million at the time of independence to a billion in a decade's time. But we shall mention some figures. The following is a list of figures (broken down by millions) worth mentioning:

	1900	1980	2025
Brazil	18	127	247
Indonesia	38	153	298
Nigeria	17	91	265
Bangladesh	?	93	230
Vietnam	11.5	60	106
Iran	10	44	99
Egypt	10	44	96

SOURCES: UNITED NATIONS AND WORLD BANK.

Every industrial region is flanked, on its immediate periphery, by a developing area in which population growth is very rapid. The United States is experiencing the pressure of Mexican labor. Mexico, which had barely 14 million inhabitants at the beginning of the century, reached 80 million in 1985 and will have over 115 million by 2000; its population has doubled in under 25 years and in a generation, by about 2025, it will have some 175 million inhabitants; the United States will by that time have some 300 million.

In 1900, the population of the three countries of North Africa (Morocco, Algeria, and Tunisia) was barely 11 million, while France—then a colonial power—had a population of 38 million. By 1960, the Maghreb had 27 million and by 1985, 52 million, while France had only 54 million. By 2000, the Maghreb will have 77 million and by 2025, 125 million, while France will increase by only 3 million in 30 years.

The ratio between the European Economic Community, made up of 12 countries, and the labor-exporting countries of the Mediterranean was 3 to 1 in 1988 (EEC: 320 million inhabitants; Maghreb and Turkey: 110 million); by 2025, it will be 330 million for the EEC and 225 million for the Maghreb and Turkey. Turkey, which had some 11 million inhabitants in 1930, reached 50 million in 1985, and will reach 70 million by 2000 and 100 million by 2025. For demographic reasons, its entry into the EEC is probably ruled out: by 2025, over one citizen of the Community in four would be Turkish.

But nothing is further from reality than the Western fantasy of starving hordes rising up to attack metropolises bursting with food. Overpopulation is a relative phenomenon: Holland, with almost four hundred inhabitants per square kilometer, is not regarded as overpopulated. However, galloping population growth is not a sign of vitality but of underdevelopment, since to control population growth is to clear the ground for balanced growth. Excessively rapid population growth is a handicap for societies struggling to emerge from underdevelopment. This phenomenon of population growth in the Third World will continue throughout the first part of the next century with a gradual slowing down. The number of unemployed and underemployed in populations with over 65 percent under thirty-five years of age will markedly increase, especially in cities. As for the industrial countries, they have no choice but to regulate more and more tightly the level at which they can agree to accept and absorb migrants without too much social and cultural upheaval.

The changes due to population growth also include religious shifts: the majority of Catholics are no longer in Europe, as they were at the beginning of the century, but in Latin America. The contrast between the demographic changes in developed countries and in those that are not is not simply a matter of numbers, but is also reflected in the age structures that it produces. In 1980, the current and predicted distribution by age group (in millions) was as follows:

| Ages | − 15 | | 15−64 | | + 64 | |
Years	1980	2000	1980	2000	1980	2000
Industrialized countries	26.7	23	63.7	65.5	9.6	11.3
Third World	40.6	39	55.7	57	3.8	4

The aging of the populations of the industrial countries—including Japan—poses serious problems for the social organization of those countries. Part of the population shortfall will have to be filled by immigration. Organizing the number of young people for whom there are no economic prospects will surely be the most acute social problem that most Third World states will soon be called upon to face.

Another phenomenon with incalculable consequences is the massive urbanization of the Third World. Whereas in 1900, the urban population there was less that 5 percent of the total, it was 25 percent by 1975 and will be 40 percent by the end of the century. And this urban growth is not slowing down the growth of the rural population. This will continue to increase substantially. Africa and South Asia are and will continue to be the regions where growth is highest. It can be predicted that the great cities of the Third World will often be the scenes of the most violent social and political crises in the coming years. Urban changes during the course of the century have been remarkable. London, which in 1900 was the most populous city in the world, and was still ranked number three in 1950, will only just be in the top twenty by the end of the century. Mexico City, with over 30 million inhabitants, will be the largest city in the world by the year 2000. São Paulo, Rio de Janeiro, Shanghai, Beijing, Djakarta, Bombay, and Calcutta will have between 15 and 25 million inhabitants. Tehran, Istanbul, Baghdad, Manila, Lagos, Cairo, Karachi, Seoul, Madras, and Dacca will all have well over 10 million.

However, at the same time that the population gap between North and South is widening, the technological gap between the industrial world and the developing world is also rapidly getting wider. The American and Japanese advance—dangerous even for the Europeans who have allowed themselves to be outstripped—in electronics, and generally what is known as the third industrial revolution, is increasing rapidly. And technological progress remains the guarantor of global power. Perhaps it should be stressed that the major lesson of the Arab-Israeli conflict is the overwhelming Israeli military superiority based on an industrial society facing several million inhabitants of developing countries.

Since the political emergence of the Third World, three themes have appeared: anticolonialism, non-alignment, and development. The first in some ways follows from the very idea of a colonial world sharing a particular heritage, a theme which had its heyday between the 1950s and the early 1960s. The second, despite the efforts of India (Bandung, 1955) and Yugoslavia (Belgrade, 1961), remains an ambiguous theme. The fact that Cuba should for several years have been able to occupy the chairmanship of the nonaligned movement is a negation of the very idea of non-alignment. After the 1960s, and increasingly urgently, the problems of development were legitimately at the center of Third World concerns. The theme of the "new international economic order"—an order in which North and South would be less unbalanced—was launched in Algiers at a meeting of seventy-seven countries. This theme was taken up the following year at the United Nations and today the so-called Group of seventy-seven in fact includes over 115 underdeveloped countries.

Following the Second World War, the colonial division of labor between the advanced capitalist countries and the countries of Asia, Africa, and Latin America was maintained: these latter exported mainly agricultural or mineral raw materials while the industrial West continued to produce manufactured goods and foodstuffs. This system was strengthened by the Bretton Woods Agreements and a series of international regulatory bodies like GATT. It was completed by a number of aid funds.

The industrial changes that took place in the advanced countries over approximately the next quarter of a century were reflected, among other things, in exports to the developing countries, accompanied by a relatively slow increase in the demand for raw materials—except for oil, which grew faster—and a high rate of investment in the industrial countries themselves. The developing countries attracted little capital and a large portion of the profits made there by foreign companies were not reinvested on the spot.

During the 1960s and 1970s, the efforts to lay the foundations of industrialization continued with widely varying results. However, there were improvements: the developing countries succeeded in securing recognition of their right to control their own natural resources. Some countries' economies grew faster than their populations and began to export manufactured goods, challenging all competition while they operated controls on their imports. The most visible result of these changes is that the differences among developing countries became sharper while interdependence between them and the developed countries grew.

However, compared to the forecasts of the first (1960–70) and second (1970–80) development decade, the overall results were thin. The projects of the second decade remained a dead letter and, in the main, the crisis engendered by the first oil shock in 1973 and especially the second in 1979 was felt above all by the countries of the Third World—except of course for a few oil-producing countries. The illusion that a different type of North-South relationship is possible—international relations, both political and economic, being determined not by moral considerations but by interests—seemed to fade away. The countries that had decided to take their destiny into their hands, and had the natural and human resources to do so, were confronted with harsh realities but succeeded in making some noteworthy breakthroughs.

Generally speaking, growth was quite satisfactory in much of East and Southeast Asia, with a few notable exceptions: Bangladesh, Indonesia, Pakistan, the Philippines, Burma, and the Indochinese peninsula. The states in the Middle East have overall progressed during the last fifteen years, especially those that have both oil and small populations. By embarking on an exhausting war against each other for regional hegemony, Iraq and Iran have wasted the industrial efforts of the previous decade. The economic future of a country like Egypt seems to be highly problematic.

Despite the size of its debts—though lending has only been to the rich since neither Brazil, Argentina, Mexico, nor Peru is short of resources—Latin America is far from being in a desperate situation. Countries like Mexico, Peru, and Argentina will almost certainly experience serious social tensions but, generally, the prospects outside Central America do not appear too bad, even though causes of tensions and crises do exist, even in Brazil. That is not the case in Black Africa where, except for a few countries like Gabon and the Ivory Coast, the continent seems destined, for an indefinite period, to have its future determined more by assistance than by development.

One of the major consequences of decolonization is that the countries of Asia and Africa recovered their *political autonomy*. In fact, the withdrawal of the colonial powers and their loss of direct influence made it possible for states, many of which preexisted the colonial period, to express their regional interests. In this respect, the Iran-Iraq conflict is a good example. When it originally intervened in 1980, Iraq was seeking to seize regional hegemony from Iran. It took some time for traditional, lazy-minded Western politicians to understand that not everything in the Third World was determined by the East-West conflict. This process was greatly aided by the Sino-Vietnamese conflict and Vietnam's invasion of Cambodia in 1978.

What Vietnam was doing was resuming, in new forms, its move, interrupted by French colonization, to bring the whole Indochinese peninsula into its orbit. This attempt at hegemony to become a regional power is largely motivated by a concern not to be weak in the face of China. China, on the other hand, is eager to have both Laos and Cambodia as states opposed to the Vietnamese presence and Vietnamese influence. It is undeniable that one aspect of Polisario's struggle was the indirect clash between Moroccan and Algerian nationalisms—Morocco having annexed the Western Sahara in 1975—the prize being leadership of the Maghreb. In Lebanon and in regard to the Palestinian movement, Syria is pursuing a project of becoming a regional power that it makes no attempt to hide. Colonel Gaddafi has always sought to act on the regional stage—and sometimes beyond—and more particularly in Chad. And the roots of the rivalry between Somalia and Ethiopia which led to war in 1977–78 go deep in history.

In reality, masked at the time by the East-West conflict

which occupied the whole political stage, the armed clashes between China and India in 1959–62, the wars between India and Pakistan, from 1947 to 1971, consequent on the formation of Pakistan, the vain efforts of Sukarno to extend the regional power of Indonesia (tension with Malaysia), and of Nasser to achieve Arab unity were already manifestations of this new political autonomy, which often takes the concrete form of attempts to achieve regional hegemony. The bipolar world of the Cold War, with its rigid assumptions on either side, has gradually given way to a complex world in which many states, even with limited means, boldly exercise their political autonomy. Conflicts of major significance, such as the Iran-Iraq war, or that are not insignificant, such as the China-Vietnam conflict, the Cambodia-Vietnam conflict, or the conflict in the Western Sahara, are outside the East-West confrontation which can be detected in Central America, Afghanistan and, to a large extent, in the Near East. That does not mean that the world has ceased to be militarily bipolar since, when a regional adversary is the ally of the United States, the sole recourse for the other party is alliance with the Soviet Union. In this sense, what other choice does Syria, for example, have to satisfy its regional ambitions than a tactical alliance with the USSR?

If we were to identify the main features of the stages of decolonization and what followed, we should have to stress two or three major topics; winning independence marked the end of humiliation. This is of vital importance, even if it is difficult for those who have never been humiliated because they belonged to a despised category to appreciate it. Of course, becoming independent did not give every class in the various societies of Asia and Africa the fruits they expected of it, nor even the dignity of being citizens. However, _identity_ almost everywhere was exalted and this process marks the end of being made to feel inferior, which was a key feature of the colonial period. This change, carried out by the modernizing elite in general, or, using religious feeling, by the advocates of a return to a purified tradition, was more directly felt by those living in urban areas than by the peasantry. Whether it was a form of therapy, a technique of manipulation, or both, it was in any event a major political phenomenon. Humiliation and identity were at the heart of the struggles waged for independence and in the years that followed.

Politically, independence was first and foremost marked by _state-building_. Everywhere, since the West defined the concept of the state and developed its structures, the number of nation-states has continued to grow. This process began in the nineteenth century and accelerated in the twentieth with the collapse of the Austro-Hungarian and Ottoman empires at the end of the First World War and even more with decolonization after the Second. While old national formations, often rooted in states that existed before the colonial period, found in it a reasonably coherent framework, other states, ones with no nation—notably, but not only, in Africa—found in this model a framework to which they adapted badly rather than well. Here and there, in Africa or the Near East, dictatorships rely on ethnic or confessional groups. In Syria, the state is controlled by the Alawites, who represent barely 15 percent of the population. In Iraq, it is controlled by the Sunni Arabs who number about one-third of the total population. Lebanon is engulfed in a multiconfessional civil war. And it is important to note that in many countries the allegiances of a group may be confessional or ethnic and that, particularly in Islam, it is not always easy to distinguish faith and the City (_Dar We Dawla_), given that Islam is both. In Black Africa, power often rests on a single individual and a very narrow clientele (almost always ethnic in nature).

Generally speaking, in all these countries, the situation of minorities is worse than during the colonial period, during which some of them had been the object of concern on the part of the rulers. But too often independence was for the majority group— or for a particular group—the occasion to stifle any minority demand, including even the most elementary rights. There are few countries in Asia, Latin America (in relation to the Indians), or Africa, where in one way or another minorities are not persecuted. The most extreme case is surely that of the Kurds in Turkey, since officially *they do not exist*. To describe oneself publicly as a Kurd is a crime.

The complexity of minority problems is considerable.[3] Some are economically privileged, like the Chinese in Southeast Asia in general, Indians in Burma, or Tamils in Sri Lanka. Others, on the contrary, are strongly disadvantaged compared to the majority, like the Baluchis in Pakistan or Iran, or the mountain people in Indochina, Thailand, or Burma. Their common feature is that they are often oppressed and discriminated against by states that accentuate their marginalization and do nothing to improve their status. These minorities are usually ethnic but they may also be religious. For a long time, the sole reference was to religious membership. In the Middle East, this continues to be sometimes more important than national identity. In the recent past or even still today, many religious minorities have been discriminated against or eliminated, like the Assyro-Chaldeans (Eastern Christians) during the First World War and again during the 1930s, first in the Ottoman Empire, then in Iraq, or the Baha'is in Khomeini's Iran. It is urgent that public opinion be alerted so as to put pressure on international institutions to put into legislation—not as a pious principle that is not applied—a set of minority rights: the right to identity, cultural rights, and the right to be heard in international forums. Denunciation of violations of individual human rights is strangely restrictive. Paradoxically, men in groups have fewer rights than individuals unless they have their own state. States jealously watch over everything concerning their internal affairs even when they are violating international laws that they have ratified. And international institutions do not utter a word about

3. G. Chaliand, ed., *The Minorities at the Age of Nation-State* (Pluto Press, London, 1988).

anything that comes under the umbrella of the internal affairs of states. It is high time that there were more initiatives like that of the UN Human Rights subcommission in 1985 or the Council of Europe in 1987, which acknowledged the genocide of the Armenians, historically and morally. This genocide, which followed a mass deportation and massacre in 1915–16, has never been recognized by the Turkish state. It is vital that, in flagrant cases of crimes against humanity and violation of elementary rights, nonpartisan agencies with moral stature be able to denounce the guilty state.

III

The states of crisis, like the state of conflict, whether latent or not, is a classic and one could almost say banal phenomenon. On the contrary, in history, stability can rather be seen as an exceptional state. Western ideology has been based for at least two centuries on the idea of progress, continuous and unending. But that ought not to conceal the breaks, destabilizations and relapses that occur along the way. The world has never ceased to be the scene of confrontations.

In the militarily bipolar world which ours has been since the end of the Second World War, East-West antagonism is central. War, the ultimate expression of relationships of force, is, for an indeterminate period, highly unlikely because of nuclear weapons and their apocalyptic prospects. So East-West antagonism has been played out indirectly, essentially in the Third World, although, in the immediate postwar period and in the 1980s, in Europe too.

These indirect strategies take the form of intense psychological warfare (ideological confrontation, propaganda, deception, disinformation), crisis management—the most serious crises being the Berlin crisis in 1949 and above all the Cuban missile crisis in 1962—and specific indirect interventions such as those in Iran against Mossadegh's oil policy in 1953 or in Guatemala against the reformist regime of Arbenz in 1954, or direct interventions such as those in Lebanon in 1958 or in the Dominican Republic in 1965, and finally, through direct but localized conflicts like the Korean War or the Vietnam War.

In this clash of wills in which the enemy is attacked at his weak points, the advantage has usually gone to the one whose determination and capacity to seize the favorable moment are based on a long-term political strategy. In this framework, what is the balance sheet of East-West antagonism? What are the midterm prospects?

The American retreat may seem considerable if the position of total hegemony in the immediate postwar period is taken as the starting point, but that concept needs to be heavily nuanced. This absolute hegemony, at the time when the United States was supplying 45 percent of world industrial output and holding a monopoly of nuclear weapons, was bound to be short-lived. The USSR was bound to make progress militarily after it had created for itself a shield to ensure its security while seeking any opportunity to weaken the adversary. Japan and Western Europe—which benefited from the Marshall Plan— once again became rival economic and trading powers. The American retreat is only relative, although it has been marked since the setback in Vietnam.

The Korean War was the first indirect confrontation between the USSR and the United States. It occurred shortly after the major event that was the arrival of China in the communist camp, which was at that time seen as monolithic, except for Yugoslavia. In the eyes of the Soviets, the Korean War moved the epicenter of the cold war from Europe to the Far East. While Central Europe was lost for the West and this fact was endorsed twenty years later at Helsinki in 1975, Greece saw the Communist Party defeated after the Civil War (1947–49). Other revolutionary wars were lost: the Huks in the Philippines, the Chinese communists in Malaya. But the Vietnam War corroded the moral energy and consumed a not insignificant proportion of American resources (1965–73), while at the same time the USSR was speeding up the strengthening of its military capabilities. The consequences of the Vietnam War[4] affected American political life for a decade and its psychological effects have been considerable, leading to a military impotence that was hardly modified by the small expedition to Grenada in 1983, the air raid on Tripoli in 1986, and above all the maritime response against Iran in the Persian Gulf in 1988.

The Vietnam War was an indirect success for the Soviets. The American failure was turned to advantage by Moscow in Angola in 1976 and Ethiopia in 1977. The unexpected fall of the Shah of Iran facilitated the Soviet intervention in Afghanistan in 1979. However, Washington's recognition of China and Nixon's visit to Beijing in 1972 revived Soviet fears for its Siberian flank. So the Soviet Union supported Vietnam in its policy of regional hegemony in Indochina, knowing that this was contrary to China's interests. Fearing the formation of an alliance between the United States, Japan, and China, the USSR supported India, another regional power, and sought to control Afghanistan, while the United States and China supported Pakistan, India's adversary and the Afghan resistants' sanctuary. Geopolitics was the name of the game, while ideological declarations were less and less successful in masking the interests of states.

For a long time, Africa remained a Western preserve where the USSR got itself into a series of unfortunate situations in Zaire, Guinea, and elsewhere. But 1975 marked the end of that period. The vacuum created by the withdrawal of the Por-

---

4. On 1 September 1966, General de Gaulle made a speech at Pnomh Penh: "France considers that the combats that are raging in Indochina are of themselves and can themselves provide no solution. In France's view, while it is unlikely that the American war machine will be annihilated on the field of battle, there is, on the other hand, no chance that the peoples of Asia will submit to the law of the outsider from the other side of the Pacific, whatever his intentions and however powerful his weapons. In short, however hard and long the trial is, France is certain that it will have no military solution."

tuguese was boldly exploited by the Soviet Union. With independence fast approaching, Nixon and Kissinger carried on an active clandestine policy with the National Security Council[5] (this also happened with the Kurds in Iraq between 1973 and 1975), and financed the National Front for the Liberation of Angola (FNLA) led by Holden Roberto, whose forces were based in Zaire. The USSR, which had broken off its aid to the Popular Movement for the Liberation of Angola (MPLA) which was torn into three factions in 1973, resumed its aid. On the proclamation of independence, the fragile compromise reached by the three Angolan movements unraveled. The third movement was UNITA, led by Jonas Savimbi, whom the United States realized too late it should have been helping rather than Holden Roberto's FNLA. The intervention of a South African column tolerated but not sanctioned by Nixon and Kissinger precipitated a crisis and enabled Moscow to react effectively. The intervention of Cuban troops was able thus both to reverse a situation in which the MPLA was caught in a pincer between the Zairian forces and the FNLA in the north and the South African column in the south and present their victory as a triumph of the revolutionary forces. In fact, what state in Black Africa could (openly) wish for the victory of the South Africans? As for American diplomacy, it was paying the combined price of the failure in Vietnam, Watergate, and a lack of knowledge of the Angolan situation. Being an expert on East-West relations does not enable one to throw oneself intelligently into the complexity of a regional reality. The Angolan government was not recognized by Washington but this non-recognition of a state did not prevent Gulf Oil and other American companies from carrying on business as usual.

After boldly exploiting the Angolan vacuum and having more discreetly moved into Mozambique at the invitation of Samora Machel's Frelimo, which began by pursuing a revolu-

---

5. John Stockwell, *In Search of Enemies: A CIA Story* (New York: Norton, 1977).

tionary policy that was beyond its resources, the USSR continued to win points. The fall of the Emperor Haile Selassie, the United States' faithful regional ally, in 1974, the consequence of ten years of social immobility and corruption, ushered in the rule of the Derg, whose policies moved further and further leftward. However, since 1972, the USSR had been linked by a treaty of friendship and cooperation to Somalia, Ethiopia's rival, which had annexed the Ogaden, inhabited by Somalians, at the beginning of the century. The unofficially declared war broke out in 1977, at a time when the Ethiopian regime was threatened in Eritrea, when the Eritrean People's Liberation Front seized Keren, the country's second town, and went on to launch an attack on Masawa, the main port. Other problems were threatening the regime just when President Carter ceased supplying arms to a country which he condemned in the name of human rights (and not because of its increasingly visible Marxism-Leninism) both in the province of Tigre and in the north by conservative forces and in Addis Ababa by a student and left-wing challenge. When Somalian troops attacked the strategic position of Dire Dawa, the USSR did an about-face: it had Cuban troops brought in and turned the situation around to the advantage of its new client. With these two states both proclaiming themselves "Marxist-Leninists," the Soviet Union with unblinking cynicism chose the regional power that could counter the Saudi project to turn the Red Sea into an Arab lake. That is why the question of the independence of Eritrea is impossible to resolve unless there is a complete collapse of the Ethiopian state.

While the Cuban intervention in Angola could be justified as a response to South Africa's, the Cubans' interference in Ethiopia was perceived very differently in Africa. Since 1966 and the tricontinental conference, Cuba had maintained relations with Amilcar Cabral's PAIGC, Agostinho Neto's MPLA, and Samora Machel's Frelimo. In the Horn of Africa, the Cubans had only had relations with the Eritrean People's Liberation Front (EPLF). By intervening on the side of Mengistu's Derg, they found themselves facing their former Somalian ally and opposing an Eritrean movement that they had formerly supported. Never had Cuba seemed to be so close to the Soviet line and Soviet interests.

In 1979, unexpectedly, at the end of a series of urban demonstrations carried on by various sectors of Iranian urban society clerics, the bazaar, the mujahidin, the regime of the Shah, formerly the United States' close ally, and a major regional power, collapsed. This blow put the loss of the Ethiopian ally in the shade. Before long, the Ayatollah Khomeini and the mullahs were establishing themselves firmly in power. They stirred up the Shiism of the popular masses, the thirst for justice of the urban poor, Persian nationalism, and the feelings of frustration towards the United States that resulted from a quarter of a century of influence. The profound political crisis into which the United States was to be plunged with the seizure of members of the embassy as hostages was to greatly facilitate the Soviet intervention in Afghanistan. This marked a turning point. Although the previous year a left-wing coup d'état had brought to power a Marxist regime which soon clashed with massive armed opposition, there was nothing to indicate that Brezhnev would send troops into Afghanistan.

This was the first intervention outside a Warsaw Pact member country. The rationale for it has not yet been established. Some experts saw in it a push towards the Gulf—but the Soviet Caucasus is equally close; others, an attempt to get closer to warm waters—but the USSR already had bases in both Vietnam and Aden and Socotra. Still others debated whether it was a defensive strategy against the rise of Muslim fundamentalism or an offensive move against Pakistan. While the reaction of the Europeans was extremely restrained, President Carter's, boycotting the Moscow Olympics, appeared moderately appropriate. Meanwhile, with often derisory weapons, the Afghans held out.

The era of detente in any case was closed with the Soviet intervention in Afghanistan which came on top of the victory of the Sandinistas in Nicaragua. Everywhere it seemed that the United States was on the defensive, while the USSR was engaging in an aggressive policy that was seemingly crowned with success. Ronald Reagan's election became inevitable, and the period of guilt that had been embraced by the presidency of Jimmy Carter was coming to an end given the new political situation. Already, during the second half of the 1970s, conservative trends were all the time becoming more important in the United States as a consequence of major changes around the world: the breakdown of the strategic balance perceived as being to the advantage of the Soviet Union; the installation of SS20s intended to uncouple Europe and the United States and push the Europeans toward neutralism; exploitation of the "vacuums" in Angola and Ethiopia, with the help of the Cubans and logistics remarkable for their scope and effectiveness; the collapse of the Shah of Iran, the Tehran hostage crisis, and finally the intervention in Afghanistan.

With the presidency of Ronald Reagan, who incarnated both the end of guilt feelings emerging from the Vietnam War an the need for new certainties about the power and prosperity of the United States, a rhetoric reminiscent of the cold war resumed in the United States. Its purpose was to signal to the adversary that the United States was once again resolute and would make the necessary effort to reestablish its military superiority. While it was consistent for the United States to seek to restore strategic parity both on the global level and in the European theater, at the world level the warlike posturing and aggressive rhetoric could not measure up to the situation. From this angle, despite all the criticisms that can be made of Jimmy Carter for his failure to understand the nature of the USSR (the problem of relations with the Soviet Union cannot be reduced to the problem of arms control), under his presidency a different approach had been tried that had positive results in the Camp

David Agreements, the settlement of the Zimbabwe crisis, and an improved image of the United States in Africa and Latin America (Panana, etc.); as for the inevitable swing against the Sandinistas, that was already happening under Carter.

But the global observation is that, thirty-five years after the United States took up the role of leading world power, it appeared in the Third World to have little capacity to handle a situation other than by blocking it, ill-equipped to exploit the chances offered, and incapable of disengaging in time from hopeless situations. Very rarely has support been given to less corrupt, less ineffective, and less conservative social forces, even when they had real chances of winning. Contrary to what some on the left think, these shortcomings are not structurally inherent in capitalism. They are above all the result of the political shortcomings of the American decision-making elite.

It is not at all surprising that the status quo policy should be constantly challenged in the Third World by conflicts that provide the USSR with the chance to use them against the interests of the United States. But instead of refining its political perspective, the United States dug in obstinately with a declared logic of using force, which resolves few crises but plugs gaps. What responses could the United States make to the global crises of Ethiopian and Iranian societies, both riven with discontent, one because of unwillingness to change and the other through excessive change? The question is worth asking.

The countries of Asia, Latin America, and Africa are the major arena of conflict in the contemporary world. The situations of internal imbalance inherent in the world economic order and the distortions bequeathed by the colonial past, and made worse by the corruption and inefficiency of most governing classes and by population growth, are further aggravated by a crisis that deals the Third World a severe blow. As the century draws to a close it has seen, and will see again, the collapse of many regimes. If the contradictions expressed in this or that Third World country can be exploited by the USSR to alter the regional balance in its favor, than the internal, social, and economic problems of the Third World are not actually the result of any action by the Soviet Union. But, in keeping with tradition that is precisely what Ronald Reagan and a large number of his advisers seemed to believe. Moreover, whatever judgement one may make about him, Richard Nixon, in the Republican camp, had an altogether different stature as a statesman. Haunted by maintaining the status quo that had been already rather eroded during the 1970s, the Reagan administration saw the Third World as a battlefield in which Latin America was reduced to Central America and the rest of the world to places that only existed when a crisis blew up.

The mediocrity and incompetence of most decision-makers and the absence of analysis of Third World problems are obvious and will continue to be so as long as every crisis, violent or not, is explained as interference by Moscow. It was in any event not possible for the United States to exorcise the complexity of the world as it tried to do under Ronald Reagan by becoming obsessed by the arms race and Nicaragua. A complex world has to be taken into account, whose problems, particularly in the Third World, have many dimensions. Demands for identity and welfare are central to them even if the solutions temporarily invoked today are no more successful than those that preceded them in resolving the crises of these societies. This is as much the case with recourse to Islam in its Shiite version in Iran as in its Sunni version in Egypt or elsewhere. Social and economic demands are the expression of the frustration felt by a large portion of recently urbanized but marginalized groups who constantly see the luxurious conditions of the rich. As for political demands, they reflect the fact that the ruling groups are, in general, thoroughly corrupt. The political tragedy of a large proportion of the developing countries is that over and beyond the revolutionary verbiage of a few elites, serious alternatives have rarely appeared over the last twenty years, because none had been prepared. This is as true for Africa as for the Middle East and a good part of Latin America.

IV

During the 1970s, the Soviet Union became a major military power. Its advances were not only in the military sphere but also in space and sea power. After a decade of efforts, the Soviet navy sailed all the oceans even though it remained decidedly inferior to the United States'. It became a true world power, a status previously denied it by Henry Kissinger when he was Secretary of State, with a proven capacity to intervene anywhere in the world. After exploiting the "vacuums" in Angola, Mozambique, and Ethiopia, it strengthened its position in South Yemen. It intervened in Afghanistan. The regimes it supported, thanks to Cuban arms or its own, cannot at present do without its support, or they would fall. But—and this is what Mikhail Gorbachev has realized—it is important not to underestimate the economic weakness of the Soviet Union, which is due to the numerous contradictions of the system. It is not possible to look only at military strength in the USSR any more than it is elsewhere, as if it had no relation to the state of its society. The USSR has had its political setbacks too: the breach with Egypt in 1972, the hostility of a China that is less and less isolated, the setback in Zimbabwe, where the movement that they backed failed to win power, military stalemate in Afghanistan, and almost permanent tension in Poland since 1980 questioning the very bases of a system that claims to be based on the working class.

During the past decade, the major crises in the Third World have affected five regions: Central America; Afghanistan; Southern Africa, and, more particularly, South Africa; the Middle East, a region of chronic instability, with the Lebanese civil war in which the Palestinians and the Shiites play a major role, Israel, whose military superiority does not resolve political problems, and the war between Iran and Iraq; and, finally, the Philippines, where the fall of Marcos and the return to democracy inaugurated by Corazon Aquino has not settled the problem of the Marxist-Leninist guerrilla movement, the New People's Army. These crises took place against a background of guerrilla activity (Afghanistan, Angola, Mozambique, Philippines, Nicaragua, El Salvador), riots (South Africa, Israel) and international terrorism aimed at the West that has grown relentlessly in importance between 1975 and 1988.

Relations between the United States and Central America go back a long way. In this respect, 1898 is an important date. In that year, having completed the conquest of its *hinterland* and extended its control over the whole of the northern Pacific, the United States removed Spain from both the Philippines and the Caribbean (Cuba and Puerto Rico). The war with Spain doubtless marked the birth of the "imperial republic." Admiral Mahan,[6] a geopolitician before the term was invented, had already stressed the vital importance for the security of the United States of control of the Caribbean basin, which he called "the American Mediterranean."

Compared to the continental mass of the two Americas, which counts only three states in the north and rather more than a dozen in the south, the proliferation of small states and the large number of islands—a minority of which are not independent—make the Caribbean basin particularly vulnerable. Geopolitically, this zone brings together a complete recipe for chronic instability.

Between 1903 and 1933, the United States intervened militarily some fifteen times in Central America and the Caribbean to defend its commercial interests. From the time it was built, the prime purpose of the Panama Canal was as a route between

---

6. See A. T. Mahan, *The Interest of America in Sea Power*, 1897.

the east and west coasts of the United States. In the name of its companies, including the famous United Fruit—the United States practiced an imperialism without responsibility. As Adam Smith said, there is no worse colonialism than that practiced by a company. The two last direct interventions, after the indirect ones in Guatemala in 1954 and Cuba in 1961, were the one in the Dominican Republic in 1965 and the one in Grenada in 1983.

The United States' strategic concern as a maritime power to exercise close control over the Caribbean basin, which it considers its backyard, has been all the greater since, twenty years ago, Cuba appeared as a troublemaker. For the United States, whose strategy is based primarily on control of its own hemisphere, the importance of the Caribbean in terms of communications and its proximity make it vital for its security.

For almost twenty years—from the aftermath of the Bay of Pigs in 1961 to the victory of the Sandinistas in Nicaragua in 1979—Latin American revolutionary movements, despite a few spectacular cases, marked time or were defeated: Venezuela, Guatemala, Colombia, Uruguay, Bolivia, Brazil, Chile, and others. The fact is that the political, organizational, and strategic weakness of the revolutionary movements, combined with the harshness of the repression and the impact of the presence of the United States, prevented any victory over these two decades. In any event, the main performance was taking place elsewhere—in Vietnam and the Middle East.

With President Reagan, whose rhetoric and language in foreign policy go far beyond his actions, the crisis in Central America became a focal point. And this was not simply because it was happening on America's doorstep but also because the new administration deliberately chose to make it a test of the determination of the United States.

In Nicaragua, El Salvador, and Guatemala, guerrilla movements grew out of local conditions: the side-effects of the world crisis, the corruption of the system, the ineffectiveness of ruling elites. But they became one focus of East-West friction. The whole balance in the Caribbean basin was at stake in the game being played between, on the one hand, the United States and its local allies, with Honduras as the cornerstone, and, on the other, the USSR and Cuba working together to support Nicaragua and the revolutionary movements in El Salvador.

Ideally, the United States would like to see regimes come to power in El Salvador and Guatemala that are open to reforms and have a democratic facade. In fact, the physical elimination of many liberals and reformists leaves the way clear above all for conservative elements who often have an extreme right breathing down their necks with its own, considerable strength. Despite José Napoleón Duarte, the Salvadoran far right is experiencing a revival.

Yet this time, on its own home ground, the United States cannot allow itself to fail. Even if public opinion and Congress have not always been aware of it, the issue is an important one. It remains to be seen, on the ground, whether the measures adopted and their implementation are effective or counterproductive.

Beyond the Reagan style and rhetoric—for there should be no need to be reminded that the United States' permanent interests do not change every four years—United States diplomacy still has to find answers to two key questions:

1. Why so often (and in the Caribbean basin more than elsewhere) does the United States support for decades regimes that are notoriously corrupt, repressive, and ineffective without ever bothering themselves about the future? If one wants to avoid the Sandinistas, the Somozas have to be removed in plenty of time. That lesson seems to have been learned in the Philippines.

2. Why does American diplomacy live in the short term structurally, which, instead of enabling it to foresee crises, leads it to make defensive responses to them, often when it is already too late?

It is simply not possible to stick to the convenient ideology of seeing the hand of Moscow and using Cuban weapons to explain everything without looking for the structural causes that make it possible for the USSR to interfere in a United States preserve.

Generally speaking, the Sandinista government has not escaped the dynamic that is peculiar to Marxist-Leninist regimes: popular mobilization made all the more necessary because of external threats, considerable restrictions on basic freedoms, causing them gradually to lose the support of large numbers of the urban population which had not hesitated to support them against the Somoza dictatorship, and deterioration of the economic situation. The latter is blamed on the difficulties created by the Contras. But two other reasons ought to be mentioned to fill out the picture: the incompetence of the Sandinista bureaucracy and its myth of the state being able to exercise effective control of the productive apparatus, and the fact that Soviet economic aid has been extremely parsimonious.

Several complex lessons can be learned from Nicaragua. The price to be paid for establishing a Marxist-Leninist-type revolution on the American continent is extremely high. If the United States no longer has the will to intervene directly, it has available a considerable panoply of indirect means to weaken experiments that it feels are contrary to its interests and security and to make them excessively costly.

For Latin American nationalists anxious to promote development and greater social justice, is the adoption of a Marxist-Leninist program, especially if it involves a Soviet presence, the best means of achieving their aim of modernizing society? Ought not the United States to contribute more to the development, modernization, and democratization of Latin America in general and Central America and the Caribbean in particular, and would it not gain from putting into effect policies that have the support and cooperation of a number of important countries in Latin America?

The support given to the Contras, christened "freedom fighters," though its initial core was made up of ex-Somozistas, would have gained if it had been more selective. In sum, while the Contras have succeeded in forcing the Sandinista regime to seek a compromise, they have also shown themselves to be the most mediocre fighting force seen in recent decades. Their motivation, compared to that of Unita and the Afghans, is slight.

V

It was not the United States that dreamed up the idea of turning the technique of guerrilla warfare against Marxist-Leninist regimes that have come to power as a result of armed struggle but, for the recent period, South Africa. In 1977–78, Pretoria offered its help to the exhausted and much diminished forces of UNITA and Jonas Savimbi who had no choice but to accept or disappear.

Today, ten years after its recovery, UNITA effectively controls over a quarter of Angolan territory. It is true that it is the southeast, the poorest and least inhabited part of the country. But UNITA carries out guerrilla actions all over the country. Its essential ethnic base is outside the territory that it controls directly, in the central highlands, and embraces about 40 percent of the total population of Angola, with its center at Huambo, the country's second city. In the shelter of its sanctuary—government offensives are launched each year during the dry season—a territory as large as Great Britain, UNITA over the years has organized itself remarkably. Since 1987 it has enjoyed American aid. UNITA's logistics are remarkable. A base situated in the province of Cuando Cubango programs and organizes the movement and transport of troops and the repair of vehicles while a system of transmissions covers all operations and passes on daily news to Jamba, Savimbi's headquarters.

UNITA, made up of a small group of men who are survivors of the anticolonial struggle who form the core of the movement, is credited with about 25,000 to 30,000 men. That is not many for a country four times the size of Great Britain, but considerable in African terms, especially as they are motivated, disciplined, and war-hardened troops. It is undeniable—the reports of priests and technicians, Western or not, taken by UNITA as far away as the northern provinces of the country confirm it—that the guerrilla forces operate virtually anywhere in Angola. Many military outposts are supplied by air, because there are no safe roads. However, government troops hold all the larger towns outside the sanctuary—plus Cuito Canavale, a forward government position in UNITA's strategic disposition which in 1988 gave rise to a battle lasting several months with the participation of Cuban and South African troops. UNITA's defensive military bases are remarkably well-equipped strongpoints: 60-, 61-, and 82-mm mortars; 75-, 76-, 82-, 108-, and 122-mm cannons (Stalin organs); 12.7-, 14.5-, and 23-mm antiaircraft guns. Since 1985, UNITA has had several SAM 7s and is said to have received Stingers in 1987. However, the government forces' military superiority (40,000 to 50,000 men and 30,000 to 40,000 Cuban soldiers[7]) is above all due to air power: Soviet helicopters and Swiss P1-7 long-range machines.

Apart from the village militias, UNITA's military organization has four levels: at the base there are guerrilla groups of 50 to 100 men equipped with individual weapons (Kalashnikovs, RPG7s); at the level above, compact columns of 150 to 250 men with three 60-mm mortars and light machine guns; at the next level, semi-regular battalions of about 500 men equipped with seven 82-mm cannons; finally, at the highest level, the regular battalion of 1,500 men equipped with considerable firepower.

---

7. And maybe as many as 40,000 to 50,000 since 1988.

All these forces operate on the six fronts into which Angola is divided.

Despite the movement's anti-Marxist ideology, Jonas Savimbi's UNITA is organized on the Leninist-Maoist model. There is a considerable amount of training in schooling and health. The sanctuary includes education centers with several thousand pupils, from nursery to sixth-form level; all the classes are in Portuguese. A technical training center includes two or three thousand boys and girls who are boarders. A school for political cadres has been running for several years and holds two two-month sessions a year. Twenty percent of cadres are women.

Relations with the population in the areas controlled appear to be excellent; the people in them belong to minority ethnic groups (Chokwe, Ganguelas and Luchazes) that UNITA, mainly made up of Ovimbundu, has organized. The other two major ethnic groups in the country are the Kimbundu and the Kongo. But, despite the voluntarist declarations of the Luanda government, which repeats that Angola is made up "of one people and one nation," ethnic problems, here in Angola as elsewhere in Black Africa, remain fundamental. Despite a very complex situation in which the East-West conflict and a regional conflict due to the impact of South Africa are involved, the war also has a strictly Angolan dimension. While the Luanda government has coopted the Kongo, who made up the ethnic base of Holden Roberto's movement, it has been unable or unwilling to absorb the Umbundu, who recognize Jonas Savimbi as their leader. Behind a Manichaean terminology, two movements, each with an anticolonialist legitimacy but a different ethnic base, are fighting for power.

Contrary to the usual techniques of Marxist-Leninist-inspired parties, UNITA does not seek to dismantle the traditional structures at the village level. The chiefs and notables are left with functions of prestige but they are assisted by representatives of the party who live in the village. The movement receives food surpluses, exchanges salt, cloths, and other basic necessities for foodstuffs and, classically, brings in the teacher and the nurse and organizes a village militia to mobilize the youth behind it.

Against it, the MPLA is holding up militarily. No town of any importance has fallen to UNITA.

Each dry season, government forces launch an offensive to try to retake control of the sanctuary held by UNITA. The economic situation, on the other hand, is mediocre. Despite oil and, to a lesser extent, diamonds, and given the war effort and bureaucratic waste in the system established by the MPLA, the country is extremely impoverished. The economic aid expected from the socialist camp has proved to be disappointing. But, like UNITA, the MPLA has no choice when it comes to military allies. And even then the Luanda government has shown itself to be increasingly flexible. American firms and their investments are welcome; Angola has joined the other African countries and signed the Lomé agreements which open up prospects with the EEC.

UNITA's strategy, in recent years, has been increasingly to paralyze the Luanda government economically, starting out from a sanctuary whose security it ensures by carrying the offensive to the enemy. To attain its objectives, it has both to strike at the diamond mines in the province of Luanda, and to try to hit the oil installations in Cabinda (sometimes using South African commandos); Jonas Savimbi's ultimate aim is to force the regime to negotiate and agree to a coalition government. But it is very difficult for the MPLA to conceive that a charismatic personality like Jonas Savimbi can be satisfied with only a part-share in power. No one can predict the outcome of this struggle in which neither side can win a military victory. One day a decision will have to be made between a war of attrition and negotiations.

South Africa is of course part and parcel of any Angolan settlement insofar as it is playing a regional game. In order to prolong the status quo for as long as possible, Pretoria is aiding UNITA, intervening with its troops in Angola whenever it deems necessary and fighting the Southwest Africa People's Organization (SWAPO) whose sanctuary is in Angola.

Despite a war that has been discreetly going on for over two decades, South Africa has not managed to eliminate SWAPO or to find a viable political solution in Namibia. Eventually, Namibia will be independent, probably with SWAPO leading it. The exploratory negotiations that took place in London and several capitals in 1988 between the parties involved (the United States, South Africa, Cuba, Angola) necessarily bore on a solution in which the independence of Namibia would be accompanied by the withdrawal of Cuban forces from Angola. But in this perspective there remains for Luanda the crucial problem of UNITA which, without the Cubans, might contemplate a military solution to the conflict that has been raging between it and the MPLA for over a decade.

In Mozambique, South Africa has backed, until 1988 at least, the Mozambican National Resistance (RENAMO) whose core of five hundred men was transferred to it by Ian Smith of Rhodesia before elections brought Robert Mugabe to power in Zimbabwe in 1979.

South Africa trained this force, topped it up and, with ten thousand or more fighters, made it into a formidable war machine. In 1984, faced with growing disorder and widespread anarchy, Samora Machel was forced to sign the Nkomati Accords. These stipulated among other things that Mozambique should cease all support for the African National Congress (ANC) fighters whose commando groups were using Mozambique as a sanctuary. In exchange, Pretoria agreed to cease sheltering members of the RENAMO. In fact, South Africa continued to supply the RENAMO with weapons and munitions and even to give it technical back-up. The situation in Mozambique did not improve. The country made overtures to the West; it joined the Lomé signatories. But insecurity reigned over most of the country. It is with great difficulty and with the help of several thousand soldiers from Zimbabwe and Tanzania that the Beira railway functions as best it can. For several years, the country has been experiencing a drought which has made the war conditions even harsher. As for RENAMO, far from being a disciplined organization like UNITA, it behaves like a group of thugs. An American State Department report in 1988 reported massive liquidations and a policy of generalized terror.

The key to the present regional balance in Southern Africa is South Africa. The export of the bulk of what is produced south of Zaire is carried by South African railways and ports. Logistically, economically, and militarily, Pretoria will be decisive.

Politically, power in South Africa is in the hands of the Afrikaners in the National Party, led by Pieter Botha since 1978. Defeated by the British in the Boer War (1899–1902) and humiliated, the Afrikaners took power in 1948 and intend not to lose it again. Apartheid is the means that has enabled the Afrikaners to retain what is their sole objective: political hegemony.

This was challenged continuously between 1984 and 1987. The riots in the black townships put the problem of apartheid at the forefront of international problems. For a quarter of a century, while the rest of Africa became independent, South Africa could be the only country in the world in which racism was institutional without being massively denounced. Between the Sharpeville demonstrations in 1960, protesting against blacks being obliged to carry passbooks, and the riots of 1984–87, only the big demonstrations in Soweto and other urban centers in 1976–77 reminded the world of the anachronism of a situation which, until 1960, had attracted very little attention from the West.

The secret of this white domination rested on a system of division and control before moving on to the use of coercion and repression and atomization of the blacks by accentuating their ethnic and linguistic divisions, and driving almost all of them into homelands (formerly Bantustans, some of which have been proclaimed "independent"). A considerable proportion of blacks thus found themselves transformed into foreigners in their own country. Information and the educational system were directed at carefully reproducing submissive blacks convinced of their inferiority. Finally, the major rift is between urbanized and rural blacks, the latter being still politically inactive. As before, control still depends on the considerable role of the state as employer: there are a million state employees in South Africa out of a working population of fewer than ten million. A whole clientele of blacks earns its living from jobs given by the state in exchange for their docility—some are even on the police force. The other aspect of control is based on a formidable network of informers. The direct use of brutal force between 1960 and 1984 was highly selective. It was designed to get at the leaders and to liquidate potentially charismatic figures such as Steve Biko who "committed suicide" in prison, as did approximately forty other detainees between 1960 and 1977.

The core of apartheid as it is today lies in two laws. One is the "Population Registration Act," which requires every individual living in South Africa to belong to one of the following four racial groups: Whites (14 percent, three-fifths of whom are Afrikaners); Blacks (73 percent); Coloured (10 percent); Indians (3 percent). The other is the Group Areas Act, which requires each racial group to live in a segregated area. Thus white cities are separated from the townships by distances of between 10 and 20 kilometers.

The riots, school boycotts, and strikes in the autumn of 1984 occurred shortly after the adoption of a new constitution coopting the "Coloureds" and Indians, but excluding the blacks. While regionally South Africa was in as good a situation as possible, its economy was going through the most serious crisis of recent decades. The riots stood in stark contrast to the military and political successes of the Nkomati Accords with Mozambique and the Lusaka Accords with Angola.

The reforms undertaken in the framework of the new constitution were very limited. But they still constituted a breach in the consistency of apartheid by offering separate parliaments without any real political rights to the "Coloureds" and Indians. This search for allies beyond the racial barrier led to a split in the National Party. Since 1984, other splits have brought to three the number of extremist Afrikaner organizations that think that Botha is pursuing an unacceptable policy of compromise.

The distinctive features of the 1984–87 riots were that they took place essentially in four highly urbanized areas: the Johannesburg–Witwatersrand–Vereeniging triangle, Durban-Pinetown, Port Elizabeth–Uitenhage, and the Cape suburbs. The majority of urban blacks, officially 4.5 million, plus two or three million illegals, are concentrated in the first three areas, the Cape being above all "Coloured." The other feature of these riots is that they soon turned against the black municipal authorities and the black collaborators with white power. Often these struggles were horribly violent (victims burned alive by "necklacing"—putting a tire filled with gasoline around the victim's neck and then setting fire to it) and involving gangs of young men. The coming conflicts of the next decade, given growing urbanization, poor housing conditions, growing consciousness, and the development of trade unions, are bound to happen in these centers. It can even be predicted with a minimal risk of error that the two most active factions of the urban, black population will be the fifteen- to twenty-five-year-old young jobless and probably a section of the unionized workers.

At present, the changes in South Africa are not enough for urban blacks who are aware of the possibility of a change— and these people are growing in numbers and are shocked by the three extremist Afrikaner movements clinging to the apartheid of yesteryear.

In the white towns, the black presence, almost unknown before 1979, has become very noticeable. The internal passbooks have been abolished. A number of relatively important segregationist laws have been repealed; for example, the laws outlawing sexual relations between the races. Obviously this changed nothing for blacks, but has led to the development of a new type of prostitution in which white men can legally have relations with black women. The ban on interracial marriages has also been lifted. Reforms have been made, the most important of which concern trade union and labor rights. In the framework of territorial segregation, the right to own property was granted.

Black demands are aimed not at the end of apartheid but at political power on the basis of one person, one vote. That is precisely what the Pretoria regime cannot concede. Thus, the situation, whatever the reforms that the Botha government may grant, is one of stalemate. A trial of strength cannot be avoided. It will be prolonged. The majority of whites want nothing to do with a change of status by which they would lose power and feel—especially among the Afrikaners—that they have no mother country to fall back on. As for the blacks, despite gaining self-confidence from their capacity to fight back, organize themselves, and force concessions and support (albeit reticent at times) from the Western states, and above all the positive sway of public opinion, they still have a long way to go. Direct confrontation is virtually unthinkable toward them and they have to prepare themselves instead for a long campaign of attrition without giving the adversary any respite. White power still has many strong cards among which divisions among the blacks are not the least. The movement that came together in the United Democratic Front (UDF) has been hit hard. Although the African National Congress, which has a charismatic leader in Nelson Mandela and plenty of external representation—as well as the support of the USSR—has largely succeeded in taking advantage of the events of the last few years, other movements are also active: the Pan-Africanist Congress (PAC) and the Azanian People's Organization (AZAPO), both advocates of a black state—and not multi-racial like the ANC; Gatsha Buthelezi's reformist Inkatha which draws its support from the Zulus, and others. The possibilities of dividing them are considerable, not to mention the black apparatus working for Pretoria. However it is hard to see how, eventually, given the spirit of the age, demography, and growing urbanization, the increasingly active role of black trade unions and, finally, international public opinion, Pretoria can indefinitely prolong white supremacy. Eventually it will have to compromise in the face of the combined pressure of urban terrorism and strikes that are bound to increase in coming years, and Botha has started to think about how to coopt blacks.

V Afghanistan

There were two surprising things about the Soviet occupation of Afghanistan: their intervention and their withdrawal. Both were unexpected.

In eight years, Soviet troops, unlike those of the American intervention in Vietnam or the French in Algeria, where over half a million troops were involved, were never more than 120,000 strong. This minimal force above all ensured control of the towns and major communications and delivered some sharp blows to the resistance. Never was counterinsurrection seriously carried out and there has been no escalation.[8] Gradually, airborne troops, well-trained parachutists—the *speznats*—made their appearance. The Afghanistan war enabled the Soviets, on the strictly military level, to train their troops. Since the Second World War, unlike American, French, and British troops who have fought in many theaters, Soviet troops, before 1980, had

---

8. The coherence of the conduct of the Soviet war in Afghanistan remains unexplained.

not used their weapons except in Budapest in 1956. The number of Soviet dead probably does not exceed 15,000–20,000, which is not high either compared to the Soviet population of 280 million or compared to American casualties in the Vietnam War (over 50,000).

The diplomatic cost of the Afghanistan war, both worldwide and in relation to the Muslim countries, was infinitely less than the Vietnam War was for the Americans. At no time did Western public opinion get very worked up about Afghanistan, as it had over Vietnam. The Muslim countries that were hostile to the USSR before the Soviet intervention naturally remained hostile, those that were favorable or played up to Moscow continued to be favorable or to play up to an ally (Syria, PLO, Iraq, etc.). For a long time, votes at the United Nations on Afghanistan called for the withdrawal of foreign troops and not those of Soviet troops by name.

The feelings of the Soviet people changed as the years passed: indifference gradually changed to hostility to an interminable war. This hostility was not peculiar to the Muslim republics as has often been said, it was widely shared by the Baltic republics (Estonia, Latvia, Lithuania) and the Caucasian republics (Georgia, Armenia). The most spectacular public demonstration against the war in Afghanistan took place in 1986 in Erevan (Armenia). In Leningrad, as in Moscow, the war was also not popular; however, opposition to the war was not such as to force a change of policy. Nor was the number of casualties. There remains the problem of the economic cost and, above all, the absence of any prospect of a military solution to the conflict and the need to modify the USSR's image in the framework of the new policy adopted by Mikhail Gorbachev. It was these last factors that contributed to the decision to withdraw Soviet troops.

But this unexpected withdrawal—which Brezhnev would doubtless not have agreed to—is a new factor in the assessment of the USSR. Hitherto, the Soviet Union's policy of force from

Stalin to Brezhnev rested on acceptance by the victim that this force was invincible. The Afghan fighters' determination has now proved the opposite. The calculation that Afghanistan would not be the Soviets' Vietnam has proved to be wrong. This calculation was based, consistently, on the fact that there is no public opinion in the USSR in the Western sense. With *glasnost*, that is less and less true. But the withdrawal was not forced by the grass roots, as would have been the case in the United States, but by those at the top. Gorbachev's global vision, that the Soviet system's need to adapt to the changes necessary to make it more efficient and competitive, is worth more in his view, than Afghanistan. By blaming the "error" of the intervention on his predecessor, Gorbachev is trying to transform a setback on the ground into a diplomatic victory.

For its part, the Afghan resistance chose not to accept any compromise with the Kabul regime. This choice is consistent, since the civil war began at the end of 1978 to bring down a regime that claimed to be Marxist-Leninist, even though, at the time, the trend in power was not the same one. The withdrawal of Soviet troops—staggered between May 1988 and February 1989—gives the war in Afghanistan back its original appearance of a civil war. This will now proceed at a much higher qualitative level than was the case in the years 1978–79 in terms of the number, effectiveness, and level of weaponry. It will doubtless be costly, and complicated by divisions and rifts, not only ideological, as it is often believed, but mostly ethnic (among pashtun and non-pashtun essentially) within the resistance itself.

This is made of half a dozen organizations, three of which are classified as "fundamentalist": the Islamic parties of Gulbudin Hekmatiar and Yunis Khalis and B. Rabani's Jamiat. Pakistan always sought to favor Gulbudin Hekmatiar's group and, in general terms, he was backed by the United States, and everything suggests that this party will seek to strengthen its position. But the Jamiat is a movement that cannot be ignored, especially in the northeast. The three traditionalist groupings, the first two led by S. A. Gailani and by S. Mojadedi, as well as the Harakat, are said to be in favor of a restoration of King Zahir, who was dethroned in 1973.

These divisions suggest that there will be bitter power struggles. As for the Kabul regime, it will not collapse but will be able to remain in power for some time, even after the withdrawal of Soviet forces. The balance sheet is already a heavy one for the Afghan people: several hundred thousand casualties and between four and five million refugees—mostly in Pakistan. The Afghan guerrillas—except for the northeast regions held by Massoud, the most prestigious leader in the resistance— remain organizationally highly traditional.

Throughout, the resistance had no other strategy than to pursue the war, no coordination, no other organization than the tribal, regional, or family ties or classic clientage networks typical of traditional societies; it had no social projects, and no program for the future. In all the guerrilla movements in Asia and Africa—except for Mau-Mau—there was always something new, and the observer was always shown it: an elected village committee, the involvement of women in the struggle, the creation of dispensaries and schools, manufacturing workshops, people's shops, and the like. In Afghanistan, except for the organization set up by Massoud, there has been nothing new to show. But the Afghans are proud of their traditions of independence, having victoriously resisted an attempted British occupation in the last century, and been shaped by a culture that holds up the model of the warrior, and they consented to fight in conditions in which most other societies would have chosen to remain passive.

The organization established by Massoud is based on the classic Leninist-Maoist model, minus the ideology. Massoud was the first to have set up a permanent fighting corps that functioned in a disciplined and coordinated way. The Panshir valley, where he has been able to hold out against a dozen Soviet-Afghan offensives, rapidly became a symbol, and its example was used to extend the organizational experience of the valley over a whole area of the mostly Tajik northeast. With its medical organization, its financial department, its system of justice, and its local militias, Massoud's model was the one of parallel hierarchies peculiar to guerrilla warfare and intended to replace the state.

The game that will be played out after the Soviet withdrawal will be a civil war that is all the more complex because there is no Afghan nation but only tribal loyalties, notably among the Pushtos, the largest ethnic group. The outcome is more uncertain than it might appear, and is geopolitically important for both the USSR and Pakistan and, to a much lesser extent, for Iran.

VI Middle East

In 1974, the representative of the Palestine Liberation Organization (PLO), Yasser Arafat, was triumphantly welcomed to the United Nations, and seemed to be at the zenith of his glory. A movement unknown before the Six-Day War, despite a crushing defeat in Jordan in September 1970, had succeeded in making the whole world aware of the cause of a dispossessed people and its demand for a homeland. Between 1976 and 1987, for more than a decade, the Palestinian national movement's chief merit was to survive and be perceived by a majority of Palestinians, including those in the occupied territories, as the representative of Palestinian national aspirations. Apart from that, after 1976, the Palestinian movement suffered direct hostility from Syria which encouraged opposition to Yasser Arafat within the PLO, and the various splits which divided the movement until the reconciliation of 1987. Meanwhile, in 1982, the PLO suffered the blows of the Israeli intervention in Lebanon and attacks by Syrian-backed organizations. The dispersal of the PLO into a series of Arab countries—some as far removed from the Near East as Tunisia—in 1982 was a severe blow to an organization whose military achievements were rather slight and whose main strength lay in the existence of a Palestinian population in the occupied territories.

The long series of disturbances that broke out in the occupied territories at the end of 1987 added a new dimension to the long conflict between the Israelis and the Palestinians. However liberal it may have been, the Israeli occupation was still an occupation. In the age of nationalism, there was every prospect that this occupation would be felt as unacceptable by a generation of young people who were not traumatized by defeat. The rise of small religious parties, and the coming to power of the Likud in the late 1970s, greatly contributed both to the establishment of Jewish settlements in the West Bank and to the strengthening of a de facto annexation.

Israel today is caught up in a dilemma: how can it remain a Jewish state when over forty percent of the population is made up of Palestinians with a higher birth rate, and how can it remain a democratic state if these Palestinians are to remain as a conquered people with no definite status? Time does not work for one side only, and the Israeli wager on making the occupation permanent was refuted by the months of disturbances in the occupied territories. For the observer who attempts to be impartial, it seems that, while there is a refusal on the part of the Palestinians to accept the existence of Israel, there is a parallel refusal of Israel among its political leaders to accept the existence of a Palestinian nation and to contemplate a withdrawal from the West Bank and Gaza. There is an increasing divergence between what the United States proposes to initiate a peace process and what the right-wing Israeli parties—such as Yitzhak Shamir's Likud—maintain is non-negotiable. Yet apart from the highly improbable hypothesis of circumstances leading to a mass expulsion of the Palestinians from the West Bank and Gaza, the political and demographic situation of the territories controlled by Israel is rather like squaring the circle. Since there is no military solution, Israel is faced, as a result of the ultra-nationalist obstinacy of some of its leaders, with a quasi-permanent crisis situation, the psychological and political repercussions of which might very well turn against it. If peace can only be the result of a complex compromise, maintaining the status quo seems to carry no guarantee of stability.

Lebanon has been engulfed in civil war since 1975, torn apart by conflicts between religious sects and political groupings—the Shiites, for example, are divided between the Syrian-backed Amal and the Iranian-backed Hezbollah. On a reduced scale, like a *bonsai*, Lebanon crystallizes in itself the whole range of crises and tensions in the Near East.

It involves a struggle between Christians and Muslims, and between Christian clans associated with various families; between Sunnis and Shiites, and between Shiites aligned politically with Syria and others aligned with Iran; and finally, between Druzes and pro-Western Maronites, etc. Lebanon has failed to build a state for the reason that the sectarian balance in the administration and in the army has always been seen as more important than the interests of the Lebanese state.

The Palestinians upset the fragile balance of Lebanon between 1970 and 1975 and this led to interference by Syria. Syria had long had regional ambitions over Lebanon—and if possible beyond. In the absence of a Lebanese state, regional anarchy and civil war transformed Lebanon into a sanctuary for trans-national terrorist groups, a free range for sectarian and political rivalries, and a major issue for Syria and a minor one for Israel and Iran.

As none of the religious sects or political factions had the means to impose their hegemony, and Lebanon appeared to lack the will to work out a viable compromise, it appeared increasingly that Syria acted as both arbiter and moderator.

The war between Iraq and Iran is a clear illustration of the growing political autonomy of Third World states formerly subject to the West. In 1975, to put an end to the conflict that had been going on since 1961 with the Kurds of Iraq seeking autonomy, Saddam Hussein of Iraq agreed to sign an agreement in Algiers with the Shah of Iran. In exchange for the termination of Iranian aid to the Kurds in Iraq, Saddam Hussein agreed to give up Iraq's claims to the Iranian Arabic-speaking province of Khuzistan and in the dispute between Iraq and Iran about sovereignty over the Shatt al-Arab waters.

Four years later, the unexpected fall of the Shah of Iran, the Khomeini revolution and the apparent weakening of Iran, the turmoil in the country, and the propaganda directed at the Shiites in Iraq—over one-third of the population—all came together to provoke Saddam Hussein to try to become the major power in the Middle East. In 1980, Iran seemed to be prey to disorder, and the army had been severely purged; since the signing of the Camp David agreements, Egypt was being held at arm's length by the Arab world; Syria, its eternal rival, was busy in Lebanon. The circumstances looked propitious.

Neglecting the fact that Iran's population outnumbers Iraq's three to one and underestimating the depth of Persian nationalism, the Iraqi regime embarked on a war that it expected to be short and limited. The Iraqi forces' initially victorious offensive was poorly followed through. What ought to have been a blitzkrieg became a war of attrition and, increasingly, after 1982–83, the war was being fought on Iraqi soil with Iranian successes such as the taking of Fao in 1986; it was retaken in 1988 by Iraq, which is now on the offensive.

The very special feature of this war is the de facto agreement between the powers to defend the status quo. This tacit agreement proved to be a success insofar as Iraq did not collapse. The reality was that Iran was put on quarantine because of fears of what would happen if it won.

The West, on the whole, supported Iraq, given that the fundamentalism of the mullahs' regime seemed to be an unacceptable regional troublemaker. Despite Soviet advances,

Iran has so far shown itself to be as hostile to the USSR as to the United States. This isolation was only broken by cordial relations with Syria, which is only too happy to help weaken its Baathist Iraqi rival. It was covertly tempered by Israeli aid, particularly military aid, given because the Israeli leaders saw Iraq as the one of the two protagonists that was an enduring adversary.

Despite numerous human losses and growing economic difficulties, the Ayatollah Khomeini proved determined to pursue the war until the summer of 1988.

Given the aid from the West—including France—and from the USSR, Iraq's superiority in weapons was considerable. And yet, despite numerous difficulties, the Iranian leaders proved to be remarkable tacticians and have been able to accentuate the populism of their revolution in order to continue to have much broader popular support than the hostility of the West might lead one to believe. In this conflict in which the great powers have used all their weight to ensure that there is no victor, there will have to be a compromise for an uneasy peace. Both countries, especially Iraq, are going to hit their Kurdish minority hard. The most tangible result of this conflict is the economic weakening of the two countries, which is likely to be a more difficult handicap to overcome than the demographic bloodletting.

VII

All through the conflicts in the Middle East, international terrorism has played a major role. It is not so long ago that the word *terror* harked back to its use during the French revolution. From the tyrannicides of antiquity to the Russian "populists," a whole tradition justified murder of crowned heads as an act of justice. Closer to our own time, in the context of liberation movements, terrorism is one of the forms of violence used in both rural and urban areas. In South Vietnam, elements of the future FLN liquidated the administrative personnel installed by Saigon village by village.

Terrorism, in itself, has no ideological connotation. As a weapon of the weak—much more so than guerrilla warfare—it has over the centuries served both the right and the left: the rise of European fascism during the 1920s and 1930s, or, closer to our own time, the OAS at the end of the Algerian War. It served the liberation struggle against the colonial order: the Cypriot EOKA against the British, the Algerian FLN, and others. Mention should also be made of state terrorism—the assassination by the Syrian secret services of the French ambassador in Beirut in 1982—or quasi–state terrorism—the death squadron in Brazil or the terrorist commandos in Guatemala today. Above all we must not forget to stress the states that practice torture, the *extreme form of individualized terror*, as Paul Wilkinson[9] has so rightly said.

What appears to characterize terrorism today compared to the past is that it is no longer the last resort, but a means of expression. The appearance of *publicity terrorism* is typical of our time, especially in its *transnational* version.

In its publicity version, contemporary terrorism appeared in July 1968 with the highjacking of an Israeli plane in Rome by elements of the Popular Front for the Liberation of Palestine. This innovation was heavily exploited in the years that followed.

In the absence of international agreement on the problems of terrorism, operating in both the West and the Muslim world, using the media to the maximum, the Palestinian commandos publicized the existence of the Palestinian national problem.

In this connection, the interrelation between the media and terrorism must be emphasized, the one feeding the other and vice versa.

In totalitarian states such as the Soviet Union, for example, neither the motives nor the courage lack for recourse

---

9. *Terrorism and the Liberal State* (New York: Macmillan, 1977 and 1987).

to terrorism; it is the fact that it is not reported. What matters in terror is its impact. In a liberal democracy, through a conception of the media perverted by the quest for commercial success, the impact of terrorist actions is disproportionate and this fuels violence. Liberation movements carrying on military struggles involving exceptional organizational qualities like the Eritrean People's Liberation Front (EPLF) are infinitely less well known than tiny, politically unrepresentative terrorist groups with no impact beyond the one they make in the media.

Publicity terrorism began in 1968 with the hijacking of planes belonging to El Al by the Popular Front for the Liberation of Palestine led by Georges Habash, but it only began to be taken seriously by the West in the latter half of the 1970s.

For a whole period, the West and more particularly the European states underestimated the importance of the phenomenon of terrorism. Conversely, it was largely overestimated by the media. In fact, one should really talk of terrorisms and establish a typology. This would include three categories:

(1) The terrorism of ideological sects in industrial countries such as the Weathermen in the United States or the Red Army Faction in West Germany, the Red Brigades in Italy or Action Directe in France.

These groups originated in the Latin American model of the Tupamaros in Uruguay and Carlos Marghella in Brazil. Initially, these groups thought they could win over the mass of the people by using violence to provoke a repression which would demonstrate to the masses the fundamentally repressive character of the democratic state. Obviously such an assumption was inevitably doomed to failure.

Without it being admitted ideologically, this failure was recognized de facto in 1985, when the Red Army Faction, Action Directe, and the Belgian Cellules Communistes Combattantes formed an alliance and announced that they would henceforth attack the European and NATO military-industrial complex.

Overall, these groups—among which the Red Brigades had been the most numerous and could boast of the assassination in 1978 of the former Italian prime minister, Aldo Moro—have been hit hard and their prospects are slight.

(2) The terrorism of minority movements, of which the most famous examples in the West are the Irish in the Irish Republican Army and the Basques in ETA. In the Third World, the two minority movements that have resorted to terrorism have been the Tamils in Sri Lanka and, above all, with a large number of casualties, the Sikhs in Punjab who are demanding a Sikh state.

(3) International or transnational terrorism, whose two main components are the groups championing the Palestinian cause and the Islamic fundamentalists, Shiite or not, who draw their inspiration from the Iranian revolution. These groups emerged chiefly in the Middle East and the eastern Mediterranean—except for the Japanese Red Army—and they have mainly operated in Western Europe: the preferred targets have been France, Italy, Spain, Greece, Great Britain, Austria and West Germany (though the United States abroad has been the main target).

In the beginning, Palestinian terrorism was both a substitute for guerrilla warfare—which the Palestinians have never been able to wage inside the occupied territories—and a means of propaganda. Broadcast by the media of the democratic countries, terrorism enhances its impact with television and exploits to the maximum its psychological aspect. Terrorism is the most violent form of psychological warfare. The publicity terrorism used by the various Palestinian groups was imitated, especially after 1975, by several other movements. The classic example of publicity terrorism is doubtless that of the two Armenian groups active between 1975 and 1983.

The mass deportation and liquidation of the Armenian population of Anatolia in 1915–16 by the Young Turk government led to 40 or 50 percent of them being casualties according to Justin MacCarthy, Johannes Lepsius, and others. This genocide, the first one of the century—imagine what the disappearance of 40 percent of the American population in a deportation would look like—is not recognized by the Turkish state. The Armenians are in the situation the Jews would be in if the German state did not recognize the genocide perpetrated by the Nazis during the Second World War. No request from Armenian political parties in the diaspora addressed to the United Nations led to any results. And in 1973–74, Turkey opposed mention of the genocide of the Armenians in a report on the prevention and elimination of the crime of genocide presented to the United Nations subcommission on human rights.

Between 1975 and 1983, two Armenian organizations, the Justice Commandos for the Armenian Genocide—close to the Dashnak Party (conservative)—and the Armenian Secret Army for the Liberation of Armenia (ASALA) assassinated twenty-six Turkish diplomats or members of their families in twenty-odd countries, including Bulgaria (1981) and Yugoslavia (1982).

These morally condemnable attacks were directed at the representatives of a state that denied the genocide of the Armenians and resisted any mention that it had happened. These attacks, which ceased after a split within ASALA, provoked by a random attack which ignominiously killed seven Turkish Airlines customers in a Paris airport, helped to bring back into the public eye a crime defined by the United Nations in 1968 to be not subject to statutory limitations. In 1985, Ben Whitaker's report on the prevention and elimination of the crime of genocide for the UN human rights subcommission mentioned that of the Armenians. In 1987, the Council of Europe recognized the genocide of the Armenians and called on Turkey to recognize it. Any other demand, apart from the recognition of the genocide, might fail, but this one, for historical reasons and as a matter of moral reparations by the international community, was vital. The demand had been given publicity in the media initially through publicity terrorism; regrettably, it alone had been able to focus attention on a crime forgotten by everyone except the Armenians.

Over the years, publicity terrorism using Europe as its stage became transformed, especially in the 1980s, into coercive diplomacy. An observer who drew up a balance sheet of international terrorism in 1982 would have concluded that it was ineffective. It is true that for the states concerned, international terrorism poses costly security problems: redesign of embassies, surveillance at airports, protection of buildings, security of political leaders, and so forth. But globally, the concessions made to terrorism until then were negligible, and the political victories—and not the noise in the media—of terrorist organizations modest in the extreme.

So long as the major objective of terrorist groups remains publicity, it represents only a limited danger. The use of terrorism as an indirect strategy becomes a much more serious matter once states try to manipulate it.

For the most part, publicity terrorism is content to publicize a cause, to win over the sympathy of public opinion (at least its own) if possible, and to remind people of its existence. As coercive diplomacy, international terrorism becomes a not insignificant means of pressure.

It is mainly four states that have used international terrorism: Iraq, in the framework of an extremist Palestinian strategy by supporting the Abu Nidal group in the 1970s, and more particularly in the framework of anti-Western strategies, Syria, Libya and Iran.

Today, the balance sheet of international terrorism is not nearly as poor as it was in the early 1980s. Two or three suicide operations with trucks loaded with explosives were enough in 1983, by killing 241 marines and 83 French parachutists—and 57 other American victims at the American embassy in Beirut and some 60 Israeli soldiers—to precipitate the withdrawal of the Western peace force. Worse, in 1987, the Irangate revelations informed the world that, despite President Reagan's bluster, he had agreed to secret negotiations with the Iranian authorities involving, among other things, an exchange of hostages for weapons. Part of the proceeds of these sales was then channeled as clandestine aid to the Contras in Nicaragua. It was remarkable behavior for a president who was given to criticizing the insufficiently intransigent attitude of his allies and boasting of his own total determination. In fact, Great Britain is the only European country that has consistently maintained an attitude that is both firm and in accordance with its statements.

International terrorism, which had long used Western Europe as a stage, took it as a target when coercive diplomacy replaced publicity terrorism. Libya took Great Britain and the United States as its targets—and in 1986 as a result suffered an air raid, the final outcome of which proved to be to the advantage of the United States. Iran, and to a lesser extent Syria, both infinitely more important but also more dangerous to strike than Libya, are particularly active through the intermediary of the Lebanese commandos. France, which pursues an actively pro-Iraqi policy and which has pretensions to be the protector of Lebanon on account of the mandate that it once held over it, was hit particularly hard in 1985–87. In practice, it negotiated with hostage-takers and the states that supported them. Thus relations with Iran were gradually normalized thanks to arm-twisting by the Iranians.

Backed and/or used by a state, international terrorism and particularly hostage-taking has proved to pay off politically with the Western democracies. Only Israel, the particular target of Middle Eastern terrorism, has essentially conceded almost nothing in two decades but, unlike the other Western democracies, Israel is in a state of war. This psychological difference is fundamental. It took the European states a long time to take the appropriate measures of coordination and fight with some effectiveness against the underground organizations installed in their capitals by the various Middle Eastern movements and more particularly in London, Paris, Rome, and Madrid. But it is still true that policies continue to vary enormously between the firmness of London and the easygoingness of Athens or Rome.

For the observer of liberation movements, the new fact is not the use of terrorism, in itself a classic phenomenon, but its exclusive use by groups which do not need a mass base of popular support but only the support of a state. In this respect, the terrorist groups of this type are tending to come closer to the image of the mercenary than that of the militant.

VIII The Philippines

Symbol and catalyst of a return to democracy, Corazon Aquino was triumphally elected President in February 1987. Her term extends until 1992.

Cory Aquino has to face three major obstacles. First a conservative ultra-right wing which is present simultaneously in the army and among civilians. Second, a very difficult social and economic situation and, last but not least, a communist insurgency now stronger than ever.

Since independence, the country has essentially been dominated by a few hundred families who have coopted those who were able to make it. The agrarian reform which has been promised for over thirty-five years remains a major aspiration for a large number of peasants. The limited reform which occurred during the Marcos era has produced little change in the countryside. The Philippines has not implemented an agrarian reform similar to Taiwan's, even though its archaic agrarian structures sorely need it. This, Aquino has promised, will change soon. But reforms are not welcomed by the oligarchy, to whom the possession of land is a sign of prestige. Until now taxation has been for all intents and purposes evaded by the wealthy.

According to official Philippine standards of living, 60 percent of the Philippines population live below the poverty level. This means that a family of six has to survive on $110 a month. Manila has the worst shantytowns east of Bangladesh. In the countryside, where 63 percent of the population is still living, more than half of the peasants have no land at all, no roads, and, in some areas, no drinking water.

During the period 1983–86, economic growth was very weak compared with that of other countries of Southeast Asia (Thailand, Singapore, Malaysia, etc.). When one considers that in Asia, three or even two decades ago, the Philippines was only second to Japan economically, the present deterioration is appalling.

Cory Aquino came to power at a time when the Philippines was suffering its worst crisis since World War II. She has aroused hopes which are probably beyond her means to fulfill. Even if she wanted to achieve the promised reforms, the conservatives would certainly oppose them or at least sabotage them. Aquino is a populist leader probably better at making generous promises than at achieving radical reforms.

Despite foreign help, mainly given by the US and Japan, Cory Aquino is facing great difficulties in trying to restore confidence among private investors. In 1986 and 1987 several attempted coups were launched. From an investor's standpoint, Singapore or Thailand appear to be much safer places to invest, despite the high skill-level of the Filipino workers. The most likely prospect for the Philippines is that the country is heading for an extended civil war.

The last obstacle for Cory Aquino is the communist insurgency. Stemming out of the Huk insurgency of the late 1940s and the 1950s, the present insurgency waged by the (new) Communist Party started in 1969 with about sixty to seventy men and it is credited today with twenty-three thousand by the government and the army.

How did we reach this point?

Jose Maria Sizon quit the Moscow-oriented orthodox

Communist Party in 1968 and created a new organization influenced by Maoism. With the help of Bernardino Buscayo—an ex–Huk guerrilla leader—they started an armed struggle in Luzon, the main island of the archipelago: the New People's Army was born. The NPA gained support and popularity after martial law was proclaimed by Marcos in 1972. Many students and members of the intelligentsia then went underground and joined the organization. From the start, the level of the NPA was intellectually higher than the Huks'. Besides, the cadres of the NPA have been able to work successfully among the peasants.

In the beginning, the model for the new organization was the Chinese cultural revolution. For some time, China even provided support in military equipment. In 1973, under the pseudonym of Amedeo Guerrero, Sizon published an essay on people's war. He emphasized the necessity to adopt *military and tactical decentralization* owing to the geographical condition of the Philippines: an archipelago of two major islands one thousand miles apart and in between them half a dozen major islands. Unlike the Huks, who were active only in Central Luzon, the NPA was to take root in Mindanao and then slowly proliferate in the middle islands (Vizayas).

While the political ideology is centralized, the military tactics to achieve the goals of the organization should be decentralized according to local needs and circumstances. Ultimately, the aim is to force the army to disperse its units on about eight islands instead of concentrating in Luzon. Besides, the NPA is indirectly helped by the Muslim insurgency in Western Mindanao (the "Moros" insurgency started in the early 1970s and is still going on). This program was fulfilled by 1980–81. By the end of 1984, Marcos himself acknowledged the NPA as a threat.

At the present stage, the NPA cannot win in the foreseeable future. But it cannot be significantly reduced or beaten. It is already too late to avoid a protracted civil war.

Above all, the NPA has had the time and the ability to

build a serious political underground infrastructure in the countryside and has gained supporters in the cities.

The insurgency is present in the north, the center, and the
south of Luzon. The NPA is active in eastern Mindanao and it
has benefited by the Muslim insurgency which, for the last
twelve years, has kept one-third of the Filipino army busy.

Generally speaking, the terrain is well suited for guerrilla
warfare. In north Luzon, the stronghold of Cagayan has resisted
all army offensives.

With the Sierra Madre on the eastern side and the Cordillera on the western side, about ten provinces of Luzon are
easily accessible. During World War II, about 150,000 Japanese
troops were severely hit in this very area by the Huk guerrillas.

Despite the fact—which seems well established—that it
has no outside help, the NPA has been able to arm its recruits.
Estimated at ten thousand in 1983, they have since more than
doubled. Ironically, many of the recruits have joined the movement since the rise of Cory Aquino.

The guerrillas, however, are not very well equipped. They
lack heavy and antiaircraft weapons, but they are highly
motivated.

Quite classically, the strength of the NPA stems from patient political work among the peasants. This has taken years.
Contact teams are first sent to inquire about the situation in
a village; later, when the report of the contact team has
been studied, propaganda teams are sent out gradually to try to
create a group of sympathizers in the village. Once a village
has been contacted, it is constantly in touch with the NPA
cadres.

Changes are brought: in coconut country, the landowner
usually gets two-thirds of the product of the harvest and the
peasant one-third. The NPA forces a share of fifty-fifty. Usury
is reduced to a lower rate. Worse for the state, which sees its
rule challenged, is the fact that, since 1983–84, the NPA has
been raising taxes. Timber companies which operate in the

countryside have to pay taxes in order to be able to operate.

The NPA is challenging the state at many levels. The controlled villages are called "barrios revolucionarios" and a beginning of agrarian reform is taking place in some areas (Luzon, Negros, and others).

On the ideological level, the models are no longer the cultural revolution or the Khmer Rouge, which were once admired for their radicalism. The Communist Party has learned to be somehow a little more empirical, though the nucleus of the movement is what may be called Stalinist. The two experiences which are the most studied and which look the most relevant to NPA cadres are El Salvador and Nicaragua. The NPA believes that its situation is not too dissimilar from that of the Frente Farabundo Marti in El Salvador. If successful, they think they would reach a result not so different from the Sandinistas with regard to the United States.

The organizational structure is classic: the nucleus of the movement is the CP; its armed wing is the NPA; the broader front, UDF (United Democratic Front), is composed of thirteen organizations with, at the center, the CP. Last, the CP tries to set up a large legal movement: the Partido NG'Bayan, which is meant to be as broad as possible.

Militarily, the Popular Army has well-trained units of about 150 men. Local guerrillas, which are semi-regular, range from 30 to 50 men. Village militias have 10 to 25 members according to the size of the village. The NPA has many young women among its members.

Members are fifteen to twenty-five years old, motivated, and disciplined. By Filipino standards (Filipinos are not so tough as the Vietnamese), they are good. Schools for cadres of different levels, ranging from two to six weeks, are held two or three times a year according to circumstances and needs.

In the cities, the NPA has sympathizers and an underground infrastructure. In Manila itself, many students and professors of the University of the Philippines are sympathizers of the movement. They like its concern for the poor, its nationalism, its stress upon reforms.

In the field, in the Visayas, the strongholds of the NPA are Samar, Leyte South, Western Negros, and Panay. In Mindanao, the eastern part of the island (with problems of leadership in 1985–86). In Luzon, which is the core area of the country, the stronghold is northeast Luzon. The south of Luzon is also well organized with two fronts (south and west). Last, the province of Bataan.

The army is 60,000 strong—and, if we count all the armed forces, 250,000 (this includes the Constabulary and the police forces)—but the anti-guerrilla forces such as the ranger type are still in limited number, though the army does not give official figures.

The first problem with the army is that it remains divided between those who are supporting Aquino's democratic experiment and those, quite numerous (especially in the air force but not only there) who think that a more energetic policy is required to fight the NPA and who trust people like General Enrile. The second problem is that, in the last fifteen years, the army has performed rather poorly. The rank and file are not motivated and, even worse, the officers too often do not fight at the head of their troops. To be an officer is, to many, less a military activity than a quick way to social promotion. The search-and-destroy has too often been a search-and-avoid. The army does not conduct night operations. Many high-ranking officers say that they have understood the causes of the insurrection among the rural population. This should normally lead to reform. But little has been done so far. The battle for "hearts and minds" has not been seriously waged. Army propaganda is poor and sporadic.

The army's best success is the establishment in several areas of the civilian "Home Defense Forces" at village level.

According to the army statistics for the year 1985–86, losses are as follows:

Army casualties	835
NPA casualties	1,145
Civilian fatalities	794

At the aforementioned rate, the battle to crush the NPA could go on ad infinitum.

Much hinges on economic growth. The ability of Aquino's government to successfully implement reforms is vital, though one could first question her chances of reaching the end of her mandate.

In the meantime, negotiations are going to be held on the issue of the United States bases (1991). There is a conviction among most Filipinos that the financial terms of the lease agreement are inadequate. Reforms and economic growth are sorely needed to successfully counter (and not only militarily) the NPA. The most likely answer of the NPA to growing pressure from the army in the coming years will be to add the use of selective urban terrorism in order to keep the armed forces busy.

The dozen years just ended have been rich in events and unexpected twists and turns.

The oil crisis was pretty much absorbed within ten years (1973–83) with a second shock in 1979 that was harder for the Third World than the first. Soon, states which had lived beyond their means for ten years were forced to resort to brutal measures; thus, Nigeria expelled some two million foreign workers. The oil crisis was accompanied by an unbalanced monetary system without provoking a world recession crisis comparable to that of the 1930s. Faced with the necessary changes, the Western economies adapted rather well. On the other hand, new industrial countries came into being in Asia (South Korea, Taiwan, Singapore, Hong Kong) and Latin America (Brazil). Their competition—including in weapons—forced the United States and Western Europe to hasten their modernization. Especially as the Japanese competitor, which arrived on the market in the 1960s, had become virtually invincible by the 1980s.

The period from 1973 to 1980 was one in which the United States faced one setback after another: Vietnam, Laos, Cambodia, the Cuban intervention in Angola and Ethiopia, the strengthening of the Soviet presence in South Yemen, the occupation of Afghanistan, the Sandinista revolution in Nicaragua, and the rise of terrorism, particularly international terrorism. But, conversely, the period that followed, especially after 1983, saw a vast counteroffensive reverse the situation on all these fronts, except for coercive diplomacy used, above all, by Iran.

IX Outlook

The technological innovations that have followed one after the other all through the twentieth century have tended in all respects, and notably economically, toward a world that is more integrated than ever, and one that is highly interdependent.

Attempts at considering the outlook should remain modest when one measures the present in the light of most past predictions. The uncontrolled variables are numerous as they are unforeseen. One factor is of utmost importance: demography, dividing the lightly populated northern part of the globe as a pole of prosperity, while the southern part erodes under an ever-growing and often impoverished population, especially in the case of Africa.

In a world in which nuclear energy rules out war for an indeterminate period, political and economic relations are carried on at several levels.

The first level is that of East-West relations, far and away the best-organized of these levels, where militarily the United States and the USSR have hitherto occupied a hegemonic position. It is highly likely that the relative superiority of these two powers will decline. Japan will surely make major progress along the path to conventional rearmament as the United States is pushing it to do. Japan, now a major power, is already playing a major economic role with the whole of Southeast Asia and doubtless China.

In the next ten years, Western Europe will either have accomplished the decisive steps on the path to political and military unity, or abdicated any will to play a role as a power for the next century. At present, the choice still appears to be uncertain. The three other regional powers that will count will be China, India, and Brazil.

China is regionally situated in an environment determined by the weight of the USSR and that of Japan. It will have every interest in having cordial relations with the United States in order to balance this environment.

India succeeded in eliminating its adversary Pakistan as a power by intervening to ensure the secession of Bangladesh in 1971. It has not only asserted itself as a regional power among the small Himalayan states but also, since 1987, in Sri Lanka by intervening in the conflict between the Colombo government and the Tamil minority calling for secession. While it needs to pay close attention to its own internal cohesion, which is perpetually threatened—currently by the Sikh nationalists—India will doubtless seek to enhance its influence in the Gulf and the Indian Ocean.

In the western hemisphere, Brazil faces a quite different geopolitical situation.

For its part, the USSR is facing a very complex situation. Gorbachev's aim is to make the Soviet system more dynamic and more competitive. This attempt to do so is running up against not only part of the bureaucracy but also the inertia inherent in the system, and the fact that the people balk at adopting a more sustained work tempo. This raises the problem of the social base of Mikhail Gorbachev's regime: is it limited predominantly to the intelligentsia and part of the bureaucracy?

If that were true, his situation would rest on a very fragile base indeed. In fact there is a considerable difference between *glasnost,* which is generally welcomed by the people, and *perestroika,* which involves changes that are bound to be painful. Thus the USSR will have to carry on a three-pronged policy of restructuring its economy, moderately adapting its nationalities policy and managing the crises which will surely arise in some of the people's democracies (Poland, Hungary, and probably Romania). All this is being pursued head-on by the dynamic Gorbachev, who appears to have the art of transforming any difficulties he encounters into diplomatic and media victories—difficulties to which he finds compromises that may well prove to be fragile. In years to come, the USSR's chief effort will consist of trying to uncouple Western Europe from the United States. This will doubtless be made easier for him by the vulnerability of West Germany and will depend on the Europeans' determination.

Up to a certain point, through the prism of the media, Mikhail Gorbachev's star looks like Henry Kissinger's in his early days (1968–71). The future will tell whether, although a man of stature, he has been overestimated, given the inertia that is beyond any leaders, whoever they may be, for it seems likely that he is heading, in his perestroika, to a semi-failure. But is there an alternative solution?

In 1945, the United States had an almost absolute monopoly of power. This was bound to be eroded by the recovery of the powers left exhausted by the war or by the rise of newcomers. But the weakening of the United States has been relatively limited, as it is still the leading power. However, the margin of error allowed over the period 1945 to 1980 has been much reduced. In the future, the United States is going to need leaders and decision-makers who will not take any chances and not commit any gross errors. Great Britain in the days of its imperial splendor did better. After forty years of apprenticeship, it is time to make better use of existing talents and for less mediocrity to be seen emerging at the top of the administration in which too often there is a mixture of ideological assumptions and ignorance of the outside world.

The United States, no longer able to assert its presence everywhere as it did during the 1947–73 period, will attempt to maintain a balance of power on the Eurasian landmass. That consists today in countering the USSR by relying on Japan, China, and Western Europe. *More and more, there will be a multipolarization of relations with the powers that count.* In all that, the necessary domestic changes must not be overlooked: restructuring of industry, savings, and the technological race. The United States seems well placed to face the twenty-first century, although there will be increasingly sharp competition with the Asian industrial pole with, around Japan, coastal China, South Korea, and Taiwan. And doubtless Western Europe.

The second level is that of the Third World, which is politically very unstable. Anti-imperialist, anti-Western rhetoric is common in a large part of the Third World, expressions of the affirmation of an identity and the resulting crises. Then there are the inequalities of development between the Asian pole, an Africa which is sinking deeper into poverty, and a Latin America that is still uncertain.

All these tensions are still being played out in the framework of the nation-state, *the* political entity of the twentieth century. In the Third World, the most unstable zones for the future seem to be in the Middle East, Africa, and the Caribbean and Central America. Most of the time, the factors conducive to upheavals lie not in relations between states but within societies.

In this respect, for the developing countries, the increase in the number of young people whose future is joblessness and the already growing urbanization in these countries suggest that insecurity, delinquency, and riots will be centered in the cities, as demonstrated in Algeria in October 1988.

On the other hand, nothing suggests that there will be fewer localized conflicts in the coming decade. In a world undergoing particularly rapid change, in which there is greater and greater awareness, above all in the urban areas in which regional ambitions are expressed more and more autonomously and in which the state is extending its control more and more, all the conditions exist for population pressure and economic and social needs to fuel violence.

The organization of the world will continue to be based on inequality, and to be moved more by the interests of states or of groups more or less justified in law than by moral considerations aiming to create a more equitable international order, so long as there are not more goods to share.

Montreal, 1988

SELECTED BIBLIOGRAPHY

The French edition of this book has a sixteen-page commented bibliography including many books in English and Spanish. The following bibliography is a very short and selected one. Excellent bibliographies can be found on Latin America, Asia, or Africa, such as *A Bibliography for the Study of African Politics* by Richard L. Sklar and Robert B. Shaw, Los Angeles: African Studies, University of California, (1973). Books which are already in footnotes have not been included.

Third World

Baran, Paul A. *The Political Economy of Growth.* New York: Monthly Review Press, 1957.

Dobb, Maurice. *Economic Growth and Planning.* London: Routledge and Kegan Paul, 1960.

Fanon, Frantz. *The Wretched of the Earth.* New York: Grove Press, 1965.

Jalée, Pierre. *The Pillage of the Third World.* New York: Monthly Review Press, 1967.

Magdoff, Harry. *The Age of Imperialism.* New York: Monthly Review Press, 1969.

Shanin, Teodor, ed. *Peasants and Peasant Societies.* New York: Penguin, 1971.

Wolf, Eric R. *Peasant Wars of the Twentieth Century.* New York: Harper and Row, 1969.

Worsley, Peter. *The Third World.* Chicago: University of Chicago Press, 1965.

Marxism, Leninism, and Soviet Experience

Carr, E.H. *The Bolshevik Revolution,* 3 vols. New York: Penguin, 1967.

Deutscher, I. *The Prophet Armed: Trotsky, 1871-1921.* New York: Vintage Books, 1965.

_____. *The Prophet Unarmed: Trotsky, 1921-1929.* New York: Vintage Books, 1965.

_____. *The Prophet Outcast: Trotsky, 1929-1940.* New York: Vintage Books, 1965.

Fainsod, Merle. *Smolensk under Soviet Rule.* Cambridge, Mass.: Harvard University Press, 1958.

Lenin, V.I. *What Is To Be Done.* London: Oxford University Press, 1963.

_____. *State and Revolution.* New York: International Publishers Co., 1932.

Marx, Karl. *Critique of the Gotha Program.* New York: International Publishers Co., 1938.

Shapiro, Leonard. *The Communist Party of the Soviet Union.* London: Eyre and Spottiswoode, 1960.

Solzhenitsyn, A. *The Gulag Archipelago,* 3 vols. New York: Harper and Row, 1974–1977.

Souvarine, Boris. *Stalin: A Critical Survey of Bolshevism.* Repr. of 1938 ed. New York: Octagon, 1972.

Tucker, R.C., ed. *The Lenin Anthology.* New York: W.W. Norton & Co., 1971.

_____, ed. *The Marx-Engels Reader.* New York: W.W. Norton & Co., 1971.

Wolfe, Bertram. *Three Who Made a Revolution.* New York: Random House, 1949.

Armed Struggle

Bambirra, V., ed. *Diez Años de Insurreccion,* 2 vols. Santiago, Chile: Prensa Latina, 1971.

Bejar, H. *Peru 1965: Notes on a Guerrilla Experience.* New York: Monthly Review Press, 1970.

Clausewitz, Carl Von. *On War,* 3 vols. London: Routledge & Kegan Paul, 1968.

Ellis, John. *A Short History of Guerrilla Warfare.* London: I. Allen, 1975.

Fairbairn, G. *Revolutionary Guerrilla Warfare.* London: Penguin, 1974.

Galula, D. *Counterinsurgency Warfare: Theory and Practice.* New York: Praeger Publishers, 1964.

Giap, Vo Nguyen. *The Military Art of People's War: Selected Writings.* New York: Monthly Review Press, 1970.

Greene, T.N. "The Guerrilla and How to Fight Him." *Marine Corps Gazette,* 1962.

Guevara, E. Che. *Guerrilla Warfare.* New York: Vintage Books, 1968.

Laqueur, Walter. *The Guerrilla Reader: A Historical Anthology.* New York: Meridian, 1977.

Mao Tse-Tung. *On Guerrilla Warfare.* New York: Praeger Publishers, 1961.

Nasution, A.H. *Fundamentals of Guerrilla Warfare.* New York: Praeger Publishers, 1965.

Osanka, F.M., ed. *Modern Guerrilla Warfare: Fighting Communist Guerrilla Movements.* The Free Press of Glencoe, 1962.

Paret, P., and Shy, J.W. *Guerrillas in the 1960s.* Rev. ed. Princeton Studies in World Politics. New York: Praeger Publishers, 1962.

Pye, Lucien. *Lessons from the Malayan Struggle against Communists.* Cambridge, Mass.: M.I.T. Press, 1957.

Thompson, R. *Defeating Communist Insurgency.* London: Chatto and Windus, 1970.

_____. *Revolutionary War in World Strategy, 1945–1969.* New York: Taplinger Publishing Co., 1970.

Valeriano, N.D., and Bohannan, C. *Counter-Guerrilla Operation: The Philippine Experience.* New York: Praeger Publishers, 1962.

Colombia

Adams, D. *Colombia's Land Tenure System.* Madison: University of Wisconsin Press, 1966.

Campos, G., and Fals-Borda, O. *La Violencia en Colombia,* 2 vols. Bogota: Tercer Mundo, 1962 and 1964.

Dix, Robert H. *Colombia: The Political Dimension of Change.* New Haven: Yale University Press, 1967.

Fals-Borda, O. *Peasant Society in the Colombian Andes: A Sociological Study of Saucio.* Gainesville, Fla.: University Presses of Florida, 1955.

_____. "Violence and Break of Tradition," in *Obstacles to Change in Latin America,* edited by Claudio Veliz. London: Oxford University Press, 1968.

Smith, C.T. *Colombia: Social Structure and the Process of Development.* Gainesville, Fla.: University Presses of Florida, 1967.

Algeria

Blair, T. *The Land to Those Who Work for It.* New York: Doubleday & Co., 1972.

Clegg, Ian. *Workers' Self-Management in Algeria.* New York: Monthly Review Press, 1972.

Etienne, Bruno. *L'Algérie: Cultures et Révolution.* Paris: Seuil, 1977.

Fanon, Frantz. *A Dying Colonialism.* New York: Grove Press, 1968.

Harbi, Mohamed. *Aux Origines du FLN: Le populisme révolutionnaire en Algérie.* Paris: C. Bourgois, 1975.

Lacheraf, Mostefa. *Algerie: Nation et Société.* Paris: Maspero, 1965.

Ottaway, David, and Ottaway, Marina. *Algeria: The Politics of a Socialist Revolution.* Berkeley: University of California Press, 1970.

Quandt, W.B. *Revolution and Political Leadership: Algeria, 1954–1968.* Cambridge, Mass.: M.I.T. Press, 1969.

Egypt and the Arab Middle-East

Antonius, George. *The Arab Awakening: The Story of the Arab National Movement.* London: H. Hamilton, 1938.

Berger, Morroe. *Bureaucracy and Society in Modern Egypt: A Study of the Higher Civil Service.* Princeton: Princeton University Press, 1957.

Berque, J. *Egypte: Impérialisme et Révolution.* Paris: Gallimard, 1971.

Gendzier, I. *A Middle East Reader.* New York: Pegasus Press, 1969.

Haïm, Sylvia G. *Arab Nationalism: An Anthology.* Berkeley: University of California Press, 1962.

Kerr, Malcolm. *The Arab Cold War: A Study of Ideology in Politics.* London: Oxford University Press, 1965.

O'Brien, Patrick. *The Revolution in Egypt's Economic System: From Private Enterprise to Socialism, 1952–1965.* London: Oxford University Press, 1966.

Rodinson, Maxime. *Marxisme et Monde Musulman.* Paris: Seuil, 1972.

Vatikiotis, V.J. *The Egyptian Army in Politics: Pattern for New Nations.* Bloomington, Ind.: Indiana University Press, 1961.

Von Grunebaum, G.E. *Modern Islam: The Search for Cultural Identity.* New York: Vintage Books, 1964.

Vietnam

Corson, William R. *The Betrayal.* New York: W.W. Norton & Co., 1968.

Fall, Bernard. *The Two Vietnams: A Political and Military Analysis.* 2nd rev. ed. New York: Praeger Publishers, 1967.

Gourou, Pierre. *Les paysans du delta tonkinois.* Paris: Hartmann, 1936.

Kahin, G.M., and Lewis, J.W. *The United States in Vietnam.* New York: Delta Books, 1967.

Marr, David. *Vietnamese Anticolonialism, 1885–1925.* Berkeley: University of California Press, 1971.

Mus, Paul. *Vietnam, Sociologie d'une Guerre.* Paris: Seuil, 1952.

Race, Jeffrey. *War Comes to Long An: Revolutionary Conflict in a Vietnamese Province.* Berkeley: University of California Press, 1971.

Woodside, Alexander. *Vietnam and the Chinese Model: A Comparative Study of Nguyen and Ch'ing Civil Government in the First Half of the Nineteenth Century.* Cambridge, Mass.: Harvard University Press, 1971.

China

Balazs, E. *La Bureaucratie Céleste.* Paris: Gallimard, 1968.

Bao Ruo-Wang (Jean Pasqualini), and Chelminski, Rudolph. *Prisoner of Mao.* New York: Penguin, 1976.

Belden, Jack. *China Shakes the World.* New York: Monthly Review Press, 1970.

Esmein, Jean. *The Chinese Cultural Revolution.* New York: Anchor Books, 1973.

Fairbank, John K., Reischauer, Edwin O., and Craig, Albert. *East Asia: The Modern Transformation.* New York: Houghton Mifflin Co., 1964.

Hinton, William. *Fanshen: A Documentary of Revolution in a Chinese Village.* New York: Monthly Review Press, 1966.

Isaacs, Harold. *The Tragedy of the Chinese Revolution.* 2nd rev. ed. Stanford, Calif.: Stanford University Press, 1961.

Leys, Simon. *Chinese Shadows.* New York: The Viking Press, 1977.

Schurmann, Franz. *Ideology and Organization in Communist China.* 2nd rev. ed. Berkeley: University of California Press, 1968.

Schurmann, Franz, and Schell, Orville. *The China Reader.* 3 vols. New York: Vintage Books, 1967.

Snow, Edgar. *Red Star over China.* New York: Grove Press, 1967.